American Awakening

"*American Awakening* is a virtuoso exercise in diagnostics. It abounds in trenchant insights drawn from Scripture and from the Western tradition of political philosophy. But the seriousness of the diagnosis underscores the difficulty of the most pressing question is raises: what is to be done?"

—*The Claremont Review of Books*

"A penetrating analysis of identity politics in the modern age.... Everyone interested in understanding the real scope of the challenge identity politics presents for the West should read *American Awakening*. Joshua Mitchell proposes that the many threads of this movement ought to be understood as a species of civic religion, carrying with it the echoes of mostly-forgotten theological longings felt by citizens yearning for liberation from the oppressive legacies of the past."

—*Law & Liberty*

"Mitchell's robust theological conservatism pinpoints that identity politics feeds our desire to be elevated above our weakness and sins, placing them on the other—but like so many other idols it only leads straight to perdition. For helping us understand the grave peril identity politics poses to America, we should be grateful to Joshua Mitchell."

—*The Public Discourse*

"Joshua Mitchell has written that rare book that captures the state of our souls and describes our situation with clarity, astuteness, and spiritual depth. *American Awakening* is a book that expertly combines classical political philosophy with penetrating cultural diagnosis in a manner that holds up a revealing mirror to the great afflictions of our time. At the same time, Mitchell admirably avoids narrow partisanship and undue polemics."

—*RealClearBooks*

"A highly original analysis of what ails America and an intriguing proposal for a biblically informed Great Awakening that can redeem us from the scapegoating now destroying the Republic's cultural fabric."

—*Catholic World Report*

"*American Awakening* is an ambitious book, seeking not only to translate the deep theological assumptions driving the woke agenda but also to draw parallels between them and older derangements in liberal democracy. Though many others have sounded the alarm, Mitchell's warning is compelling."

—*City Journal*

"*American Awakening* is essential reading. Joshua Mitchell exposes the spiritual disorders that are paralyzing public life. An ersatz politics of innocence has replaced our liberal politics of competence."

—R. R. RENO,
editor of *First Things*

"At last—a sophisticated and articulate theological/philosophical/political critique of the intellectual incoherence, bad faith, and internal contradictions that mark today's identity politics. Its appropriation of a religious rhetoric of transgression and innocence makes a civil politics of liberal competence impossible. Allied to a new and schizophrenic world of national administrative elites, global economic managers, and isolated 'selfie' individuals, the future of American democratic social and political life is at stake."

—ELDON J. EISENACH, professor emeritus of political science,
the University of Tulsa, author of *Sacred Discourse and American Nationality*

"There is no more trenchant analyst of postmodern democracy and its discontents than Joshua Mitchell. This courageously argued manifesto is spring water in the desert of an American politics reduced to fusillades of sound-bitten and tweeted idiocy. Read it and be chastened. Read it and find hope."

—GEORGE WEIGEL, distinguished senior fellow and William E.
Simon Chair in Catholic Studies, Ethics and Public Policy Center

"If you, like so many others, are bewildered by what is taking place in our streets today, *American Awakening* is for you. It will provide you with the tool kit needed to sift through the wreckage. It will also be good for your soul."

—MIKE GONZALEZ, Angeles T. Arredondo
E Pluribus Unum Fellow at the Heritage Foundation
and author of *The Plot to Change America*

"From identity politics and the Alt-Right to the opioid crisis and coronavirus lockdown, Joshua Mitchell is the master diagnostician of the philosophical and spiritual errors behind our country's critical condition. And best of all, he shows us how to correct them."

—DANIEL McCARTHY, editor of
Modern Age: A Conservative Review

"*American Awakening* is a tour de force: it is the deepest and yet the most accessible analysis of the political and intellectual movement which may yet undermine our civilization, identity politics. Mitchell has a capacious and original mind, and his book is an unmatched resource for understanding our confused and confusing times."

—ARTHUR MILIKH, executive director, Center for the
American Way of Life, the Claremont Institute

AMERICAN AWAKENING

JOSHUA
MITCHELL

AMERICAN
AWAKENING

Identity Politics and
Other Afflictions of Our Time

ENCOUNTER BOOKS   NEW YORK · LONDON

First American edition published in 2020 by Encounter Books, an activity of Encounter for Culture and Education, Inc., a nonprofit, tax-exempt corporation. Encounter Books website address: www.encounterbooks.com.

Manufactured in the United States and printed on acid-free paper. The paper used in this publication meets the minimum requirements of ANSI/NISO Z39.48—1992 (R 1997) (*Permanence of Paper*).

First paperback edition published in 2022. Paperback edition ISBN: 978-1-64177-282-2

LIBRARY OF CONGRESS HAS CATALOGUED THE HARDCOVER EDITION AS FOLLOWS

Names: Mitchell, Joshua, 1955- author.
Title: American awakening : identity politics and other afflictions of our time / Joshua Mitchell.
Description: First American edition. | New York City : Encounter Books, 2020. | Includes bibliographical references and index. |
Identifiers: LCCN 2020008204 (print) | LCCN 2020008205 (ebook) | ISBN 9781641771306 (cloth) | ISBN 9781641771313 (epub) |
Subjects: LCSH: Identity politics—United States. | Political culture—United States. | Religion and politics—United States.
Classification: LCC JK1764 .M57 2020 (print) | LCC JK1764 (ebook) | DDC 306.20973—dc23

LC record available at https://lccn.loc.gov/2020008204
LC ebook record available at https://lccn.loc.gov/2020008205

1 2 3 4 5 6 7 8 9 20 22

For Reagan Alice and Harper Hope,
the first two of the next generation

Contents

PREFACE TO THE
PAPERBACK EDITION
xiii

PREFACE TO THE
2020 EDITION
xxix

PART ONE

Identity Politics:
Transgression and Innocence

2

PART TWO

Bipolarity and Addiction:
Further Obstacles to the Retrieval
of Liberal Competence

134

CONCLUSION

Patient and Unending Labor

188

EPILOGUE

American Awakening: Wuhan Flu Edition

228

ACKNOWLEDGMENTS

241

INDEX

243

Preface to the
Paperback Edition

§1. The seemingly novel developments of the last several years have not taken me by surprise. When I completed *American Awakening* in May 2020, the national election was still five months into the future, and the stringent measures ostensibly instituted to hold the Wuhan Flu at bay had just been implemented. I thought then that a Democratic Party victory in November 2020 would *promise* the American electorate a return to normal politics, but in fact would operate on the basis of what, in *American Awakening*, I called the politics of innocence and transgression; and that if Joe Biden became the Democratic Party nominee, in order to demonstrate that he was the-right-kind-of-white-man, he would double-down on this sort of politics. The veneer of moderation, of adult politics, would not long conceal the inner logic of identity politics, according to which white heterosexual men—the current prime transgressors in the identity politics dystopian moral economy—must adopt *every* species of political madness offered up by identity politics or suffer social death. That has indeed come to pass in the Biden Administration, leaving the Democratic Party in a position from which it is hard to imagine it can recover in the near future. To argue against identity politics in the Democratic Party today is to invite the charge of being "racist," "misogynist," "homophobic," "transphobic," etc. Comply or be expunged. Who, within the Democratic Party, might be capable of turning it from its present, self-destructive and nation-destroying, course?

§2. One group might be members of the 1960s left who have, over the course of the intervening decades, retained their commitment to addressing race in America, to defending the middle class, and to warning about the unreasonable use of U.S. military power abroad. All good ideas. Alas, members of this group have fallen into two categories: those who naively think the Democratic Party has *not* defected from the path it walked in the 1960s; and those who are well aware that it has, but who are frightened to speak up for fear of being scapegoated and purged. Neither of these contingents from the 1960s left will likely alter the current state of things.

§3. The second group, some of whose members should be counted among the 1960s left, are black Americans who, as I have argued elsewhere, have the necessary moral authority in America today to put an end to identity politics with a single declaration. Identity politics parishioners use the wound of black America to go further—to women's rights, gay and lesbian rights, and more recently, transgender rights. In a world oriented by liberal pluralism, these groups can and will make their claims. A liberal society will respond soberly but generously that exceptions to the rule are not ruled out. In a word, a liberal society will, within bounds, be a tolerant society. Identity politics does not operate according to this liberal paradigm. From its defenders, we hear of the pressing need for "diversity," and are perhaps seduced into thinking that diversity is contiguous with earlier liberal ideals. It is not. Identity politics proceeds on the basis of the illiberal claim that the exception *is the rule*. To make room for the transgendered, for example, identity politics parishioners claim that those who believe that "man" and "woman" are natural categories, that sex matters, must be regarded as guilty of a thought crime, of *heteronormativity*, and therefore must be purged. This is anti-liberal lunacy. How far we have come since the 1960s. Then, the Reverend Martin Luther King argued that the state could appropriately *supplement* the vibrant and necessary mediating institutions of family and church, but not be a substitute for them. In the world identity politics constructs, however, the world where transgenderism is not the exception but rather the rule, the family that Reverend King had in mind—the generative family of a man and a woman—would today be charged with the thought crime of heteronormativity; and the church he had in mind—the patriarchal Christian Church—would be charged with being homophobic. Is this really where the civil rights movement takes us? Can it really be the case that the latest identity politics cause of transgenderism, whose adherents today dare claim the mantel of black America, should require that we ostracize and purge the very institutions that black America, indeed all Americans, needs to thrive? Black America endorses those institutions, in their historically inherited form, by a sizable margin. Yet black America under the tutelage of the Democratic Party that today promulgates identity politics must do as it did under the Democratic Party in the 1950s, namely, go to the back of the (figurative) bus, as more important riders take the front seats—first feminists, then gays and lesbians, and now the transgendered. Organized segregation was once visible. Today it is invisible. If you are black in America today, and want to live without fear of cancelation, you *must* support the social movements that came after yours and which trade on your wound. If you do not, the Democratic Party and the Institutions of Higher Stupification that inflame it—our colleges and universities—will ostracize you. Do you doubt this? Peruse the course catalogs of Black Studies Programs around the country; look at recent hiring; seek to discover the direction these programs intend to take. You will learn that not an insignificant number of these programs have courses on feminism, gays and lesbians, and transgenderism. Black Studies Programs were instituted a half-century ago with a view to redressing the unbalanced account of American history, and for that, they would have been a valuable and necessary undertaking. Today, they seem to have another purpose: to demonstrate, through curriculum and pedagogy, solidarity with causes that a vast majority of black Americans think have no right to draw their moral authority from the historical wound black America endured. Elite blacks *must* support these causes. Asked in her Senate confirmation testimony what the definition of a woman is, Harvard-trained black Supreme Court woman nominee Judge Ketanji Brown Jackson said she does not know. We should not be surprised. Black Americans have the moral authority to begin to cure our country from the identity politics madness that consumes us like a plague. But if they wish not to be cast into the pit with the rest of the irredeemables, both black and white, elite blacks who should be at the forefront of the effort to heal our country are instead compelled to accept a terrible bargain with the defenders of identity politics. Instead of challenging identity politics, instead of declaring with a firm and unwavering voice, "No, your cause may not invoke our wound," they are the very agents who permit and authorize identity politics to invoke ever-new victim groups, whose interests are increasingly anathema to those of black America. No small part of *American Awakening* chronicles the respect in which identity politics betrays black America. Here is but another sickening example. Defenders of identity politics are quick to call out so-called *cultural* appropriation; but without compunction, they support ever more marginal causes, whose moral authority rests on *wound* appropriation.

§4. I gave some consideration in the first edition to the inability of the conservative movement to comprehend, let alone push back against, identity politics. Identity politics I characterized as a deformation of Christianity and, more provocatively, as a deformation of the Reformation Christianity of our Puritan originaries. I suggested that free market conservatives who defend the American regime understood debt in terms of the ledger book of monetary payment, and that cultural conservatives who defended the American regime understood debt in terms of what we owe to the tradition of our forefathers. Identity politics, I suggested, attends to what I called spiritual debt, which is akin to the deep *internal* debt Christians call original sin. Call it spiritual debt, call it something else, but whatever we call it, we should understand that one of the reasons why conservatives do not understand identity politics is that they understand the first two kinds of debt, but not the third. Speaking generally, the default account from both sorts of conservatives is that identity politics is a further outworking of cultural Marxism, whose long march through our institutions they have long fought. How convenient if that were the case, for no additional work would need to be undertaken to understand identity politics; and critics could continue to bemoan the ongoing losses on the various battle fronts of the culture wars. Alas, identity politics has required no long march through our institutions. It has been met with no resistance—indeed, it has been welcomed—as Marxism never was. Cultural Marxism has been working away at American institutions for three-quarters of a century; identity politics has taken only a few years to penetrate those same institutions. Tocqueville's framework, so often invoked in *American Awakening*, helps us understanding the bigger picture. In his last great work, *The Old Regime and the French Revolution*, Tocqueville called the French Revolution an "incomplete religion," by which he meant that it less destroyed Christianity than replaced it with fragments of Christianity. "Liberty, equality, fraternity"—were these not the promise of a post-lapsarian order, complete with a new calendar, and without the social stratification that sinful human societies always produce? The French Revolution: the brotherhood of saints, without God the Father. Marxists, no less contemptuous of Christianity than the French Revolutionaries, also promulgated an incomplete religion. Because of the productivity unleashed by cruel capitalism, man, cast out of the Edenic splendor of primitive communism, stands now on the threshold of ending his long labor amid the thorns of creation to secure his daily bread. When Christianity falters, one or another incomplete religion will step in to fill the vacuum. You do not get religion-free secularism after Christianity falters, you get distorted, fragmentary, remnants of Christianity, which, like secularism, purport to have transcended Christianity, yet whose revolutionary fer-

vor disrupts rather than contributes to the tranquility that defenders of secularism claim emerges once Christianity no longer reigns in
the souls of men.

§5. The conservative movement in America has focused a great deal
of attention on the first two incomplete religions. Indeed, from its
beginning to the present day, they have been its target. On the one
hand, we see the stringent defense of "tradition" against the equal-
izing tendencies of French Revolution and of Progressivism—that
American movement also dedicated to the destruction of mediating institutions. On the other hand, we see what was, before 1989,
a counterbalancing libertarian contingent, hostile to Marx's vision
and thoroughly modern, which hallowed Smith and Hayek and the
"free markets" they thought important supports for liberty. I do not
say anything new here by noting that the current reconfiguration
happening within the conservative movement has involved the rise
of the traditionalists and the fall of the libertarians—which is to say
the rise of those whose fight is with the first incomplete religion, and
the fall of those whose fight is with the second incomplete religion.
Those in the former camp have found renewed confidence, after decades in which the *free market veto*, to use my friend Yoram Hazony's
memorable phrase, prevailed against them. This shift has satisfied
a long-suppressed contingent of the conservative movement, but it
will not in the least help conservatives understand the *third* incomplete religion that is now upon us, the incomplete religion of identity
politics. Today, America faces a far greater challenge, its gravest to
date. Conservatives who have battled the first two incomplete religions of the French Revolution and Marxism have little understanding of what is now upon them. They employ their old weapons. They
declare we are facing an outbreak of cultural Marxism. Their weapons are useless against this new enemy. This new enemy has captivated one portion of America by its promise of a spiritually purified
world, at which it will arrive by finally solving the problem of spiritu-

al debt—the unpayable debt owed by the white heterosexual male to everyone else, against whom he has perennially transgressed. Free market conservatives and cultural conservatives *do* talk about debt, as I have said; but to parishioners in the church of identity politics, what they offer seems hopelessly superficial, even childish. "Do you not see that the problem of debt is deeper than you imagine—that free markets and your hallowed traditions *are themselves stained* and deplorable," they say. The insight that identity politics is, in fact, a third incomplete religion to emerge since the French Revolution helps us understand why conservatives do not understand identity politics, and do not know how to defend themselves against it.

§6. Along what lines *can* conservatives push back? On theological grounds. More precisely, on the basis of the theological observation that identity politics is a deformation of the Christian insight that a scapegoat does indeed take away the sins of the world, and the warning that there will be no end to trouble if that scapegoat is mortal rather than Divine. In the *vertical* relationship of innocence and transgression proffered by Christianity, Christ alone is the innocent victim, and all of mankind is guilty. In the *horizontal* relationship of innocence and transgression that identity politics offers, the white heterosexual male is the transgressor, and all those who are *not* him are the innocent voiceless victims—hence the insidious phrase, "people of color" (POC), which ignores the historical antipathies chronicled by the barbarism, wars, and mutual enslavement perpetuated among "colored" peoples, and which supposes instead a unity among them by virtue of their common aggrievement against Whiteness. Whiteness is the original sin in comparison to which their never-ending violence toward one another is rendered invisible. Alas, conservatives are embarrassed by talk of original sin, and as a consequence have no way to respond to the various fictions that identity politics sets forth. Original sin is, let us face it, too much of a Reformation trope. That is why conservatives will continue to write and talk about free markets and tradition, and make no headway against identity politics. I do not say that America must become a nation of Reformation Christians to overturn identity politics. That would be illiberal. But I do say that parishioners in the church of identity politics who are *currently* captivated by the idea of irredeemable stain will only find what they are really looking for—a deep account of sin—in Reformed theology, however enfeebled it may be, and unable to deliver such an account at the moment. While this conclusion may seem to be quite a departure from what I wrote in the first edition, it follows from the claim I made in Part One, §23. If a social pathology emerges from a deformation of religion, that pathology does not heal without a return to healthy religion. There are no secular solutions to religious problems—or more precisely, the relationship between the two is not as we imagine.

§7. In Part I, §§59–63, I suggested that the liberal politics of competence, of the American sort that the conservative movement has heretofore defended, is not possible without the solution to the problem of the scapegoat that Christianity offers. That is because if we wish to build a liberal world together, a world of competence, we cannot continuously gaze upon at each other, and at the "group identity" that purportedly predestines us to be pure or stained, as possible objects of cathartic rage. Another way to put this would be that a *secular* liberal society is, in fact, precisely a society in which the Christian understanding of the scapegoat *has won*, and has receded into the background of public life without wholly disappearing.

§8. This may seem like arcane theoretical wandering, but it is not. Almost all conservative defenders of liberalism in the academic world proceed on the basis of the claim that liberalism *is* secular, and that religion is but a private *preference* or, perhaps more strongly, a private *value*. Holding fast to this impoverished view, and unable to understand that, like Christianity, identity politics is also concerned with irredeemable stain and the scapegoat who takes away the sins of the world, these defenders can defend neither liberalism nor themselves against the indictments that identity politics levels. Responding to this impotence, a growing chorus of young conservatives, too many of whom are unable to secure positions within the academy because of identity politics hiring practices, have become disgusted with the failure of the old guard to repel the assault. They ponder and plot a new path, toward an *anti-liberal order*, in which a pre-liberal form of Christianity arrests our civilizational decay, guiding and informing it at every level, assisted by the enforcing power of the state. Roman Catholic integralism is currently the leading contender.

§9. There is more. In our mixed-up world, another quite different path is also being explored, within and without the academy, namely the one cleared by Nietzsche. By this, I mean the path I illuminated in Part One, §58, the path of *forgetting*. Can we really be surprised by this development? When young men are told they are irredeemably stained, that they have a debt they cannot pay, sooner or later they will stumble upon Nietzsche, who declared that we can have a to-morrow only through forgetting. So here we are: liberal competence requires that the scapegoat problem be solved—and not in the way identity politics proposes. For liberal competence to prevail, a Divine scapegoat who takes away the sins of the world is needed. Defenders of liberalism, insistent that liberalism is a secular project, have no place in their conceptual armory for the Christian understanding of the scapegoat or for the identity politics deformation of it. As a consequence, they have no understanding that the former makes possible the liberal politics of competence, while the later will destroy it. Young conservatives see the feebleness of these secular defenders of liberalism, and are opting for pre-modern Roman Catholic integralism or post-modern Nietzscheanism. The one rejects the radical notion of sin that inheres in identity politics, and adopts, instead, the semi-Pelagianism of the Roman Catholic Church; the other rejects the radical notion of sin that inheres in Reformation theology and in identity politics, and casts off the idea of sin altogether. No one can predict how the current confusion will be resolved or further jumbled, or how many rounds this brawl will go. Three groups of contenders for the soul of the West are in the ring: Roman Catholic integralists; secular liberal heirs of the Reformation and the latter's religiously deformed children, the identity politics New Elect; and Nietzscheans, who are sickened by guilt in all of its forms, and wish to start over. We will see whether a fourth group—Reformation thinkers who understand and can defend the theological precondition for liberalism, as WASPs once did—make an appearance. When I wrote *American Awakening*, I was concerned that conservatives did not understand, and could not fight back against, identity politics. Now I am concerned that their response to it may involve an endorsement of anti-liberal, pre-modern or post-modern politics.

§10. An author has the opportunity in hindsight to form new judgments about which portion of what he has written may be most attended to in the future. My conclusion now is that the portion of *American Awakening* pertaining to identity politics will have a shorter shelf life than the portion concerned with the problem of substitutism. Substitutism is that malady which arises as a result of man's perennial search for shortcuts (see Conclusion, §§91–98). On his watch, supplements to our difficult labors are turned into substitutes for them. The instances I considered in the first edition of *American Awakening* were varied and seemingly unrelated. If I had seen things a bit more clearly at the time, I would have added an obvious instance of substitutism that we see all around us every day, namely, that pets have become a substitute for children rather than a supplement to them. But here, I want to move away from the whimsical to the serious, and consider a recent development of substitutism that is as pernicious and it is emblematic of the disease, namely, the hype around the metaverse, the purported full extension of digi-verse that social media only begins to reveal. A better case study of substi-tutism—which is to say a more delusional one—I can hardly imagine. To review terrain covered in *American Awakening*, Part Two, §82, so-cial media *can* supplement our existing friendships; it can be a stim-ulant, which helps us keep *in touch* with old friends when we are not able to confirm, through a handshake, a pat on the back, or an em-brace, that we are indeed friends. We feel the presence of our friends through this supplement; but the supplement by itself, without the preexisting competence of friendship, cannot *produce* the feeling of presence. That is why we are comfortable having Skype or Zoom calls with friends and family members who are far away, but not with strangers. I use the word "presence" because it is a term on the minds of many of our Tech Elect these days. Facebook has changed its name to Meta, and Mark Zuckerburg and his "metamates," for-merly known as his "employees," are betting that the future lies in the metaverse, a digital platform that, he acknowledges, can *only* work if it is able to deliver the experience of "presence." Today, bil lions of dollars are being spent on this project, by Meta and other digital media companies, with a view to building a Tower of Babel with digital high-tech bricks (Gen 11:3–4) that will lift us altogether beyond the need for actual competence. They want to re-create the presence we feel through the social media supplement to friendship, but in the form of a substitute for the hard and patient labor—on the playground, in school, after school, in our families, in our churches and synagogues, in our civic groups, and in and through our local po-litical affiliations—that friendship takes to develop and flourish. The mediating institutions through which we form friendship need no longer trouble us, they proclaim. The age of lived competence has now passed. Friendship once had to be formed in institutional set-tings where noise and signal could not be disentangled, where filth and festering wounds were always near. Places; always places—places of institutional and bodily *regeneration*, where man and women were *sexed*, not *gendered*; places where we must labor, by the sweat of our brow, to develop competence, or die. The metaverse will relieve us of a double burden: the burden of long labor in a place, and the burden of the transgressions that attended those labors. Digital substitutism will solve the theodicy problem that embodied life found intractable. This prideful delusion is a violation of the very order of things. When supplements are turned into substitutes, they make us ill. The competences we develop can be supplemented, but there is no substitute for them. Early forays into the metaverse *have* yielded the "high" that has been promised, the addictive release from the burdens of mortal life; but it has also yielded the "lows," like virtual rape, virtual violence, verbal cruelty, etc., in short, *all* the horrible things that the world offers, but now without the competences we learn through our mediation institutions that alone can attenuate those horrors. Just as the "highs" of opioid addiction *go with* the "lows" when drugs become substitutes rather than mere supplements, so, too, the metaverse will bring soul-crushing lows if it becomes a substitute for competences we can only develop through our mediating institutions. In the metaverse, rape, violence, and cruelty *seem* to be ruled out because we have purportedly left behind the world of filth and festering wounds where that sort of thing *does* happen. In truth, the only way to attenuate rape, violence, and cruelty is to develop the competences that humanize man. To put the matter in terms of recent events (using the example I gave in Part Two, §86): You do not get rid of Harvey-Weinstein-toxic-masculinity by *purging* masculinity, by building a de-sexed digital alternative; you do it by assuring that *healthier* versions of masculinity are around to quash pernicious versions—something every man either did learn or should have learned in his youth on the playground. It is healthy *men* who keep *unhealthy* men in check. Those healthy men are formed through the competences we develop in our mediating institutions. If we were to formulate this problem in terms of evolutionary biology, we would say that mediating institutions humanize the primitive, reptilian impulses in man. The metaverse *promises* transhuman man, but in bypassing the competences that humanizes the reptile in us all, the *twofold* result will be the "high" of transhumanism and the "low" of prehuman barbarism. That is what happens when supplements are turned into substitutes. There are no shortcuts. Alas, everywhere we look, we and our fellow citizens are trying to find them, and stumbling as we go, over the terrible cost associated with the drug-like "highs" that attends them. The competence called friendship forms locally, in mediating institutions. Extend the range, the "presence," of friendship with social media, and *eureka*, our friendships seem to have no limits. That is only the half of it, however; the other half is that if we lose sight of the competence we call friendship, a loneliness that digital substitutism causes and cannot cure will become a central feature of our life, as it has throughout America. Like a crashing opioid addict, our Tech Elect seek now to give us the ultimate drug, to lift us from the stupor of loneliness to which their corporations have contributed immensely. The metaverse—the "high" that never lets you down. This will not end well. Unlike identity politics, the pathology of which our fellow citizens are recognizing with ever-greater clarity with each passing day, substitutism is not really yet understood as a comprehensive problem. Indeed, I have struggled to find an adequate name for it. What appears before us today is a vast and seemingly unrelated set of temptations whose danger lies in their undeliverable promise of a shortcut that bypasses life's difficult labors. For the moment, we see only the promise. A clear understanding of the danger lies off in the distance. I suspect that everyday life will look very different than it does today after we determine how to protect ourselves from it. The image of a drug addict returning to a life of sobriety gives some indication of the magnitude of the change that will be needed.

§11. A few words, finally, about Wuhan Flu, the subject of the Epilogue. The initial confusion about what to name the pandemic provided evidence that what would follow would involve more than medical science. One of the suppositions held by many who have fought in the culture wars over the last three decades has been that although the humanities might fall, the hard sciences would never succumb. The advance could proceed only so far. Although hinterland skirmishes might be lost, the home terrain—the hard sciences—were fortified or self-protecting. The claim made in *American Awakening* is that identity politics turns *every* domain of human life into a venue for innocence-signaling. Absent the once-and-for-all-time Divine scapegoat who takes away the sins of the world, every domain of human life becomes a battleground for establishing wherein stain and purity lie. Identity politics does not stop with the humanities; it comes for the sciences, too (see Conclusion, §94). The "fact-value" distinction, so often invoked to delineate the humanities from the hard sciences, did not—cannot—save us. In fairness to the World Health Organization (WHO), the outbreak of the recent pandemic was not the first occasion for its defection from its scientific mission. An extract from a May 2015 WHO memo reveals that the identity politics mindset had been established years before. It reads:

> In recent years, several new human infectious diseases have emerged. The use of names such as 'swine flu' and 'Middle East Respiratory Syndrome' has had unintended negative impacts by stigmatizing certain communities or economic sectors.... This may seem like a trivial issue to some, but disease names really do matter to the people who are directly affected. We've seen certain disease names provoke a backlash against members of particular religious or ethnic communities, create unjustified barriers to travel, commerce and trade, and trigger needless slaughtering of food animals. This can have serious consequences for peoples' lives and livelihoods.

Is this hard science or identity politics platitudes about innocent victimhood? History will establish if the virus now officially named COVID-19 is traceable to a laboratory in Wuhan, China, in which case the designation "Wuhan Flu" *will be* appropriate, because it will contain pertinent political information obscured by the designation "COVID 19," and because if there is guilt, it ought to be located, addressed, and remembered by history. Irrespective of history's judgment, this episode in virus-naming reveals that the hard sciences are being penetrated by identity politics. Is it any wonder, then, that more than half of our fellow citizens hear sentences that begin with, "The science says," and become suspicious? They have had their doubts about so-called "clean energy" science and its war on "dirty" fossil fuels for some time. "Clean" and "dirty" are not scientific variables; they are religious descriptors. The global pandemic further eroded the trust of our fellow citizens in the hard sciences. And now, not to be outdone, Departments of Physics, Chemistry, Biology, Mathematics, and Astronomy in almost all of our colleges and universities are scurrying around trying to purge the "Whiteness" that inheres in their scientific disciplines, and which *must* be the cause of the disproportionate representation of peoples of European and Anglo-American descent. All together, these developments are accelerating public distrust of the hard sciences. Identity politics parishioners dismiss these concerns as the rantings of anti-science irredeemables. They do not understand the catastrophe that is already underway. The hard sciences, one of the great jewels in the crown of Western civilization, are not going to be destroyed by hordes of deplorables who ride in from fly-over country on their Silverado, F-150, and Ram steeds of iron. They are going to be destroyed by the scientists within, who have become fixated on the identity politics categories of purity and stain, which tempt them into thinking—most unscientifically—that the world is divided into The Elect and the reprobate, and that they are clearly the former. In such a world, truth succumbs to the dogmas the incomplete religion

Joshua Mitchell

of the moment establishes. The record of the fate of the sciences under Marxism in the twentieth century, the second incomplete religion, is well documented. Today, a third incomplete religion is upon us, and we can anticipate that historians of science will look back at the early twenty-first century with incredulity and disgust.

Preface to the 2020 Edition

If humanism were right in declaring that man is born to be happy, he would not be born to die. Since his body is doomed to die, his task on earth evidently must be of a more spiritual nature.[1]

§1. This book is about three separable but ultimately related ailments from which we suffer immensely in America today: identity politics, bipolarity, and addiction. Should these three ailments be gathered together in one book? I think they should be, because although identity politics is the more immediate threat, our republic cannot be healthy if we do not also understand and address bipolarity and addiction. The latter two are generally treated as behind-the-scenes psychological or physiological problems about which only trained experts are authorized to write. I have no such authorization. I write as a political philosopher, attentive to what the great authors of the West have written about the human condition; and I write as an observer of, and in, our times. Because of my training, I will consider both bipolarity and addiction in an unorthodox, and I hope, more capacious way than our psychologists and medical experts generally allow. I will look at bipolarity and addiction as existential, political, social, and theological issues that the pharmacology recommended by experts cannot cure. All this, in due course. First, I will make a few observations about identity politics, to give some sense of its contours and of the danger that it poses. Unlike bipolarity and addiction, which seem to belong to our

1. Alexandr Solzhenitsyn, "A World Split Apart" (commencement address, Harvard University, Cambridge, MA, June 8, 1978), https://www.solzhenitsyncenter.org/a-world-split-apart.

quiet private affairs, identity politics is a very loud public affair. Moreover, it is a loud public affair that is making constructive public life increasingly difficult if not impossible. That is why more than half of *American Awakening* is concerned with this affliction. To wrestle with the quiet, seemingly private problems we face, we must first take care of the loud public problem. To start our longer journey to recovery, let us start with what is right in front of our nose.

§2. By so many measures, life is getting better all the time. There have been no global wars in the last seven decades. Standards of living have increased nearly everywhere, well beyond anything imaginable at the end of World War II. Many diseases have been eradicated. Starvation is rarer. Drinking water is more readily available. Housing stock has multiplied and modern conveniences have grown exponentially. Travel by every means is safer. International communication is instantaneous and inexpensive. The computing power of a common smartphone exceeds the computing power the astronauts of Apollo 11 had at their disposal during the first manned landing on the moon in 1969.

§3. Alongside the visible material economy that has made these improvements possible lies another economy that is also concerned with weighing and measuring. In this economy, however, we do not weigh and measure empirical things like money, time, and materials. Rather, we seek to measure *transgression and innocence*—sometimes with a view to the mystery that no balance of payment between them is possible, and sometimes with a view to the demand that all accounts be settled. I will say more about both of these views in a moment. For now, I will say that this invisible economy is uncorrelated with the economic advances we make and, therefore, with the happiness and well-being that is supposed to be ours. Strangely enough, this invisible economy also seems to obtrude all the more as our standard of living increases. Perhaps this is because when we attempt to build a world in which the only things we weigh and measure are money, time, and materials, we momentarily deceive ourselves that this is the only economy in which we are involved. Then, because we can never escape its primordial tug, the invisible economy concerned with weighing and measuring transgression and innocence disrupts and mocks the well-measured world of money, time, and materials that we have constructed and demands our full attention. Alexis de Tocqueville, the great author of *Democracy in America*, seemed to think this twofold economy was always going to haunt us. In 1840, he wrote:

> The soul has needs that must be satisfied. Whatever pains are taken to distract it from itself, it soon grows bored, restless, and anxious amid the pleasures of the senses. If ever the thoughts of the great majority of mankind came to be concentrated solely on the search for material blessings, one can anticipate that there would be a colossal reaction in the souls of men. They would distractedly launch out into the world of spirits for fear of being held too tightly bound by the body's fetters.[2]

In the United States, material prosperity was measured and loved more than anywhere else at that time. Because this was the case, there would be periodic and enthusiastic irruptions of the invisible economy. Religious enthusiasm—here understood as the acute awareness of our transgressions, and the frenetic search for the cover of innocence— goes with material opulence. From the vantage point of the material world, as many economists remind us, we should be happier by the day. But because the economy to which they point is not the only one in which we live, we are not happier. Man: the material being who knows the material world is not the only measure of who he is. Furnished with material advances that lift him to unimaginable heights, and haunted by unpaid or unpayable debt from his transgressions, which draw him into wretched darkness from which he cannot escape—that is man.

2. Alexis de Tocqueville, pt. 2, chap. 12 in *Democracy in America*, vol. 2, ed. J. P. Mayer (New York: Harper & Row, 1969), 535.

§4. The twofold economy of ours, the one visible and the other invisible, is quite clearly on display these days, if we know where to look. I mentioned a moment ago that sometimes the invisible economy is understood in light of the mystery that no balance of payment is possible, and sometimes in the light of the belief that a full account can be given and the demand that all accounts be settled. The former understanding is inscribed into Christianity, and the latter is the viewpoint of identity politics. Consider the former first. A mass shooting occurs somewhere in America. Christians offer up their "thoughts and prayers." They do this because they understand that in the invisible spiritual economy, prayers for the deceased innocents are heard by God—and not just prayers for the recently dead but for the dead of ages past. That is why in the invisible spiritual economy, prayers for the recently deceased are as efficacious as are prayers for African slaves who died on their way to, or on, American soil hundreds of years ago. For those oriented only by the material economy, this is senseless gibberish. A transgression has occurred, and it must be paid for—say, by changing gun laws or, if it were 1865 and we could actually count the cost, by making reparations for slavery. Material suffering requires a material recompense. The balance of payments in the visible economy must be observed. In the invisible spiritual economy, on the contrary, payments never quite balance—at least not in our lifetimes. The innocent suffer, and we do not know why. Good people die, and bad people live. Christian prayer begins and ends with the incontrovertible fact of the imbalance of payments. Innocent people were gunned down. Where were the scales of justice? Innocent slaves died wretched deaths. Where were the scales of justice? The material economy promises much, but because of the incontrovertible fact of the imbalance of payments, the invisible spiritual economy can never be supervened by the visible economy. Money, time, and materials render a portion of our life visibly coherent and manageable, but not all of it. The justice of payment alone does not fully comprehend the world; uncompensated suffering and mercy, too, have their place on the invisible balance sheet of life that only God understands. So declares the Christian. We live within two economies. The one involves payments made and payments received; the other involves something deeper and more impenetrable—an economy within which we are to prayerfully abide, but which we cannot alter. The betrayal of Christ by Judas in the Gospel of Matthew illuminates the collision between these two economies. Judas, the treasurer for the disciples, the one who weighs and measures in the visible economy, is incensed that expensive ointment has been poured out on Jesus's head. The ointment could have been sold, and the proceeds given to the poor. Jesus replies: "The poor will always be with you"—which is to say there is an invisible economy in which the scales of justice do not balance in the way that Judas wants them to. Concluding that Jesus is not the revolutionary Judas had expected Him to be, he betrays Jesus for silver coin, which he presumably wants to use to help balance the scales of justice in the visible economy.[3] For the Christian, man, try as he may, cannot resolve the imbalance of payments in the invisible economy. Only God can; and He will not do so until the end of history. A no less remarkable distinction between the two economies occurs at the beginning of the Gospel of Luke: "And it came to pass in those days, that there went out a decree from Caesar Augustus that *all the world* should be taxed."[4] Joseph and Mary go to Bethlehem to be counted and taxed—to be included in the bookkeeping of payments that "the world" records. The birth of Jesus does not happen at the Inn, however, but rather in a sheltering place for animals—probably a cave—where Mary lays Him in an animal food trough (a manger).[5] Jesus is invisible to the world that payment records; He comes to give relief in the other economy that is beyond price, the economy that man cannot control.

3. The entire scene plays out in Matt. 26:7–15. Doubt is cast on Judas's deeper motive in John 12:6, where it is suggested that he is a thief.

4. Luke 2:1 (emphasis added).

5. See Luke 2:7.

§5. Identity politics is also concerned with the invisible spiritual economy that dwells alongside the visible economy. Much has been written about identity politics, but little of it comprehends identity politics as an attempted exposition, distorted though it may be, of the mysterious invisible economy that we cannot escape. Identity politics comprehends this invisible economy in terms of a relationship between transgression and innocence, between purportedly monovalent groups—white, heterosexual men, on the one hand; and blacks, women, persons who identify as LGBTQ, and persons who identify with still other identity groups, on the other. These groups are, of course, visible. This makes the calculus complicated. Identity politics is concerned with the invisible economy of transgression and innocence, but seeks to understand that invisible economy in terms of the relationship between visible groups. In the world that identity politics constructs, for example, it is axiomatic that the "systemic racism" of one visible group toward another runs so deep that it cannot even be measured. Although it is invisible, it is real. On the one hand, therefore, we are asked to ignore the visible economic relations between members of visible groups when, say, white, heterosexual men are considerably poorer than members of groups that identity politics declares to be among the innocents. On the other hand, when the economic relations are reversed, and white, heterosexual men are the economically wealthier group, identity politics declares that the deeper cause of the visible imbalance is the systemic racism in the invisible economy of transgression and innocence in which both groups are involved. Identity politics *always* maintains the purity of those it considers innocents and the stain of those it considers transgressors, regardless of any visible evidence to the contrary. White, heterosexual men, who are "the least among us,"[6] are therefore invisible within the world identity politics constructs. That is why the devastation of the opioid crisis among whites in

6. Luke 9:48 and Matt. 25:40.

America has not captured the attention of those who live within the world identity politics constructs, and why Hillary Clinton ignored or castigated a vast swath of the American electorate and lost the 2016 presidential election. Adherents of identity politics are untroubled by the necessity of oscillating back and forth between ignoring the visible evidence, in the case of poorer white, heterosexual men, and singularly fixing on it, in the case of richer white, heterosexual men. In the world identity politics constructs, the visible economy either tells us nothing or is invested with a significance that the visible facts do not warrant. That is one of the consequences of attempting to render an invisible economy of transgression and innocence in terms of the relationships between visible groups. White, heterosexual men are either invisible or they are the hidden cause of every visible transgression in the world. The Democratic Party cannot win national elections if its candidates continue to think this way.

§6. This paradox and its political implications aside, the identity politics fixation on the invisible spiritual economy has not received the attention it deserves. The predominant account of identity politics today treats identity as if it pertains to differing *kinds* of people. This sort of analysis misses much. It has been long understood—as early as the 1830s, when Tocqueville wrote about it—that as we become more disconnected and our lives get smaller in the democratic age, the temptation to make distinctions between others and ourselves grows. When we are lost in the lonely crowd, we look for ways to distinguish ourselves. Our imagination wanders, and our pride demands more than numbing anonymity. Surely, we are more than a flickering soliloquy that emerges out of nothing and returns to the dust. To escape this fate, is it any wonder that so many Americans today turn to genetic-testing services like 23andMe in the hope of discovering who they really are? We do not want anonymity; we want to be somebody. Services like 23andMe tells us who we are. We are a little of this *kind* and a little of that *kind*.

§7. This need to have something that defines us and distinguishes us from the crowd is an important development, and certainly contributes to the fracturing of our politics. Loneliness and anonymity, however, are not the only reasons for the popularity of services like 23andMe. In addition to telling us about the larger kind of which we are an instance, we also want the assurance that some marker of our inheritance provides immutable proof that in the invisible economy from which we cannot escape, we can be counted among the innocents rather than among the transgressors.[7] The need, so amply documented since the 1960s, to stand out from the lonely crowd,[8] to express our individuality, is today intermixed with—if not eclipsed by—another need: the need to be counted as a member of an innocent group within the invisible economy of transgression and innocence on which identity politics fixes. Identity politics is not about who we are as individuals; it is about the stain and purity associated with who we are as members of a group.

§8. Identity politics is not satisfied with the Christian account that there will always be an imbalance of payments that only God can redress through His infinite mercy. Identity politics demands a complete accounting, so that the score can be settled once and for all—or, if it cannot be settled, then held over the head of transgressors like a guillotine, in perpetuity. That is why establishing what one group owes another is central to the identity politics enterprise. The complete accounting that is needed requires ongoing investigations that clarify just how stained the transgressors are, and how pure the innocents are. This now seems to be the singular task of our colleges and universities, which have thoroughly renounced their ancient charge,

7. See "Holiday Special," YouTube video, 1:11, posted by South Park Studios, September 25, 2017, https://www.youtube.com/watch?v=gKxtXzAgGew.

8. See David Riesman, *The Lonely Crowd: A Study of the Changing American Character* (New Haven, CT: Yale University Press, 1963).

dating from the founding of Plato's Academy in 387 BC, of assisting students in ascending from mere opinion to knowledge and wisdom. Once many of our American colleges and universities were Christian. Increasingly embarrassed by this, over the course of the nineteenth and twentieth centuries, they adopted the Greek ideal of knowledge and wisdom. Now in the twenty-first century, they have returned to the Christian fixation on transgression and innocence.[9] The new version of this Christian fixation, however, makes no allowance for the long-standing Christian way of understanding either transgression or innocence—namely, as a relationship first and foremost between God and man. God is nowhere to be found in the identity-politics accounting scheme. Neither is forgiveness, which would erase the score altogether, and leave us with no scores to settle. Defenders of identity politics often claim to be egalitarians concerned about existing inequalities; yet who among them, I wonder, could actually endure the radical equality that would result if we were to erase the debt and innocence points that we are now told, in the most precise terms,[10] we owe or are owed, and meet one another unencumbered, face to face? Perhaps Christians who actually understand the fantastic claim that regardless of their kind, they are all equally *adopted sons and daughters of God* could do that.[11] Identity politics, notwithstand-

---

9. See Steven B. Gerrard, "The Rise of the Comfort College: At American Universities, Personal Grievances Are What Everyone's Talking About," Bloomberg, "Opinion," September 9, 2019, https://www.bloomberg.com/amp/opinion/articles/2019-09-09/free-speech-is-no-longer-safe-speech-at-today-s-elite-colleges?__twitter_impression=true.

10. See "Intersectionality Resources," Intersectionality Score Calculator, n.d., https://intersectionalityscore.com/lcarn. The site states: "We encourage you to learn more about the growing movement of intersectionality and how to use it in your daily lives. It is also important to teach our young people how to categorize people quickly by their intersectionality. This way, they won't become racist, homophobic, Islamophobic, sexist, or have other undesirable thoughts."

11. See John 1:12; Gal. 4:4–5; Eph. 1:15; and Heb. 2:10–13.

ing its debt to Christianity and its surface profession of faith both in equality and in the sanctity of the individual, wants only a hierarchy of transgression and innocence. Here is the tribalism that awaits us, based on our purportedly permanent inheritance of stain and purity. Christian radical equality—hoped for but not yet implemented on Earth—is, through its identity politics stepchild, currently being supplanted by a strange sort of antiegalitarian *spiritual eugenics*, according to which the pure and innocent groups must ascend and the stained transgressor groups must be purged.

§9. Other religions also use the language of purity and stain, of transgression and innocence, but our long familiarity with Christianity in America means that the invocation of these categories within identity politics derives from Christianity, and from Protestantism in particular. Most of this book is concerned with the deeply deformed relationship between identity politics and Protestant Christianity. Surveys may indicate that Americans have lost or are losing their religion; however, the fever of identity politics that now sweeps the nation suggests these surveys are looking in the wrong place and asking the wrong questions. Americans have not lost their religion. Americans have relocated their religion to the realm of politics.[12] The institutional separation of church and state may be largely intact, but the separation between religion and politics has largely collapsed. More precisely, with respect to the matter of presumption of guilt and innocence, they have traded places. Once, because of the doctrine of original sin, there was a presumption of guilt in the churches, and because of our legal history, a presumption of innocence in the realm of

12. An excellent treatment of the way in which American Protestant culture has not disappeared but rather taken up residence elsewhere can be found in Joseph Bottum, *An Anxious Age: The Post-Protestant Ethic and the Spirit of America* (New York: Random House, 2014). See also James A. Morone, *Hellfire Nation: The Politics of Sin in American History* (New Haven, CT: Yale University Press, 2004).

politics. Today, the abandonment of the doctrine of original sin has had the curious effect of lifting the burden of guilt in the churches—and of shifting it to politics. Whatever the law may say about our innocence, the presumption of identity politics is that man—or rather the white, heterosexual man—is guilty.[13] This is a dangerous reversal of legal norms that in the Anglo-American world took centuries to develop and take hold.

§10. The "identity politics of innocence," as I call it throughout this book, has transformed politics. It has turned politics into a religious venue of sacrificial offering. Ponder for a moment the Christian understanding of sacrificial offering. Without the sacrifice of Christ, the Innocent Lamb of God, there would be no Christianity. Christ, the Scapegoat, renders the impure pure—by taking upon Himself "the sins of the world." In purging the Divine Scapegoat, those for whom He is the sacrificial offering are purified. Identity politics is a political version of this cleansing, for groups rather than for individual persons. The scapegoat identity politics offers up for sacrifice is the white, heterosexual man. If he is purged, its adherents imagine, the world itself, along with the remaining groups in it, will be cleansed of stain. Without exception, every major action item of the Democratic Party today is traceable to this supposition. The Democratic Party pushback against national borders; its unwavering insistence that fundamental political and economic transformations are necessary to address climate change; its disgust with "dirty" fossil

13. See Wesley Yang, "America's New Sex Bureaucracy," *Tablet*, September 24, 2019, https://www.tabletmag.com/jewish-arts-and-culture/291105/americas-new-sex-bureaucracy: "[We have before us today an] ideology [that] is a successor to liberalism. It brandishes terms that superficially resemble normative liberalism—terms like *diversity* and *inclusion*—but in fact seeks to supplant it. This new regime, in which administrative power has been fashioned into a blunt instrument of deterrence, marks off a crucial distinction—between the liberal rule of law, and the punitive system of surveillance rooted in identity politics known as 'social justice.'"

fuels; its demand for wealth redistribution; and its resolve that every mediating institution in which citizens gather must be altered so as to become "inclusive"—all of these have at their root the supposition that the nation-state, market commerce, the petrochemicals that fuel it, the conventional generative family, our civic institutions, and our religious institutions are unclean or obsolete because of the hand white, heterosexual man has had in building and maintaining them.

§11. We can and should talk about the pressing issues before us. Self-government requires nothing less. Substantive deliberation cannot occur, however, if adherents of identity politics are animated by the angry need for *catharsis*, as the desire to scapegoat always involves. Calling someone a "racist," "misogynist," "homophobe," "transphobe," "Islamophobe," "fascist," "Nazi," "hater," "denier," or any such name *is* cathartic. These words carry with them the power to banish and to exile. Once they have been uttered, the comportment of both the accuser and the accused visibly changes. The accuser beams with the iridescent light of discharged rage; the accused slinks into the darkness, shamed by the leprosy of his irredeemable stain. An unbridgeable chasm between the two has opened; they now stand on opposite sides of an impenetrable border wall within a community they were both members of a few short minutes ago. Identity politics adherents declare that *visible* borders between nations should be abolished. There will always be borders, however; abolish them in one place and they will emerge in another. Identity politics erects *invisible* borders between the pure and the stained. Too many of the political declarations we hear today intend only to banish fellow citizens. Neither conversations about nor actions taken in response to our pressing problems are possible if the deeper purpose of a political program—perhaps even more important than the political program itself, *which is but a pretext*—is to purge a group or humiliate its members into silence. However enfeebled today, Christianity has burned itself into the soul of Western man and, for now at least, holds us back from the real impetus beneath identity politics, which is actual group purgation. We will see what the future brings. Christianity's deepest insight, perennially violated by Christians themselves, is that no mortal group can cover over the sins of another group. Historically understood, this insight is a staggering breakthrough, so rare as to be exceptional, since most of human history bears witness to the conviction that the catharsis of group scapegoating *does* restore the cleanliness of the community. Writing nearly a century before Tocqueville, Jean-Jacques Rousseau noted in 1759 that prior to the advent of Christianity,

> political war was also theological war: the dominion of the gods were, so to speak, determined by the boundaries of nations. . . . Far from men fighting for gods, it was, as in Homer, the gods who fought for men.[14]

By this, Rousseau meant to give some indication of the rage that scapegoating another nation once involved. So cathartic was its ecstatic revelry that gods had to be invoked as a cause. Christianity, he mournfully declared, put an end to that, and had diminished politics ever since. Perhaps Rousseau was premature in his assessment that the ancient gods have died away.[15]

§12. We find ourselves at a remarkable impasse. Identity politics wishes to return us to the unexceptional condition, the pre-Christian condition: One group—in its current formulation, the white, heterosexual man—is avowed to be *the* transgressor. All others—women, blacks, Hispanics, LGBTQ persons—have their sins of omission and

---

14. Jean-Jacques Rousseau, bk. 4, "The Social Contract," chap. 8 in *The Major Political Writings of Jean-Jacques Rousseau*, trans. and ed. John T. Scott (Chicago: University of Chicago Press, 2012), 264–65.

15. See R. R. Reno, *Return of the Strong Gods: Nationalism, Populism, and the Future of the West* (New York: Gateway Editions, 2019).

commission covered over by scapegoating this group. Set against this is the exceptional Christian understanding that man's transgression, his "sin," is "original." This means it is always-already-there *before* any lineage or inheritance constitutes him as a *kind*, and therefore that group scapegoating cannot absolve him of his impurity. Hide quietly behind your "identity" if you wish; your anxiety about your own transgressions will not dissipate. Displace your anxiety by relentlessly aiming the arrow of accusation outward at other groups; the haunting specter of transgression will not disappear. Its source is deeper than identity politics comprehends.

§13. The arrangement that identity politics specifies has placed the scapegoated white, heterosexual man in a curious position, indeed. In order to escape cathartic rage, he must prove his innocence by virtue-signaling[16]—or more accurately, by *innocence*-signaling—his support for various social justice causes, so that he, like other groups of innocents, can be covered with righteousness. Only when covered in this way does the cathartic rage that brings social death *pass over* him and settle elsewhere, as it must. The Hebrews of ancient times were told by God that death would pass over their houses, and no one in their households would die, if they marked their front doors with the innocent blood of a slain lamb.[17] Today in America, the white, heterosexual man must reenact a version of that innocence-signaling liturgy if social death is to pass over him. Jews in America celebrate Passover once a year; if cathartic rage is to pass over the white, heterosexual man, he must celebrate the identity politics version of that liturgy daily, by displaying signs of inno-

16. The term "virtue-signaling" does not capture what is really occurring. The task within identity politics is not to demonstrate virtue but to demonstrate innocence. Virtue is a category of Greek origin; innocence is a category of biblical origin.

17. See Exod. 12:13: "And the blood shall be to you for a token upon the houses where ye are: and when I see the blood, I will pass over you, and the plague shall not be upon you to destroy you, when I smite the land of Egypt."

cence on his front door—or, more likely, his office door—for all to see. If you doubt this, wander through the university and college buildings in America that house the offices of our professors. You will soon discover ample evidence of this strange identity politics Passover ritual. Decals that declare, "This office is Green"; pictures of Foucault; dated posters announcing Martin Luther King Jr. Day celebrations; an announcement about upcoming "Diversity Training"; yet another *New York Times* article taped to a professor's office door that thinly masks its hatred of President Trump—if you display these symbols of your innocence, or of your sympathy with the innocents, social death will surely pass you by. The displays on the office doors of corporate America are no different.

Try as he may, however, the circumstance that the white, heterosexual man can never alter is this: because of his permanent transgressive status, he begins with a deficit of "innocence points," and must fight his way back to a zero balance, which is as far as he can ever advance. In the Garden of Eden, Adam hid behind a fig leaf. In identity politics, the white, heterosexual man can attempt to hide behind the fig leaf of social justice to find temporary reprieve; but the leaf is see-through, and his nakedness is always visible for all to see. In the Garden of Eden, God could see Adam's nakedness. So, too, can members of groups that identity politics counts among the innocents see the nakedness of the white, heterosexual man. Like God, they also declare his irredeemable guilt.

§14. By alerting the reader to the theological perversity of replacing the Divine Scapegoat of Christianity with the all-too-mortal white, heterosexual man as the scapegoat, I am *not* saying that the white, heterosexual man is innocent, as many who claim they are on the Alt-Right declare. Far from it. If anything, as the careful reader has already discovered, I wish to save the category of transgression, in all its depth, and I fear that both identity politics and the Alt-Right will end up stripping the category of its profound Christian significance, which will deprive us of hope. On the contrary, I am saying that in the world that identity politics constructs, the white, heterosexual man becomes more than who he really is. He becomes a member of a scapegoated group that takes away the sins of the world, rather than being a mortal of mixed inheritance, like everyone else, involved in transgression and searching for redemption. The deepest mystery of transgression and innocence cannot be understood by focusing our attention on groups. That is the Christian claim. That was Martin Luther King Jr.'s claim. That is the claim made in this book as well. No one group is unequivocally pure or stained; and without the ability to establish such purity, just who the transgressors are and who the innocents are is impossible to determine. Identity politics stands or falls on the claim that groups are unities of transgressors or innocents; and that the invisible spiritual economy from which we cannot escape can be understood in terms of the purity or stain that inheres in each visible group.

§15. Throughout this book, I contrast the identity politics of innocence with "the liberal politics of competence." Over the years, my colleagues at Georgetown and elsewhere have reminded me that the term "liberal" now belongs to the political left; and that the only political alternative to the Left in America today is captured by the term "conservative." I stubbornly refuse to heed their admonitions because I think retrieving the liberal alternative to the identity politics of the Left and to the conservative politics of the Right can provide the only way out of our current morass. Since the French Revolution in 1789, the Left has wished to start over; hence its relentless attack on *inheritance*, broadly understood. Identity politics is the latest version of that attack. Edmund Burke's *Reflections on the Revolution in France* (1790) is the founding text of the conservative movement in America, precisely because of its compelling defense of inheritance. There is much to recommend in Burke, his book, and the conservative moment. Contrary to the claims of the Left, we cannot live without our inheritance.

Something is missing, however, in setting the French Revolution against Burke, and leaving it at that. Are these the only two alternatives: either an infinitely plastic world that has no necessary continuity and that man shapes in the image of his dreams (and his nightmares), or a fixed and identifiable inheritance from which man can securely build a durable world and which is free enough from fault that he can sleep well at night? Before the French Revolution prompted Burke to give the self-conscious defense of inheritance that is today the basis of conservatism, there was a nascent body of liberal thought that had a more mysterious and providential view of human affairs. In this view, historical development and inheritance are not so adamantly opposed. Here, man sees his past, present, and future "through a glass darkly."[18] He does not have the power or authority to shape history according to his will, nor can he fully understand the mixed inheritance that binds him. On this view, we build *from* our mixed inheritance *toward* a historical culmination we can neither wholly understand nor control. This humility about what we can know and what we can do has important liberal institutional implications. Because the institutions of society are the places where our inheritance is both fortified and challenged, the power of the state should intervene rarely, as its interventions are invariably heavy handed and clumsy, even when undertaken with the best of intentions. In the institutions of society, citizens develop the competence they need to fortify those societal institutions and to modify them. Our mixed inherited past and any number of possible futures converge in the deliberations and actions of competent liberal citizens, who build a world together. When the state steps in too often or too strongly, it undermines or destroys the liberal competence that we today so earnestly need.

§16. Many writers in the last half century have seen the danger that the administrative welfare state poses to liberal competence. They

18. 1 Cor. 13:12.

have proposed political and legal remedies to address it: free markets, small government conservatism, a return to federalism, a judiciary steeped in an understanding of the original intent of the Founders, and so forth. My approach stands apart in that it reckons that there is no expressly political or legal remedy to our problem. Identity politics reflects a confusion in our understanding about where the categories of transgression and innocence may properly be worked through. The identity politics of innocence is a wager that these categories belong in politics, and that the liberal politics of competence, now over three centuries in development and possibly at its end, which would attend to merit and developed competences alone, has conscience against it. How such a conclusion has been reached, and the implications of that conclusion, not least for black Americans, who are betrayed by it, occupy a significant portion of this book. This sort of investigation, more than prescriptive political or legal remedies, is the antidote needed to overcome the immense temptation of identity politics today. When our understanding changes, our politics will change.

§17. Upon completing what would have been a short, dense book on the inner logic of identity politics, it became apparent that merely proclaiming the need to return to the liberal politics of competence would not be enough. Identity politics is a formidable impediment to the return of liberal competence; but even if the fervor and enthusiasm of identity politics were to dissipate tomorrow, and Americans were to wake up and discover that they had been deceived by it, they would not return to health. Two immense obstacles would remain. Here, too, there is no expressly political or legal remedy for these obstacles. Citizens themselves are going to have to awaken to the challenges these obstacles pose—or not.

§18. The first obstacle that stands in the way of the return to liberal competence is what our psychologists and medical experts call "bipolarity." In the twentieth century, it was known as "manic depression." Long before the invention of the field of psychology at the end of the nineteenth century, or before medical science concluded that man can be understood in terms of his brain chemistry, there were other ways of understanding the problem. I will say more about them later in the book. For reasons I will explain, I consider man's bipolarity within the framework of what I call "management society and selfie man." Liberal competence is undermined by the former because of its presumption that all or our problems are too big for man to solve with his neighbors, and must be handed over to the global managers of his fate. In such moments, man feels small, impotent, and worthless. Liberal competence is undermined by the latter because selfie man has no neighbors with whom he *needs* to solve his problems. He is unfettered and alone. In moments like these, he feels grand, indefatigable, immune from harm, and so invincible that he is reckless in what he says to and about others. This, too, is a threat to liberal competence, which can only be developed with others, in real time. The configuration of management society and selfie man presumes that such competence is not necessary for man's health and well-being. Management society and selfie man is an arrangement, anticipated by Tocqueville long ago, in which democratic citizens feel themselves to be "greater than kings and less than men."[19] This bipolar arrangement—in which, in exchange for the freedom we gain through social media to become selfie man, we renounce our liberty to address problems with our fellow citizens—is one of the defining characteristics of the post-1989 experiment. An entire generation of young Americans has grown up oscillating back and forth between feelings of extraordinary grandeur and utter impotence. One minute they make plans to "change the world" or "save the planet." The next minute they are overwhelmed by a world so frightening and difficult to negotiate that they text message their friends rather than call them—in fear that an unscheduled call will

19. Tocqueville, pt. 4, chap. 6 in *Democracy in America*, vol. 2, 694.

be too much for either party to endure. This bipolar arrangement, increasingly lived out by the young and old alike, can be ameliorated only by face-to-face, real-time relations between citizens in the institutions of society. Drugs that treat bipolar disease or manic depression or whatever our healthcare professionals will call it next can mask the symptom, but they cannot cure the disease. We do not have a brain chemistry problem; we have a problem of human association. Pharmacology can offer supplements that help us begin to confront the disease, but we go too far when we believe that pharmacological remedies can substitute for a cure. "Pharmacological substitutism," to coin a phrase, was the world Aldous Huxley gave us in his 1931 novel, *Brave New World*.[20] We would do well to go back and reread the book. Citizens enthralled by management society and selfie man, however, will likely see the real antidote they need—building a world of liberal competence together with their fellow citizens—as a poison from which they must flee. When we are ill, we are seldom drawn to the antidote that cures us, and instead seek palliatives that keep us alive without really bringing us back to life. This is a problem with no straightforward remedy.

§19. The second obstacle that stands in the way of the return to liberal competence is addiction. Here, too, I will sidestep the assessments offered by our psychologists and medical experts and treat this illness as more ancient and venerable authors did—as what I will call, "the problem of supplements becoming substitutes." No recent writers have written about this as a general problem, though very many have written about its myriad, seemingly unrelated manifestations. These include: the opioid epidemic that is ravaging America; the exponential explosion in the number of empty plastic water bottles that will soon overwhelm us; the uptick in global obesity rates; declining birth rates and the increasing attentiveness to sexual

20. See Aldous Huxley, *Brave New World* (New York: Everyman's Library, 2013).

substitutes for the generative family; the empty promise of social media; the demolition of brick-and-mortar retailers by Amazon; the dubious value of online education; our fixation with Google Maps and driverless cars; the claim that the digital world can fully supplant the analog world; the empty hope that government alone can heal the wound of slavery and its aftermath, can guide the relations between the sexes with Title IX legislation, and can supplant citizen stewardship with environmental regulations; the dreamy view that national borders need no longer be observed; the belief that fiat currency does not invite staggering debt; and the misplaced longing to become global citizens. Every one of these developments, and more, should be understood as an instance in which a supplement has been turned into a substitute, an *addiction* in a more capacious sense. There is an immense temptation to turn supplements into substitutes, which cannot be overstated. When we succumb to this temptation, liberal competence is lost or degraded. Here, too, there is no political or legal remedy that will cure the general problem or its specific manifestations. The cure requires the sober recognition that when citizens turn supplements into substitutes, our immediate, ecstatic, addictive satisfaction is soon met—as the opioid addict well understands—with an emptiness that always follows. There are no shortcuts. Political and legal action may temporarily block us from taking them, but without getting to the root of the problem, closing off one shortcut will be followed by taking another.

§20. In the course of writing *American Awakening: Identity Politics and Other Afflictions of Our Time*, the one image that has illuminated the whole is that of *homo, ex ingenio celeritas quaesitor*: "the creature man, who always looks for shortcuts." This problem had already been identified in the Hebrew Bible.[21] Readers of Plato's *Republic* may also recall that Socrates tells his impatient interlocutors that there is no

21. See Exod. 13:17.

shortcut to the Good.[22] We only get to where we really need to go by taking the longer way. Eight hundred years after Plato, St. Augustine, one of the great Christian fathers, noted that because of his transgression, man could not by himself return to God—but that through Christ Incarnate, man was granted a shortcut back to God the Father.[23] In a historical irony befitting the creature man, who always looks for shortcuts, identity politics finds the Christian shortcut *too difficult to endure*, for it demands that man be hard on himself and admit both his stain and his inability to remove it without Divine assistance. The various shortcuts identity politics offers do not require that man be hard on himself; they only require that the white, heterosexual man be hard on himself.[24] The rest are innocents, who find a shortcut to purity by scapegoating him. Alas, once he has been purged, someone else—a former innocent—*must* take his place.

That is not the end of the matter, however. Management society and selfie man is a shortcut as well. The difficult labor of liberal citizenship can only be performed in community with others—not the

22. See Plato, bk. 6, 504b, 504c, and 533a in *The Republic*, trans. Richard W. Sterling and William C. Scott (New York: W. W. Norton, 1985).

23. See St. Augustine, bk. 9, chap. 15 in *City of God*, trans. Henry Bettenson (New York: Penguin Books, 1984), 361.

24. White, heterosexual men of the Left, who manage to feign guilt but expect others to pay the price, are the exception to this requirement. See William Voegeli, "Their Sin, Your Penance," *American Mind*, April 22, 2019, https://americanmind.org/features/justice-that-aint-it-chief/their-sin-your-penance/: "There are no known examples of any white liberal giving up a tenured professorship or syndicated column so that the vacancy may be filled by a member of an oppressed, under-represented minority group. Though tormented by complicity in the oppression of victims, white liberals reliably devise penances that will be performed by other people. Their ferocity in denouncing housing discrimination, for example, is matched by their resourcefulness in keeping low-income housing out of liberal enclaves like Marin County, California." See also Zach Goldberg, "America's White Saviors," *Tablet*, June 5, 2019, https://www.tabletmag.com/jewish-news-and-politics/284875/americas-white-saviors.

abstract universal community that is effortless to join, but the everyday community in which we actually live. The thoughts, words, and deeds we undertake in our actual communities offer ample evidence that we are less pure and more stained than we would like to imagine. The shortcut offered by management society and selfie man allows us to avoid that demoralizing realization. Through this shortcut, we achieve repose not by the hard work of building a world with others, but by bypassing that difficult labor altogether.

By turning supplements into substitutes, we find a shortcut, too. The problem of replacing supplements with substitutes, we will discover, is akin to the problem of replacing the meal with vitamins. We can take the latter to supplement the meal, but not as a substitute for it. We always must return to the meal, to the hard work of developing competence—whether it be the literal competence of cooking for and with our family or the development of competence beyond the confines of the household.

That we hunger for this meal is beyond question. Liberal competence alone can provide the meal and sate the hunger. The vexing question is why we nevertheless continue to opt for the hollow, addictive satisfactions associated with turning supplements into substitutes.

§21. Readers of *American Awakening: Identity Politics and Other Afflictions of Our Time* may wonder if I despair of the future after writing a book declaring not only that America is in the midst of an identity politics religious fervor that imperils it, but also that even if identity politics died down tomorrow, two immense obstacles would remain. To despair would be to admit that liberal competence is irretrievably lost. If I despaired, I would not have written this book in the first place. The title, *American Awakening*, in fact, carries a double meaning. On the one hand, it suggests that we are in the midst of a faux religious revival that can no more cure our illness than our exponentially increasing dependence on drugs can cure us of bipolarity and addiction. On the other hand, it suggests that we may be on the verge of awakening from the slumber into which we have fallen as a result of identity politics, bipolarity, and addiction, and retrieving the satisfactions of liberal competence toward which I have pointed in these pages. I am hopeful—indeed, expectant—that the latter possibility is the real state of things.

PART ONE

Identity Politics:
Transgression and Innocence

A. THE STAIN OF OUR INHERITANCE

§1. Americans are a rough-knit community of individuals, forever re-inventing ourselves and losing sight of our past. Taking the long view, this is a rather exceptional state of affairs. For the most part, the human race has divided into nations, with long and binding histories. In the Hebrew Bible, there is mention of seventy nations.[1] Ancient history is the tale of heroic actions, undertaken with a view to defending the nation.

§2. In America, we often confuse the terms "nation" and "state," and lose sight of the meaning of nation altogether. The state we understand; we call our state our own because we are citizens within it, who have never-ending arguments about representation, law, policy, consent, voting, legitimate authority, and so on. To bring the state to life and to sustain it, we must constantly think and talk about these issues. Because of the ongoing need among citizens to think and talk with one another, the state is a fragile affair, held together moment to moment, as the long and turbulent history of the United States attests. The state can be undone. That is why we have laws against sedition.[2]

§3. The nation is different. The Latin word *natio*, from which we derive "nation," literally means "birth," which is to say, that from which

1. See Gen. 10:1–32.

2. The Alien and Sedition Acts were passed by the Federalist Congress in 1798, and signed into law by President John Adams. The Sedition Act of 1918 covered a broader array of offenses of speech deemed threatening to the government.

we receive our inheritance. We consent to being a citizen of our state, but we consent neither to being born nor to the time and place of our birth.[3] Some of us were born here in the United States, for example; others were not. Some of us can trace our lineage back many generations in this country. Those of us who cannot—I count myself partly among them[4]—often carry the weight of our more ancient inheritances from another nation or nations for several generations, which, with the passing years, is lifted as we come to feel ourselves more and more "American." In three generations or so, the work is generally done.[5]

§4. Exactly when the weight of an inheritance lifts from our shoulders is not easy to establish. Reasonable people will disagree on this point. One of the main characteristics of modern life, in fact, is that our inheritance is in perpetual danger of being overshadowed by the anxious light we shine on the present and the future. Alexis de Tocqueville, the great French philosopher who visited America in the early nineteenth century, saw the problem long ago. Americans flee their inheritance and rush headlong into the future:

3. Like our genetic makeup, along with all the visible markers of that makeup, our initial membership in a nation is not a matter we agree to but rather abide by.

4. My father's family were immigrants from what is now Lebanon in the 1890s. My mother's family were immigrants from Wales, Holland, and Germany in the 1730s.

5. The Hebrew Bible seems to confirm this figure. See Deut. 23:7–8. The exceptions to this rule are members of second- and third-generation diaspora communities who have not assimilated in their host countries. Never having lived in the nations from which their families emigrated, they tend to develop enchanted understandings of those nations; and dreamy, dangerous critiques of their host country. The most insightful work on diasporic communities remains that done by Yossi Shain: *Marketing the American Creed Abroad: Diasporas in the US and Their Homelands* (Cambridge, UK: Cambridge University Press, 1999).

Americans cleave to the things of this world as if assured that they will never die, and yet are in such a rush to snatch any that come within their reach, as if expecting to stop living before they have relished them. They clutch everything but hold nothing fast, and so lose grip as they hurry after some new delight.[6]

§5. It is worth remembering, especially in America, that in other parts of the world, nations—inheritances—are still very much alive and binding. Because equality is so important to us in America, we tend to think of other people around the globe as *persons*, without predicates, who have no inheritance, and who are "just like us." The most important work of political theory in the second half of the twentieth century—*A Theory of Justice*, written by John Rawls—is premised on our American intuition that we can build a just political community with citizens who have no history.[7] Only in America. In the rest of the world, on the contrary, most citizens acknowledge that the inheritance of their nation still binds them. Reasonable people will disagree about how intact that inheritance is, and even about what that inheritance is—but in America we often unreasonably conclude that inheritance is not binding at all.

§6. Throughout history, then, the human race has divided itself into nations, into different *kinds* of peoples, having different inheritances. As recently as the 1960s, we identified ourselves as distinct kinds of people, without the need to use additional terms. "He is Lebanese." "She is French." This was not limited to political distinctions alone; we also treated religion this way. "He is Protestant." She is "Roman Catholic." Ethnic distinctions—prone to historical drift and imagi-

6. Tocqueville, pt. 2, chap. 13 in *Democracy in America*, vol. 2, 536; cf. Prov. 22:28: "Remove not the ancient landmark, which thy fathers have set."

7. See John Rawls, *A Theory of Justice* (Cambridge, UK: Cambridge University Press, 1971).

native construction—were handled in the same manner. "He is Phoenician." "She is Viking." Racial distinctions, too.

§7. As we entered the 1990s, however, a new term became ubiquitous in our everyday vocabulary: "identity." As a philosophical term,
identity has a long history. David Hume famously wrote about it in
A Treatise of Human Nature (1739),[8] with a view to showing just how
transitive personal identity was. Sigmund Freud, whose monumen-
tal book *Civilization and Its Discontents* (1930)[9] is a classic in the academic literature of psychology, would seem to be a work very much
concerned with identity. He, like Hume, saw the fragility of human
ego, but never once uses the term identity. In Freud's framework,
the agonistic wrestling match between the id, ego, and superego,
which raised doubts about where the self begins and ends, seemed
not to require the term at all. Erik Erikson's *Identity and the Life
Cycle* (1959)[10] is among the first works in which the term identity is
used systematically in the psychological literature; but there, too,
his concern was the *instability* of the self throughout the life cycle,
especially in the transition from adolescence to adulthood. Our
use of the term during the 1990s and since that time has not indicated something transitory and fragile, but rather something firm
and irrefutable. The term now has this more self-assured meaning
whenever it is used. Instead of being "Lebanese," I might instead
proudly announce, "My identity is Lebanese"; "my gender identity
is male"; "my religious identity is Protestant"; "my ethnic identity is

8. David Hume, "Of Personal Identity," bk. 1, pt. 4, sec. 6 in *A Treatise of
Human Nature*, ed. David Norton and Mary Norton (Oxford: Clarendon
Press, 2007), 164–79.

9. Sigmund Freud, *Civilization and Its Discontents*, trans. and ed. James Stra-
chey (New York: W. W. Norton, 1961).

10. Erik H. Erikson, "The Problem of Personal Identity," chap. 3 in *Identity
and the Life Cycle* (New York: W. W. Norton, 1959), 108–76.

Phoenician"; and so on. What is going on here? Why add the term identity at all, when to a generation before, it seemed so unnecessary—indeed inappropriate, since it indicated something unstable rather than firm and irrefutable?

§8. The first answer is that in its more innocent and innocuous usage today, the term "identity" is simply the verbal upgrade and fashionable equivalent of what we once recognized the term "kind" to mean. Because the meaning of identity morphed from referring to something unstable to referring to something stable, we can understand why it came to be synonymous with the notion of a stable kind. On that basis, many Americans today declare that they have an American identity. Bearing this meaning in mind, when critics suggest that the term identity is unnecessary or pernicious, the response often heard is that people have had identities for all of human history, and that it is therefore impossible to eliminate the word. This response is understandable—but only when identity is synonymous with kind, and has no further meaning.[11]

§9. The second answer is that the term "identity" has another and more radical meaning, which is fundamentally different from "kind." Without this more radical meaning, the term probably never would have taken hold in the 1990s in the first place. I am speculating here, but it seems plausible that the innocent usage of the term identity, which today pertains to relatively stable kinds, is downstream of its more radical meaning, because it was only through its

11. See Mark Lilla, *The Once and Future Liberal: After Identity Politics* (New York: HarperCollins, 2017). Lilla's account of identity politics is of this sort. His complaint to the left is that the Democratic Party has fractured into multiple kinds, and that, unlike the old (pre-1968) Democratic Party, there is no longer anything that can gather these kinds together. Lilla's courageous internal critique is among the most earnest attempts on the left to figure out where the Democratic Party went awry.

radical meaning that the term identity came to mean something stable rather than unstable, which is in keeping with the domestication that generally happens to all radical ideas.[12] This evolved meaning of identity involves not so much a specification of a *kind* but a specification of a *relationship*. More importantly, the relationship is of a specific type, with discernible religious overtones: the unpayable and *permanent* debt one kind owes another. In America and in Europe, we know which groups identity politics declares to be the debtors and which groups it declares to be the creditors. To think clearly about the framework of identity politics, rather than becoming overwhelmed by the current attributions that haunt us all, I will use the more exotic examples I have thus far relied on for illustration. When identity is a mere proxy for kind, Lebanese identity might be considered one kind and French identity might be considered another kind, and nothing more need be said. A distinction is made, and that is all. When identity takes on this second meaning, something fundamentally different is involved. Lebanese and French identities now stand in a relationship to each other: one is the offending transgressor; the other is the innocent victim.

---

12. A good example of the domestication of a radical idea is what happened with the term "value." Today we accept that everyone has "values," and that no one person's values—religious or otherwise—are superior to another person's values, because everyone is essentially equal. Yet Friedrich Nietzsche introduced the term in the late nineteenth century to *undermine* the idea of equality that Christianity upheld. He did this by attacking the Christian claim that there is an objective order that authorizes the equality of all persons (see Friedrich Nietzsche, 3rd ess., sec. 27 in *On the Genealogy of Morals*, trans. Walter Kaufmann and R. J. Hollingdale [New York: Random House, 1967], 160). No revolutionary author wholly transforms society; to the contrary, the society in which he operates generally ends up appropriating his terms and warping his meanings, sometimes even to the extent that the terms come to mean the opposite of what he intended. Many of those who follow Nietzsche today are, unwittingly, *halfway revolutionaries*, who draw heavily from him—and misunderstand him. The same is true for those who claim to follow Karl Marx.

Moreover, the transgressor and innocent victim confront each other with these standings not just for the moment of their current encounter, but *permanently*. Like the stain of original sin that marks Adam and all his progeny, the transgressor is permanently marked. He himself may have done nothing to contribute to transgressions that predated him by decades or even centuries. Little matter. He *stands for* the sum of the transgressions linked to his identity. Pressing Christian imagery further, though distorting it immensely, like Christ, the transgressor *stands in* as a scapegoat[13] for those who purport themselves to be innocent, but who know in their hearts that they are not wholly so. The transgressor thereby covers over[14] their stains, so that no judgment against them may be rendered.

§10. This second understanding of identity is more often what we mean today when we speak about identity politics. Identity politics has no single proponent; it is less a single theory than a large genus within which all theories of innocent victimhood are species, because all of them invoke the relationship between transgression

---

13. The social and theological ramifications of the "scapegoat" have been developed and illuminated nowhere more profoundly than in René Girard, *I See Satan Fall like Lightning*, trans. James G. Williams (Maryknoll, NY: Orbis Books, 1999). Much of what follows relies on the framework Girard lays out. The Hebrew root of the idea warrants our immediate attention. Lev. 16:1–34 are the passages in which the scapegoat first appears. The scapegoat takes upon itself the sin of the entire community, and is then sent out into the desert so that the community may be reconciled and made pure.

14. "Covering over" has biblical overtones that cannot be ignored. See Ps. 91:4: "He shall cover thee with his feathers, and under his wings shalt thou trust." God "covers" the brokenness of man. In the New Testament, the covering takes the form of the blood of Christ, which by virtue of covering the sinner, washes his sins away. See 1 John 1:7: "And the blood of Jesus Christ His Son cleanseth us from all sin." In identity politics, the offering is the white, heterosexual man, whose symbolic sacrificial blood covers the sins of all others, so that they may be seen as innocents.

and innocence.[15] Identity politics began penetrating our vernacular in the 1990s, and since that time, and at an ever-escalating pace, more and more groups have self-consciously claimed that they, too, have an identity—with a view to revealing the transgressions that they, the *invisible innocent ones*, have suffered. Had Hillary Clinton won the 2016 presidential election, it is not improbable that she would have followed through with the Obama administration's plan to recognize MENA—people, like members of my father's family, of Middle Eastern and North African descent—as a group identity, distinct from whites, and therefore to be counted among the innocents rather than among the transgressors. By definition, we cannot now imagine the groups who will be counted among the innocents in the distant future, because the nature of the undertaking involves making visible a currently invisible group. The exercise is instructive, however, not least because it lays down a marker by which we can measure how unawares we will be caught in the future.

In the quasi-religious world of identity politics, innocent victims alone are hallowed; they alone receive what could be called debt-point recognition, by which I mean credits in the invisible economy of transgression and innocence. The rest of us—however much our legal, economic, or social status might otherwise indicate—have no legitimate voice. Indeed, our penance as transgressors is to listen to the

---

15. See Martin Buber, pt. 1 in *I and Thou*, trans. Ronald Gregor Smith (New York: Macmillan, 1987), 3: "Primary words do not signify things, but they intimate relations." Buber's distinction is helpful. The term "identity" signifies *things* when used as a proxy for "kinds." The term signifies a *relationship* within the rubric of identity politics. In Buber's framework, identity is sometimes a primary word and sometimes not. Buber distinguished between things and relations, with a view to indicating that justice between men exceeds any calculus of payment. Identity politics, as I indicated in sec. 5 of the preface, recognizes the invisible economy of transgression and innocence, but applies it to groups, which are things.

innocents,[16] and our lay responsibility in the identity politics liturgy is to assent to the right of the innocents to tear down the civilizational temple they say we the transgressors have built over the centuries—paid for, as it has been, not simply with money but with the unearned suffering of the innocents. Whatever the innocents wish to accomplish in politics is legitimate because the *real basis* of political legitimacy now is innocence.[17] The past belongs to the transgressors, who today

16. Emblematic of this *demand* for recognition by innocent victims is an exchange chronicled in the Yale University courtyard on November 15, 2015. See "Public Shaming MOB Demand Groveling Apology from Yale Professor," YouTube video, 12:32, posted by Gravitahn, March 5, 2017, https://www.youtube.com/watch?v=iAr6LYC-xpE. See also Michael Brendan Dougherty, "The Church of Grievance," *National Review*, April 26, 2018, https://www.nationalreview.com/magazine/2018/05/14/victim-mentality-identity-politics-dominate-modern-left/.

17. What made political arguments so charged during the Obama administration is that those who opposed the president's policies were often called "racist." What does the term mean? Through reckless use, it has become almost useless. It has had no stable meaning over time, which makes an easy answer impossible. In the American context, the term first appeared in 1902 in a report written by Richard Henry Pratt for the twentieth annual meeting of the Lake Mohonk Conference. Pratt, a founder and longtime superintendent of the Carlisle Indian Industrial School in Carlisle, Pennsylvania, used the term to indicate a detrimental separation of the races. He proposed to erase this separation by immersing the American Indian fully into the broader Anglo culture. A decade earlier, he had famously declared, "Kill the Indian in him, and save the man" (*Official Report of the Nineteenth Annual Conference of Charities and Correction*, reprinted in Richard H. Pratt, "The Advantages of Mingling Indians with Whites," in *Americanizing the American Indians: Writings by the "Friends of the Indian," 1880–1900* [1892 (report); Cambridge, MA: Harvard University Press, 1973], 260–71, at 260.) For us today, the term "racist" has a very different, quasi-religious meaning. Thinking about the term with a view to the issues I hope to clarify here, a racist is *someone who scapegoats a victim*, in the belief that by directing his cathartic fury toward the victim, the society of which he is a part will purge itself of its poison and return to health. Political argumentation is difficult if not impossible when it is unclear whether what is at issue are "interests" or the will to scapegoat a victim. For the most part, the mainstream media treated criticisms of President Obama's plans and policies

are an archaic holdover and an embarrassment. The future—politically, economically, and socially—belongs to the innocents. Little wonder
that the prime transgressors—white, heterosexual men—who, in the
world that identity politics constructs can have nothing important to
say,[18] eventually wonder if *they, too,* have been victims, and begin cata-
loging their own wounds. Hence, the recent emergence of what might
be called a "men's Me Too movement," which presumes that the right
to speak to and with other innocent victims hangs on the unearned
suffering men have also endured through the ages.[19]

---

as the scapegoating of an innocent victim—as an act of racism—rather than
as postracial disagreements with a president and his administration about
what courses of action to take. The difficulty of distinguishing political argumentation from scapegoating an innocent has increased during the Trump
administration. This debilitating situation in which political argumentation
is no longer possible will end only when the identity politics of innocence is
replaced by the liberal politics of competence. President Obama was, in a
way, correct: We must become a postracial society. He thought that arrangement would usher in a postpolitical society, as well. Instead, a postracial society—a post–identity politics society—is what will make it possible to return
to properly political argumentation.

18. In 1988, Stanford became the first top-tier US university to remove the
works of "dead white men" from its core curriculum. Other universities followed. Today, teaching the Western canon remains under assault, because
of the writings of the dead white men in it. See part 1, n. 61.

19. The emerging grievances that men list are legion. With respect to the
criminal justice system: men have a lower chance of posting bail than
women; men go to prison at a higher rate and are treated worse in prison
than women; men are punished more harshly for the same crimes; men
have higher rates of solitary confinement; men serve a higher percentage
of their prison sentence. With respect to divorce: adjusted for income,
men make higher alimony payments; men receive a lower rate of custody
of children after divorce. With respect to education: men underachieve
in their K–12 education; men attend college at a lower rate, and graduate
at a lower rate. With respect to death: men have a lower life expectancy,
by five years, in most developed countries; men are more likely to engage
in "risky" behavior (cigarette smoking, heavy drinking, gun use, employment in hazardous occupations); men are twenty times more likely to die

§11. I will offer more nuanced accounts later (in sections 23, 26, and 27), but looking back at the period from the 1960s to the 1990s, and painting with a broad brush, a number developments contributed to the emergence of identity politics in America. First, the collapse of the mainline Protestant churches shunted the idea of transgression and innocence from religion into politics. Second, the extension of the black American template of innocence[20] to other groups after the civil rights era served a growing class of political brokers, who benefited from speaking on their behalf. Third, the discovery by the academic left in America of European postmodern thought

---

in a work-related injury; men have a higher rate of suicide; men are more likely to die from a violent gun or knife crime; men "suffer" because tobacco and alcohol are marketed more toward them. With respect to physical violence: men endure a higher rate of corporal punishment in childhood. With respect to war: men are forced by law and by societal pressure to fight and die in war; male "gendercide" has been practiced throughout history as a way of subduing populations. As veterans: men suffer higher rates of homelessness, suicide, PTSD, and drug addiction. With respect to employment: men are "forced" to work for pay in capitalist economies more than women are; women might be paid lower rates for the same work while being concerned with breaking through the glass ceiling, yet almost all of the thankless work done "below ground"—in mining, utilities, fishing, and excavation—is done by men. For an even more comprehensive account of the victimhood of men, see RealSexism.com.

20. By "template of innocence," I mean not simply the *fact* of black American slavery, but the long invisibility of black Americans that took place after the Civil War put an end to legal slavery, followed by their emerging visibility—due in no small part to television—during the civil rights era. The innocent suffering of the invisible ones *was finally made visible*. I will consider the Christian basis for this template in due course. Here, I am noting that this most egregious instance of invisibility in American history became the basis for subsequent groups to make their own claims, as logical extensions of the black American case. On the matter of visibility and invisibility, see Ralph Ellison, *Invisible Man* (New York: Random House, 1952). See also Joshua Mitchell, "Seizing the Crown of Thorns," *First Things*, January 2020, https://www.firstthings.com/article/2020/01/seizing-the-crown-of-thorns.

provided a framework more powerful than Marxism for attacking the legitimacy of historical inheritance and for distinguishing who is stained from who is pure.[21] Identity politics has now incorporated itself into the heart of the Democratic Party. The Democratic Party is not, however, the source of identity politics. To justify being heard in America today, you and I must demonstrate our special standing as innocent victims. Having demonstrated that, we can take our place in the political firmament and become activists, committed—in our hearts, but seldom in our recurrent daily actions—to "social justice."

There is much to say about this, but before delving more deeply into why identity politics has taken hold, and what it does to and in the body politic, I will pause to consider what identity politics purports to repudiate—namely, the liberal idea of the competent citizen. This brief historical excursion into liberal thought will help bring to light the stark difference between what I will call the "liberal politics of competence" and the "identity politics of innocence." Through the former, we can build a world together; through the latter, we cannot. Liberal thought has been more than three centuries in the making. Identity politics has been with us for less than a generation. We need to keep this in mind as we ponder the future. The liberal politics of competence requires our never-ending difficult labor in a mixed world of purity and stain; the identity politics of innocence asks only that we cover ourselves with the fig leaf of innocence, and leave it to the state to allocate resources to the innocents and their causes.

---

21. The metahistory that Marx proposed, which declared that the historical stage of capitalism would be replaced by the posthistorical stage of communism, could no longer be defended after the fall of the Berlin Wall in 1989. Postmodernism *denies* that there is a metanarrative of history, and in its stead gives us only contesting narratives without a larger meaning. In postmodernism, everything is contested, and those who defend the idea of a grander historical coherence illuminated by their inheritance do so from positions of usurped power.

B. THE COMPETENT LIBERAL CITIZEN

§12. Our current experiment with identity politics departs significantly from the earlier liberal idea of who citizens are and what
they do to build a community with others. Much criticism has been
heaped on liberal thought right from its inception because it aims
too low—because it rests, more or less satisfied, on the idea that we
must build a political and economic community not on the foundation of the noble virtues espoused in the ancient world, but on
self-interest, and the everyday citizen competence it presupposes.
Jean-Jacques Rousseau offered the first scathing criticism of this liberal idea in 1751.[22] Contemporary critics have not let up.[23] Set against
noble virtue, modest self-interest seems the clear loser. We should
not forget, however, that liberal thought did *not* emerge from the
search to replace virtue, but from the search for an alternative to the
untamed, disruptive, cathartic passions of religious war. In the aftermath of the violence of the sixteenth and seventeenth centuries,
early liberals concluded that setting their sights lower would bring
peace and a measure of prosperity. As Voltaire put it in 1733:

> Go to the London Stock Exchange—a more respectable place than
> many a court—and you will see representatives from all nations
> gathered together for the utility of men. Here, Jew, Mohammedan
> and Christian deal with each other as though they were the same
> faith, and only apply the word infidel to people who go bankrupt.[24]

22. See Rousseau, "First Discourse," in *Major Political Writings of Jean-Jacques
Rousseau*, 26: "The ancient politicians spoke constantly of morals and virtue; ours speak only of commerce and money."

23. See Patrick J. Deneen, *Why Liberalism Failed* (New Haven, CT: Yale University Press, 2018). Deneen is among the most trenchant of cultural critics
writing today.

24. Voltaire, letter 6 in *Letters on England*, trans. Leonard Tancock (New
York: Penguin Books, 1980), 41.

A few years later, in 1748, Baron Charles de Montesquieu published *The Spirit of the Laws*, the first truly modern book of political science, and the one most cited by the American Founders.[25] He, too, saw the capacity of commercial self-interest to tame and civilize man:

> Commerce cures destructive prejudices, and it is an almost general rule that everywhere there are gentle mores, there is commerce and everywhere there is commerce, there are gentle mores.[26]

In his 1814 essay "The Spirit of Conquest and Usurpation," Benjamin Constant elegantly articulated the liberal idea that self-interested commerce can supplant the aristocratic longing for glory. Here, a world exhausted by the cathartic ecstasy of war chooses a more pacific course.

> We have finally reached the age of commerce, an age that must necessarily replace that of war, as the age of war was bound to precede it. War and commerce are only two different means to achieve the same end: that of possessing what is desired. Commerce is…an attempt to obtain by mutual agreement what one can no longer hope to obtain through violence.… War then comes before commerce. The former is all savage impulse, the latter civilized calculation. It is clear that the more the commercial tendency prevails, the weaker must the tendency to war become.[27]

---

25. See Donald S. Lutz, "The Relative Influence of European Writers on Late Eighteenth-Century American Political Thought," *American Political Science Review* 78, no. 1 (March 1984), 189–97.

26. Charles de Montesquieu, pt. 4, bk. 20, chap. 1 in *The Spirit of the Laws*, ed. Anne M. Cohler, Basia C. Miller, and Harold S. Stone (Cambridge, UK: Cambridge University Press, 1989), 338.

27. Benjamin Constant, pt. 1, "The Spirit of Conquest and Usurpation and Their Relation to European Civilization," chap. 2 in *Political Writings*, trans. and ed. Biancamaria Fontana (Cambridge, UK: Cambridge University Press, 1988), 53.

Finally, in 1835, in the capable hands of Alexis de Tocqueville, we find, under the broad heading of democratic government, the definitive understanding of the liberal commercial and political aspiration, juxtaposed to its alternative:

> What do you expect from society and its government? We must be clear about that. Do you wish to raise mankind to an elevated and generous view of the things of this world? Do you want to inspire men with a certain scorn of material goods? Do you hope to engender deep convictions and prepare the way for acts of profound devotion? Are you concerned with refining mores, elevating manners, and causing the arts to blossom? Do you desire poetry, renown, and glory? If in your view that should be the main object of men in society, do not support democratic government; it surely will not lead you to that goal. But if you think it profitable to turn man's intellectual and moral activity toward the necessities of physical life and use them to produce well-being, if you believe that reason is more use to men that genius, if your object is not to create heroic virtues but rather tranquil habits, if you would rather contemplate vices than crimes and prefer fewer transgressions at the cost of fewer splendid deeds, if in place of a brilliant society you are content to live in one that is prosperous, and finally, if in your view the main object of government is not to achieve the greatest strength or glory for the nation as a whole but to provide for every individual therein the utmost well-being, protecting him as far as possible from all afflictions, then it is good to make conditions equal and to establish democratic government.[28]

Liberal thought *does* aim lower. The turn to self-interest nevertheless makes possible something undreamed of in an earlier age: a modest

---

28. Tocqueville, pt. 2, chap. 6 in *Democracy in America*, vol. 1, ed. J. P. Mayer (New York: Harper & Row, 1969), 245.

middle-class commercial regime attentive to well-being, in which the people, rather than a war-craving monarch or aristocracy, are sovereign.[29]

§13. Many critics note this lower aspiration of self-interest, and pronounce summary judgment against liberal thought on that basis. They miss the larger picture. Self-interest does more than tame man's passions; it brings him into a new and creative relationship with others. Voltaire's observation that people of different religious *kinds* need not clash if they lower their sights and find common ground based on their interests announced the new liberal aspiration. Man can rise above his kind just enough to build a world with others, who (whatever their kind may be) also have interests—something that would have been impossible to accomplish if kinds were the only thing that mattered. Some liberals have gone too far, and claimed that man can rise above his kind altogether.[30] Their claim has obvious political implications for us today. In modern-day America, we argue, for example, about the legitimacy of borders, and about what sort of immigration policies we should have in place. Many of us presuppose that there are no kinds at all, just universal humanity. The sober liberal will acknowledge the constraint that inheritance imposes—yet also not lose hope. A vast collection of different kinds cannot move from their home nation into another without

29. See Immanuel Kant, sec. 2 in "Perpetual Peace," in *On History*, ed. Lewis White Beck (New York: Macmillan, 1963), 94: "If the consent of the citizens is required in order to decide that a war should be declared (and in a [republican] constitution it cannot but be the case), nothing is more natural that they would be very cautious in commencing such a poor game."

30. The line of liberal thought that emerges from Immanuel Kant's sharp distinction between autonomy and heteronomy makes this sort of claim. The most notable twentieth-century work that traces this line of thinking is John Rawls's *A Theory of Justice*. Later in life, Rawls came to understand that kinds cannot be completely done away with. See John Rawls, *Political Liberalism* (Cambridge, MA: Harvard University Press, 1993) for a consideration of the sort of understanding of justice that is likely to be plausible among the Anglo-American people.

confusion, adjustment, and—yes, some measure of *forgetting* the national inheritance each of them leaves behind. Assimilation not only takes
time; it requires a host of formal and informal institutional provisions
to ease immigrants into their new national life.[31] Liberal thought nevertheless holds to the hope that there is a workable policy, somewhere between maintaining a porous border and maintaining an impermeable
one, that will allow and encourage citizens within the borders of a liberal state to rise *just enough* above their still-lingering inheritances to build
a world together, through self-interest. We can argue about how much
is just enough, but it seems clear to me that without this sort of understanding, a workable immigration policy will evade us and we will be
enticed by extreme and untenable alternatives: on the one hand, having
no borders, because there is no such thing as kinds; on the other, having
impenetrable borders, because kinds are so different that they cannot
develop relationships based on liberal self-interest at all.

§14. We should be clear eyed about what this liberal aspiration to
self-interested citizenship requires of us, for I fear we have lost sight
of it. Already, as early as the mid-seventeenth century, when it became obvious that the ancient virtues were dangerously intermixed
with the violent passions of war, liberal thinkers understood that if
the self-interest with which they wished to replace ancient virtues
was to be salutary, it had to involve something more robust than
self-satisfied citizens who imagine themselves to be the center of the

---

31. Aside from state-sponsored programs, in America these provisions
include churches and synagogues, religious schools for children, worker
unions, immigrant enclaves that provide an initial "safe space" for those
who have no working knowledge of English, informal lending organizations for small business start-ups, and more. Together, such provisions in-
augurate the type of transformation that no one fully understands but that
everyone feels when they undergo it—namely, the replacement of one home
with another. For a sober assessment of the costs to immigrants of replacing their ancient home with a new one, see Norman Podhoretz, "Making It:
The Brutal Bargain," *Harper's Magazine*, December 1967.

world and who feel good about themselves just the way they are.[32] *That, alas, is what the liberal aspiration has been transposed into for so many today*. Had that been all that self-interest involved when it emerged centuries ago, the liberal aspiration would have never succeeded in the fantastic way that it has. Early liberal thinkers who defended self-interest understood that mere self-satisfaction would be fatal to the body politic. The self-interested citizen had to be pulled out of himself, so to speak, so he could build a world with others.

§15. Attempts within liberal thought to address this issue abound. Because man always thinks that his own estimation of justice is inerrant, and therefore wants others to accede to his prideful judgments, Thomas Hobbes wrote in 1651 that a powerful sovereign must arbitrate between citizens who live in their own self-referential worlds.[33] Because man wishes not cooperation and compromise but rather "subordination and subjection," John Locke wrote in 1689 that men must attend to the law of nature that declares their natural equality, and that binds them to obey it.[34] Because man prefers the self-satisfied life of an "Arcadian shepherd," Immanuel Kant wrote in 1784 that, against his will, man has been thrown into never-ending competition with others—the end of which is *not* happiness but rather

---

32. Friedrich Nietzsche, whose loathing for liberal thought is evident on nearly every page he wrote, agreed with more thoughtful liberal thinkers in one decisive respect: along with them, he observed the decay and degeneracy of the self-enclosed citizen who is content with himself. See Friedrich Nietzsche, sec. 5, "Zarathustra's Prologue" in *Thus Spoke Zarathustra*, trans. Walter Kaufman (New York: Modern Library, 1995), 16–19; this section discusses "the Last Man," who longs for nothing, endures no hardship, and cannot imagine taking great risks.

33. See Thomas Hobbes, pt. 1, chap. 5, sec. 3 in *Leviathan*, ed. Edwin Curley (Indianapolis: Hackett, 1994), 23.

34. See John Locke, secs. 4–5 in "Second Treatise of Government," chap. 2 in *Two Treatises of Government*, ed. and intro. Peter Laslett (Cambridge, UK: Cambridge University Press, 1988), 269–70.

an achieved competence that alone grants him the dignity he earns.[35] Because man in the democratic age is prone to isolation and withdrawal, Tocqueville wrote in 1840 that without local, face-to-face relations that draw him out of himself, liberty will be lost.[36] In these cases and more, *isolated citizens are understood not to be citizens at all*, but rather subjects of pride, solipsism, and self-aggrandizement.

§16. These examples, to bring this brief historical excursion to a close, suggest that liberal self-interest is much more capacious than its critics allow. Liberal citizens are oriented by self-interest; but liberals immediately add that because isolated citizens are not citizens at all, their self-interest must be fashioned in and through relations with others, in the fora of family, religious institutions, voluntary associations, local political life, and civil society. This, Tocqueville called, "self-interest properly understood." In his words:

> I am not afraid to say that the doctrine of self-interest properly understood appears to me the best suited of all philosophical theories to the wants of men in our times and that I see it as their strongest remaining guarantee against themselves. Contemporary moralists therefore

35. See Kant, 3rd and 4th theses in "Idea for a Universal History with a Cosmopolitan Intent," in *On History*, 13–16. This attention to competence, increasingly absent in us today, is probably what Tocqueville (pt. 1, chap. 3 in *Democracy in America*, vol. 1, 57) had in mind when he wrote, "There is indeed a manly and legitimate passion for equality which rouses in all men a desire to be strong and respected." Tocqueville's concern in that passage is the *other* form of equality he worried would befall America in the future: the equality in servitude, in which willingly infantilized citizens renounce their liberty in preference for an all-providing state that makes them feel good about themselves.

36. See Tocqueville, pt. 2, chap. 5 in *Democracy in America*, vol. 2, 517: "[In America] knowledge of how to combine is the mother of all other forms of knowledge; on its progress depends that of all others. . . . If men are to remain civilized or to become civilized, the art of association must develop and improve among them at the same speed as equality of conditions."

should give most of their attention to it. Though they may well think it incomplete, they must nonetheless adopt it as necessary.[37]

Because the success of liberalism hangs on this idea, we cannot parse these sentences too carefully. Self-interest properly understood is "best suited" to liberal citizens. That is, we can argue interminably about whether this statement is *true*; what we cannot argue about, however, is that we live in a world now where man is self-referential, and that, as a consequence, self-interest is what we have to work with. It is "the strongest remaining guarantee against themselves." That is, self-interest properly understood, *not virtue*, is the best way to avert the peril of individualism. "They may well think it incomplete." That is, let us admit, with the ancients, that virtue may have produced a higher man. "They must nonetheless adopt it as necessary." That is, ancient virtue is no longer available to the inhabitants of our age, so let us do what we can in this diminished age to build a world with what is at hand.

For the liberal, the task is not to distinguish among the transgressors and the innocents, as identity politics does, but to recognize the limits by which the democratic age is constrained, and to work within them to allow neighbors and fellow citizens to build a world together. Identity politics, in fact, *allows and encourages* citizens to withdraw into themselves—to become "selfie man," as I will describe this condition later (in entry N). The contrast could not be starker: within the liberal politics of competence, citizens *need* one another; in the identity politics of innocence, they do not.

C. MODEST LIBERAL ASPIRATIONS

§17. So just what *is* at hand? For the liberal, what is at hand in this diminished age, in which self-interest properly understood must be

37. Pt. 2, chap. 8 in ibid., 527.

our guide, is our fellow citizens and the natural world from which together we wrest what we need to build a middle-class regime, dedicated to well-being.

§18. *Can liberal citizens know the future?* No, they cannot. That is why there must be interminable arguments about its content and contour—and why markets, elections, and vibrant social institutions provide them with provisional answers about the present and future, but no final verdict. Justice is *an ongoing question*, not a definitive answer that closes off further argument, as "social justice" has become today. For the liberal, each and every moment, no matter how fixed it may seem, is a temporary equilibrium inviting adjustment, compromise, and action—after which liberal citizens resume arguing, without end, and improving their lot as they go. The future *emerges*. Because the future cannot be known until it actually arrives, liberal citizens doubt that the farseeing plans of "experts" will get them there any better, or get them there at all.[38] Liberal citizens are even more dubious of claims by these so-called experts that no further improvement is possible because the cost to the planet of these endless and inefficient small steps forward is too high. For the liberal citizen, there is no postcompetitive, post-political age in which the global task is to redistribute wealth and political power under a settled but never defined schema of social justice, overseen by global managers.[39] The version of social justice set forth by global managers, no matter how comprehensive, will always be sterile. Tocqueville saw already in 1840 that in the dem-

---

38. See Adam Smith, bk. 1, chap. 2 in *The Wealth of Nations*, vol. 1 (Chicago: University of Chicago Press, 1976), 17: "[The production of wealth is] not the effect of human wisdom." That is, no person or small group can know, in advance, how to employ capital and labor most productively.

39. See Joshua Mitchell, "Age of Exhaustion," *American Interest* 11, no. 2 (Nov./Dec. 2015), 53–64, https://www.the-american-interest.com/2015/10/10/age-of-exhaustion/.

ocratic age, comprehensive schemes intended to bring about the end of history would emerge, and that these schemes would seek to gather all the disparate threads of humanity into one great whole:

> Men think that the greatness of the idea of unity lies in the means. God sees it in the end. It is for that reason that the idea of greatness leads to a thousand mean actions. To force all men to march in step toward the same goal—that is a human idea. To encourage endless variety of actions but to bring them about so that in a thousand different ways all tend toward the fulfillment of one great design—that is a God-given idea. The human idea of unity is almost always sterile, but that of God is immensely fruitful. Men think they prove their greatness by simplifying the means. God's object is simple but His means infinitely various.[40]

The liberal citizen understands that man's far-reaching schemes always end in wretchedness, because they supplant, with abstract theories, the living facts on the ground through which the plurality of human associations has emerged and actually operates.[41] The

40. Tocqueville, app. 1, Y in *Democracy in America*, 734–35.

41. The wreckage from twentieth-century social-engineering schemes is well known. The most fragile communities are the first ones to succumb. According to Robert L. Woodson: "There are powerful social, economic, and political institutions that have a proprietary interest in continued existence of the problems of the poor, the denial of solutions, and the portrayal of low-income people as victims in need of defense and rescue. These powerful interest groups include members of the civil rights establishment, a massive poverty industry that owes its existence to the problems of the poor, and politicians who are aligned with them. They are the modern-day equivalents of the Pharaoh's court counselors who view . . . Joseph's ability to heal people and solve their problems as a threat to their domain of 'expertise'" (Robert L. Woodson Sr., chap. 1 in *The Triumphs of Joseph: How Today's Community Healers Are Reviving Our Streets and Neighborhoods* [New York: Free Press, 1998], 12). Woodson's argument is that local communities have within themselves the resources to heal their wounds.

world is comprised of many nations and states, each of which is *a competing wager about the future*. There is plurality within these nations and states as well. That is why liberal citizens defend market commerce, federalism, and social institutions that are relatively independent of both commerce and politics. In these different domains—society, commerce, and politics—competing wagers about possible alternative futures *emerge*. Liberal citizens understand that they cannot know the future in advance. That is why they organize their social, economic, and political institutions the way they do.

§19. *Can liberal citizens know themselves?* No, not really. They always remain "a problem to themselves,"[42] sure of who they are at one moment, unclear or lost the next, guided more often than not by their habits and familiar interests rather than by self-conscious ideas. Compounding this problem of an absence of true internal harmony and self-clarity is the blur of the world around them. If life stood still, if roles in society were fixed, some measure of assurance would be theirs; but when life is constantly on the move, and roles are treated with irony or scorn, liberal citizens are left disoriented and often without compass. They long for an assurance that exceeds their grasp.

In the swirl of a life always in motion, citizens are tempted to withdraw into the secure confines of their undisturbed imagination, and from there invent distinctions that cordon them off from others, so that they may establish a fixed frame of reference that no worldly commotion can dislodge.

> In democracies, where there is never much difference between one citizen and another, and where in the nature of things they are so close that there is always a chance of their all getting merged

42. St. Augustine, bk. 4, chap. 4 in *Confessions*, trans. Henry Chadwick (Oxford: Oxford University Press, 1991), 57. See also bk. 10, chap. 33, 208, in ibid.: "I have become a problem to myself"; and Tocqueville, pt. 1, chap. 17 in *Democracy in America*, vol. 2, 487.

in a common mass, a multitude of artificial and arbitrary classifications are established to protect each man from the danger of
being swept along in spite of himself with the crowd. . . . However energetically society in general may strive to make all citizens
equal and alike, the personal pride of each individual will always
make him try to escape the common level, and he will form some
inequality somewhere to his own profit.[43]

Surveying the broad sweep of Western history, for centuries God
gave man a fixed point of reference, and national inheritance did as
well. Tocqueville understood that when God and nation recede, as
they do in the modern age,[44] a stand-in would likely emerge. "Imagined and arbitrary classifications" with ready-made, bullet-point[45]
attributes provide that stand-in. "My identity is American, male, of
Lebanese and Phoenician origin. My afflictions and foibles, around
which you must orient yourself in order for me to recognize you, are
this, *this*, and *this*."

Once tariffs were a material affair, intended to protect a nation's
interior commerce. Identity politics spiritualizes the ancient practice of collecting tolls; it establishes interpersonal tariffs, intended
to protect the identity bearer's fragile interior.

The liberal citizen is impatient with this imaginary indulgence.
Imagined markers are, at best, a shorthand and a convenient point

43. Tocqueville, pt. 3, chap. 13 in *Democracy in America*, vol. 2, 605.

44. For Tocqueville, God recedes because middle-class anxiety (about
which, more in sec. 21) fixes the attention of citizens in the modern age on
the material world (see Tocqueville, pt. 2, chap. 11 in *Democracy in America*,
vol. 2, 533). The idea of the nation recedes as well, because of the general
suspicion of inheritance in the modern age (see pt. 1, chap. 1 in ibid., 429).

45. Nothing more distinctly characterizes young adults who have been im-
mersed, Achilles-like, in the River Styx of identity politics than that the
first thing so many of them do to disclose their invulnerability to argument
is confess the bullet-point attributes they think define them.

of departure, perhaps a way to begin a conversation, not a way to end one—as identity politics almost invariably does. Once liberal citizens enter into conversation with their fellows, they discover that their shorthand account of themselves is woefully inadequate; and that shorthand accounts are generally obstacles to improving their lot together, because they declare not what citizens might do together but rather why they are separate and must remain so.

Speaking theologically for a moment, confessions of this sort are not made for the benefit of fellow liberal citizen-parishioners at all; they are, instead, supplications to the higher power of the state, offered up as evidence of a suffering that is deserving of relief. This arrangement does not presuppose that liberal citizens work together in freedom, but rather that isolated citizen-subjects, servile and floundering, must ask the state for mercy, which identity politics promises to deliver, through governmental assistance earmarked for just them, the sanctified. The liberal citizen looks outward to his fellows to build; the citizen-subject looks upward to the state to receive.

§20. *Can liberal citizens know one another?* No, not really. Unless they engage in regular, real-time conversations, a caricatured depiction of their fellow citizens will emerge in their imagination,[46] which will grow proportionally more egregious the more that citizens grow apart. When they do not need one another to secure their well-being, when the state promises cradle-to-grave security,[47] or when social media provides virtual communities that insulate them from

---

46. So subject to corruption is man's imagination that the Hebrew Bible offers it as the cause of the Great Flood. See Gen. 6:5: "And God saw that the wickedness of man was great in the earth, and that every imagination of the thoughts of his heart was only evil continually." See also Rom. 1:21.

47. See the Obama-era video "Life of Julia" (YouTube video, 2:10, posted by Stina Starry-Eyed, June 13, 2015, https://www.youtube.com/watch?v=o-qBjXP8RKho).

one another, what reason do citizens have to cast the caring glance toward other people and to rein in the ideas of their fellow citizens that exist in their imagination? Without that glance, political polarization increases. By every measure where imagined distinctions could become more acute—political, economic, religious, cultural, ethnic, national, sexual—they do become more acute. Without *practical* engagement, citizens lose the art of engaging; if their imagination temporarily rests, it is not because they have been put at ease by the work they are doing with their fellows, but because they have excised their fellows from their lives altogether.

Citizen-subjects today are burdened with the caricatured categories that have developed and calcified. The more they are "cared for," cradle-to-grave, by the helicopter parent–like state, the more their imagination is bound to wander. Isolated and on their own, of course, no two citizen-subjects will imagine their fellows in quite the same way. There may be a real world out there, but alone and isolated, they will not see it in the same way. Under these circumstances, "human opinions are no more than a sort of mental dust open to the wind on every side."[48] Their imaginings will therefore be inchoate and ephemeral—unless and until they are named, given form, and brought to life by the opinion shapers of the world: family, educational institutions, political parties, the news and entertainment media, special interests, authoritative leaders, and the state itself.[49] And brought to life they

48. Tocqueville, pt. 1, chap. 1 in *Democracy in America*, vol. 2, 433.

49. See James C. Scott, pt. 1, chap. 1, in *Seeing like a State: How Certain Schemes to Improve the Human Condition Have Failed* (New Haven, CT: Yale University Press, 1998), 22–23: "No administrative system is capable of representing *any* existing social community except through a heroic and greatly schematized process of abstraction and simplification. . . . State agents have no interest—nor should they—in describing an entire social reality. . . . Their abstractions and simplifications are disciplined by a small number of objectives." As citizens, our question should be: To what end does the state settle on its set of abstract categories?

have been. For Americans today, "white," "black," Hispanic,"[50] "male," "female," "*the* rich," and "*the* poor" are far from ephemeral dust. They are electrified categories, having immense, opposing charges. In contrived public settings, conversations between members of these groups are often painfully scripted, for fear that any departure will unleash misunderstanding or rage. Having few occasions actually to work together on matters of common concern, citizens say what is expected of them, then return to their private worlds, relieved that the awkward encounter is now behind them. Today, far too many citizen-subjects have passively settled in, strangely satisfied with the caricatured categories contrived on their behalf,[51] not because they know them to be true, but because the cost of undoing them is too high. They ask only that the awkward encounters they have with members of other groups be kept to a minimum, so that they only occasionally have to endure the painful disjunction between the ideas and feelings they know and feel but must muzzle, and the words they are compelled to publicly utter, in order to keep the peace. Like members of a deeply dysfunctional family, the chasm between their own inner life and the words they must say to hold together the fragile social unit that nominally nourishes them grows by the day.

50. See, for example, G. Cristina Mora, *Making Hispanics: How Activists, Bureaucrats, and Media Constructed a New American* (Chicago: University of Chicago Press, 2014), 159: "A sort of collective amnesia sets in as organizations begin to refer to the new category's long history and develop narratives about the rich cultural basis of the classification. By then, the category is completely institutionalized, and the new classification is, like other classifications, *assumed to have existed*" (emphasis added). For a comprehensive account of how government categories of persons have been invented for political purposes, see Mike Gonzales, *The Plot to Change America: How Identity Politics Is Dividing the Land of the Free* (New York: Encounter Books, 2019).

51. Plato described the mortal situation in a similar way in one of the most compelling fables of Western civilization, "The Allegory of the Cave." See Plato, bk. 7, 514a–520d in *The Republic*, 209–14. Unless the light of the Good illuminates man's vision, the opinion shapers, who convince man of what he is seeing by their lesser light, will enslave him.

Liberal citizens know better than to settle for such illusions. Liberal citizens are *active*, not passive. That is their antidote to caricatured categories. Like knowledge of the future, knowledge of their fellow citizens *emerges*, in this case, through actual face-to-face engagements with them. Formalities can and should inform their engagements. No choreographed plot, with characters imagined in advance, can anticipate how engagements will develop or what their conclusion will be.[52] As Tocqueville put the matter: "Feelings and ideas are *renewed*, the heart *enlarged*, and the understanding *developed* only by the reciprocal actions of men, one upon another."[53] Renewal, enlargement, expansion—by virtue of these, liberal citizens come to know and see one another in a new and unanticipated light. The categories "white," "black," "Hispanic," "male," "female," "*the* rich," and "*the* poor" are invariably *exceeded* by face-to-face encounters. Such encounters alone dispel the imposing power these categories hold over the isolated mind for as long as the memory of the encounter lasts or as long as the newfound association endures. Through these encounters, the world is made new. Somewhere between the inchoate caricatures invented by, and formed for, the passive solitary citizen-subject and the perspicuity, authenticity, and transparency for which romantics and lovers long, there lies the ever-developing knowledge liberal citizens can *actually have* of one another—which though incomplete is nevertheless workable and just enough to build a world together.[54]

52. See Michael Joseph Oakeshott, "The Voice of Poetry in the Conversation of Mankind," in *Rationalism in Politics: And Other Essays* (1947; London: Methuen, 1962), 488–531.

53. Tocqueville, pt. 2, chap. 5 in *Democracy in America*, vol. 2, 517 (emphasis added).

54. Tocqueville's treatment of poverty illustrates the limit and promise of what liberal citizens can know about one another. See Alexis de Tocqueville, pt. 2 in *Memoir on Pauperism*, trans. Seymour Drescher (Chicago: Ivan R. Dee, 1997), 60: "Individual alms-giving established valuable ties between rich and poor. The deed itself involves the giver in the fate of the one whose poverty he has undertaken to alleviate." Here, face-to-face relations attenuate the categories of "*the* rich" and "*the* poor," and humanize both parties, without asking that they become abiding friends.

D. WHO SHOULD BE HEARD?
OF COMPETENCE AND INNOCENCE

§21. *Should all liberal citizens be heard?* If politics is concerned with calling out transgression and declaring innocence, as is the case with identity politics, a great many will have to remain silent or be silenced. In such a politics, only the innocent really have a voice. Liberal citizens answer the question differently. They are concerned with building a world with others—from the local to the national level. Therefore, *all* who speak with a view to that project should be heard, without impediment or prejudice. Whatever *kind* they may be, their credibility as fellow citizens depends on the ideas and interests they bring to the ongoing conversation about how to build a world together.

Why, we should ask, is the liberal citizen so intent on building a world?[55] Tocqueville's account remains among the most compelling. When people are stratified by money and not patronage, as they are in America, something new under the sun appears: *middle-class anxiety*. In the aristocratic age, under a patronage system in which everyone had reciprocal obligations to those above and below them, subjects had some small assurance that they would not fall too far. They may have had various fears, but they did not have class anxiety. When patronage disappeared, this changed. Because in the democratic age nearly everyone will taste enough of the goods of life to know what it means to enjoy them, but almost no one will be secure enough in their possession of them that they will not fear losing what they have, anxiety is the great disease of our day. As Tocqueville saw it:

---

55. The theological answer is that man, having been implicated in the corruption of God's creation, wishes to actively participate in its stewardship and renewal. This kind of answer is especially important in the covenantal theology of the American Pilgrims and their heirs. Nowhere is this more apparent than in the American proto-environmentalism of the nineteenth century. See Mark Stoll, *Inherit the Holy Mountain: Religion and the Rise of American Environmentalism* (Oxford: Oxford University Press, 2015).

When distinctions of rank are blurred and privileges abolished, when patrimonies are divided and education and freedom spread, the poor conceive an eager desire to acquire comfort, and the rich think of the danger of losing it. A lot of middling fortunes are established. Their owners have enough physical enjoyments to get a taste for them, but not enough to content them. They never win them without effort or indulge them without anxiety.[56]

To ameliorate this anxiety, liberal citizens know they must turn toward their fellows with an outstretched hand. Manners between liberal citizens therefore must be "natural, frank, and open."[57] These manners, in turn, reinforce the trust without which a liberal polity devolves into despotism. The disposition to withdraw into the solitude and safety of the imagination I have already considered. The charge given to liberal citizens to actively build a world with others counteracts it. Liberal citizens accomplish this through self-interest and through labour,[58] the immediate objective of which is the manipulation of the material world for the sake of well-being, and the profound inner mission of which is the development of the problem-solving competence citizens need to exercise their liberty well with others.

§22. Identity politics is for many today the compelling alternative to competence-based, self-interested, world-building liberal citizenship. Identity politics proclaims that innocent victims must be heard, and that historical perpetrators of transgression must listen, regardless of the competences they possess. While seldom attacked directly, this

56. Tocqueville, pt. 2, chap. 10 in *Democracy in America*, vol. 2, 531.

57. Pt. 3, chap. 2 in ibid., 567.

58. See Locke, sec. 34 in "Second Treatise of Government": "God gave the world . . . to the use of the industrious and rational (and labour was to be his title to it), not to the fancy or covetousness or the quarrelsome and contentious."

fixation on innocence quietly undermines and supersedes the idea of liberal competence by altering our understanding of who can speak and why.[59] If the proportion of those who labor in a particular field does not correspond to the demographic make-up of America, the explanation must be that one or more identity groups has been scapegoated, silenced, and excluded.[60] In the world identity politics constructs, the appropriate question posed to and within a field is not how to recruit the most competent practitioners, regardless of their innocent victim status, but how to modify, or even erase, the field to achieve proportional representation.[61] We must, after all, avoid *embarrassment*—and too many transgressors in any one field is a moral embarrassment hard to publicly justify. When identity politics prevails, the legitimacy of a field is not correlated to its accomplishments, but rather to whether proportional representation has been achieved. That *is* its accomplishment.

59. In many translations of the New Testament, the words of Christ—the scapegoated Innocent One—appear in red, and require attentive listening to be truly heard. Identity politics is akin to a church service: silent listening to the "red letter" testimony of the innocent ones is required.

60. See Heather MacDonald, *The Diversity Delusion: How Race and Gender Pandering Corrupt the University and Undermine Our Culture* (New York: St. Martin's Press, 2018).

61. Within the broad field of political theory, the fate of the subfield of history of political thought is illustrative. Since its inception, that subfield has largely involved the study of Western political theory, the shorthand designation for which today, among its critics, is the study of "dead white men." It does not matter that Plato was Greek, that Aristotle was Macedonian, that St. Augustine was from present-day Algeria, that Hobbes was English, that Rousseau was Swiss, that Tocqueville was French, or that Nietzsche was German—or that each of these nations were at one time or another at war with each other. Western political theory is about dead white men. That is why in almost every university in America today, hiring in the subfield of the history of political thought is difficult to justify. The reason given is that "the voices of the silenced need to be heard." The subfield itself is unlikely to survive, not because there are not supremely competent scholars within it, but because the subfield is an embarrassment to those who wish to reorganize the entire university with identity politics in mind. See part 1, n. 18.

§23. It is important to pause here to ponder more deeply the conditions under which the criteria of innocence offered up by identity politics *could* supplant the liberal criteria of competence. Under what conditions might this novel account of who may be heard and who must remain silent emerge and be justified? Four considerations immediately come to mind, which build on observations I made earlier in section II. The first consideration of why identity politics has gained prominence, as I mentioned there, is that the collapse of the mainline Protestant churches shunted the idea of transgression and innocence from religion to politics. This intermixing and confusion between political and religious categories was an error that Tocqueville thought the Americans had avoided. In his words:

> In the moral world everything is classified, coordinated, foreseen, and decided in advance. In the world of politics, everything is in turmoil, contested, and uncertain. . . . Far from harming each other, these two apparently opposed tendencies work in harmony and seem to lend mutual support.[62]

This passage is worth attending to carefully. Religion and politics are not the same; they pertain to different domains of experience, and each has their own distinct grammar, categories, and vocabulary. They work well together when religion binds the moral imagination, by specifying how transgression and innocence operate in the invisible economy, and what we must do to abide by it. This then frees the practical imagination of liberal citizens to experiment and build in the visible economy. In mixing religion and politics together, the result is an unseemly and confused mess. When politics becomes a venue for establishing which groups are the transgressors and which are the innocents, we can expect that liberal citizens who believe that politics is a venue through which we may build a world

62. Tocqueville, pt. I, chap. 2 in *Democracy in America*, vol. I, 47.

33

together will be silenced—unless, of course, they can count themselves among the innocents.

It would stretch credibility to claim, as Tocqueville does, that America has ever completely separated religion and politics. Every upheaval of American society—the American Revolution, the Civil War, the social gospel movement, progressivism, the civil rights movement—has been inaugurated or assisted by religion. It stretches credibility even further, however, to claim that since the collapse of the mainline Protestant churches in the aftermath of the Vietnam War, America has "lost its religion." A 2012 Pew Research Center report concludes that religious "nones" are on the rise.[63] Going back further, Reinhold Niebuhr had already seen in 1941 that his life's work of bringing an understanding of original sin back to the mainline churches had failed.[64] What is missing from the analysis of this seemingly inevitable trend line pointing toward an America devoid of Christianity is the fact that although the dying mainline churches have increasingly abandoned the idea of original sin and the sacrificial atonement of the Innocent Lamb of God, the categories of transgression and innocence have migrated into politics and taken up residence. Identity politics *is* that migration. An ever-growing number of "nones" no longer attend church. Why should they, if they can find a seemingly compelling account of transgression and innocence in identity politics? Christianity has not disappeared from America; rather, the Christian categories of transgression and innocence have moved into politics—a development Tocqueville thought would lead to the complete paralysis of both politics and religion. Exactly this

63. See Pew Research Center, *"Nones" on the Rise* (Washington, DC: Pew Research Center, October 9, 2012), http://www.pewforum.org/2012/10/09/nones-on-the-rise/.

64. See Reinhold Niebuhr, preface in *The Nature and Destiny of Man*, vol. 2 (New York, Charles Scribner's Sons, 1941), 8. On why he failed, see Joshua Mitchell, "Is Christian Realism Enough?," *Providence*, July 19, 2019, https://providencemag.com/2019/07/is-christian-realism-enough/.

has happened. Politics in America today is haunted by the question, Are microaggressions or unconscious bias (if not overt racism) toward the innocents lurking in or beneath the so-called interests that liberal citizens—especially white, heterosexual male citizens—profess? There will be no return to the politics of competence, through which liberal citizens build a world together, as long as the religious categories of transgression and innocence that identity politics promulgates overwhelm the political category of self-interest, as they now do.

The second reason identity politics has become so formidable is that after 1989, it has appeared to many that the long labor of history, with its never-ending competition and war between nations, is at an end, so that we may ease up, or let off entirely, on the disciplining demand for competence. For all of history, as nation fought nation, the innocent have suffered and endured heartless cruelty. Now, at history's end, the lion must lay down with the lamb[65] and confess his transgressions. The final reckoning is at hand. In the 1989–2016 period from which we are now beginning to awaken, the nation was cast as an archaism, and an army of "conflict managers" emerged with a promise that great wars between nations need no longer break out.[66] The West, in short, entertained the illusion that history had ended and, *still under the sway of the Christianity it thought it had repudiated*, concluded that all the historical transgressions the West had incurred had come due and had to be judged. We need only slightly contort St. Augustine's prefatory remarks, written in 426 AD in his great work *City of God*, for identity politics to reveal itself as the twisted heir of his thought: "We, the innocent, await in steadfast patience, until justice returns in judgment; then, we will ascend over our enemies as the final victory is won and

65. Isa. 11:6.

66. For the sober-minded counterargument that few wanted to hear at the time, see Edward N. Luttwak, "Give War a Chance," *Foreign Affairs* 78, no. 4 (July/Aug. 1999), 36–44.

peace established."[67] Little wonder that in the Middle East, in South Asia, and in China—that is, in those places that Christianity never really cast its shadow—identity politics is something of a curiosity, because its end of history redemption-of-the-innocents seems quaint or foolish. Alternatively, in those regions, identity politics is an irksome reminder that any end-of-history thinking is a luxury in which only a hegemonic power can indulge. Only victors dream that history has culminated—*with them*.

The third reason identity politics has supplanted the liberal criteria of competence, at least in some portions of America, is illustrated through demographics. A scan of the 2016 electoral map on the next page reveals two Americas.[68] The division between the two sides has deep cultural roots, but the relatively recent advent of digital technology and communications networks has exacerbated it. There are any number of distinctions we can invoke to understand the division between the two sides. As shown on the demographic map, on the one hand, America has a "densitarian"[69] blue region. This region is well integrated into the global digital economy, with an hourglass pattern of wealth stratification and contains affluent "anywheres"[70] and low-wage service support workers, but few citizens in

67. St. Augustine, preface of *City of God*, 5. Any serious effort to untangle identity politics will require comparing the transliteration given here to what St. Augustine wrote and believed.

68. A more recent Brookings study suggests that the problem has only worsened since 2016. See Mark Muro and Jacob Whiton, "America Has Two Economies—and They're Diverging Fast," Brookings, September 19, 2019, https://www.brookings.edu/blog/the-avenue/2019/09/10/america-has-two-economies-and-theyre-diverging-fast/.

69. Michael Lind has put forward the helpful distinction between "densitarian" and "posturban." See Michael Lind, "The Coming Realignment: Cities, Class, and Ideology after Social Conservatism," *Breakthrough Journal*, April 28, 2014.

70. David Goodhart has put forward the helpful distinction between "anywheres" and "somewheres." See David Goodhart, *The Road to Somewhere: The New Tribes Shaping British Politics* (New York: Penguin Books, 2017).

County-Level Results of the 2016 Presidential Election

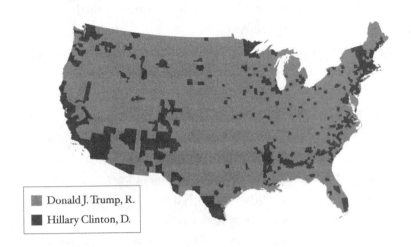

Donald J. Trump, R.
Hillary Clinton, D.

Source: Mark Newman, Center for the Study of Complex Systems, Department of Physics, University of Michigan, December 2, 2016.

the middle. This is "front row" America.[71] Anywheres are content to live...anywhere. They need live in no particular place to feel at home. On the other hand, there is a "posturban" red region, only partly integrated into the digital economy, with a diamond-shaped wealth stratification pattern, largely containing "somewheres." As the term indicates, they find their home in one place but not in another. This is "back row" America. Oversimplifying the matter somewhat, the blue regions are predominantly "digital" and the red regions are predominantly "analog." I will consider the relationship between digital and analog in detail in section 85. This relationship is important not least because liberal competence is first and foremost

Anywheres are those cosmopolitan travelers who need no home to feel at home; somewheres are those who are at home only when living in one place.

71. See Chris Arnade, *Dignity: Seeking Respect in Back Row America* (New York: Sentinel Books, 2019).

analog rather than digital. Little wonder that the liberal politics of competence prevails in the posturban zone among the somewheres who are part of back-row America. The identity politics of innocence, on the other hand, prevails in the digital regions where normalcy consists of products ordered on Amazon Prime; of temporary work assignments and long-distance relationships (and/or Tinder); of rental apartments and Uber; of episodic political activism posted on Facebook and Twitter; of vicarious screen entertainment (most notably, Netflix); of music downloads; of e-mail; of Instagram, and so on. These front-row Americans, enthralled by digital technology, as so many in the blue region are, easily imagine a perfection of which the lived-in world is incapable. Theirs is a timeless world freed from the burden of generation; a spaceless world freed from the need for borders; and a world in which it seems plausible to imagine that the inevitable sufferings and injustices of life need no longer be endured. If, to the dismay of your pride, it has dawned on you that the professional work you *really* do consists of being a "data-entry worker" for Google, Facebook, Amazon, and Microsoft—which for the rest of your life will gather, codify, and store *all* of your "inputs" at massive data storage facilities for *their* future use—you live in digital America. To put the matter in its starkest and most uncharitable light, if you live in digital America, *you* are the commodity. In analog regions, these cultural accoutrements and these sorts of jobs are less prevalent, though still widespread. If you know someone without an e-mail account, who does not own a smartphone, who pays with cash, or who has never lived more than twenty-five miles from his childhood home, you know someone in analog America. The two regions shade into each other, to be sure; but the cultural division, which now appears also as a class division,[72] is real. No return to the analog world

---

72. See Darel E. Paul, "Culture War as Class War: How Gay Rights Reinforce Elite Power," *First Things*, August 2018, https://www.firstthings.com/article/2018/08/culture-war-as-class-war.

Party endorsement. To cover herself anew with the mantle of innocence, she declared: "We live in a country now where the president is advancing environmental racism, economic racism, criminal justice racism, health care racism."[126] Incoherent as this statement seems on the surface, it reveals the strategy the Democratic Party has adopted since the civil rights movement: invoke black American moral authority for every cause you wish to advance—and expect black America to sit still and say nothing. Her invocation of "everything racism" failed to bolster her standing as an innocent, and among the innocents. Before she departed the race, Marianne Williamson at least had the good sense to know she is white, and offered public prayers seeking forgiveness for that unpardonable sin.[127] The attention given by Democrats to long-departed (Robert Francis) Beto O'Rourke was disproportionate to his demonstrated competence, and is explained by the *need* Democrats had, after President Obama's ascendance, for O'Rourke to not be *just another white man*. Then there was candidate Pete Buttigieg, who, while white and gay, might have been too white and not gay enough.[128] For the most part, the agents of the first phase of iden-

126. Elizabeth Warren, quoted in Matthew Rozsa, "Democratic Candidates Shine a Light on Racial Disparities while Trump Doubles Down on Racist Remarks," Salon, July 31, 2019, https://www.salon.com/2019/07/31/democratic-candidates-shine-a-light-on-racial-disparities-while-trump-doubles-down-on-racist-remarks/. In response, see Robert Woodson interview of July 31, 2019, on *Tucker Carlson Tonight*, in Charles Creitz, "Bob Woodson: Warren's Claims of Trump Racism on Health Care and Environment Are 'Insulting and Condescending,'" FOX News, July 31, 2019, https://www.foxnews.com/media/bob-woodson-warrens-claims-of-trump-racism-on-health-care-and-environment-are-insulting-and-condescending.

127. See "Marianne Williamson Leads a Prayer Apologizing for Being White," YouTube video, 3:01, posted by Daily Caller News Foundation, July 19, 2019, https://youtu.be/cvBPwDIRgYU.

128. See John Aravosis, "The Insanity of Democrats Attacking Buttigieg—for Not Being Gay Enough," *Daily Beast*, updated March 31, 2019, https://www.thedailybeast.com/the-insanity-of-democrats-attacking-pete-buttigiegfor-not-being-gay-enough.

tity politics in the Democratic Party were white brokers who spoke on behalf of the innocents. In the second phase, the innocents speak for themselves. The oscillating status of Elizabeth Warren and Beto O'Rourke—alternatively white broker and innocent—confirms the entrance of the Democratic Party into this new phase. Kamala Harris, a "woman of color" would have been the candidate most listened to within the Democratic Party in the run-up to the 2020 election if her heavy-handed prosecution of innocents during her stint as attorney general of California had not placed her among the transgressors. In the world identity politics constructs, mercy trumps justice. A woman of color who prosecuted criminals and showed no mercy does not fit in to the identity politics narrative. She sided with the transgressors—something too jarring to comprehend. President Bill Clinton was elected, in part, because he was "tough on crime" while he was governor of Arkansas (1978–80; 1982–92). His legacy within the Democratic Party today has been besmirched because of that stance, among other reasons. Once politics pertained to justice; henceforth, the only Democratic candidates who will be given serious consideration by the party faithful will be those who substitute mercy for justice.

A final caveat on the upcoming November 2020 election: While the logic of identity points to the disappearance of white brokers who speak on behalf of the innocents, if white candidates *do* prevail, their success will hang on the extent to which they can escape the cathartic rage that would otherwise settle on them for being white. They will do this by innocence-signaling their support for various social justice causes, so that they, like other groups of innocents, can be covered with righteousness. Perhaps, as has been proposed, the unspoken agreement that they must have a vice-presidential running mate who is not a white, heterosexual man will prevail. In these ways, as I indicated in section 13 of the preface, the cathartic rage that otherwise brings social death will *pass over* them and settle elsewhere—likely on middle- and lower-class whites, without whom the Democratic Party cannot win the presidency.

H. THE PURGE

§41. Proceeding from the premise of identity politics that it is both possible and desirable to cleanly distinguish between transgressors and innocents, we can imagine a Democratic Party in which the innocents finally replace the white brokers who once spoke for them. To understand the inner logic of identity politics, however, we must go further and imagine a world in which not only are the white broker-transgressors replaced by the innocents within the Democratic Party but also a world in which transgressors themselves disappear from view altogether. This is already starting to occur. Held responsible for transgression because of who they are, yet not authorized to act in accordance with who they are, an entire generation of boys and young men are already so benumbed and befuddled that they regularly withdraw into the video universe—or, all too often, explode outward in violence.[129] There, hidden from a world that declares, "The future is female," they live vicarious lives of conquest, command, protection, and competence. Because in the world identity politics constructs, there can be no wars in defense of noble causes, no new horizons to explore, no wives and children to protect,[130] these young men are of no use—except as a scandal providing orientation for the innocents. Held responsible for the sins of the world and at the same time accorded no author-

129. See Mark Meckler, "Of the 27 Deadliest Mass Shooters, 26 of Them Had One Thing in Common," *Patheos*, February 20, 2018, https://www.patheos.com/blogs/markmeckler/2018/02/27-deadliest-mass-shooters-26-one-thing-common/. The one thing these mass shooters had in common is that they came from fatherless homes, which is to say that they grew up in a world in which men had no real place.

130. See Geoff Dench, "Reversing the Descent of Man," *Quillette*, December 28, 2018, https://quillette.com/2018/12/28/reversing-the-descent-of-man/. This essay was extracted and reproduced from Geoff Dench, *Rediscovering Family* (London: Hera Trust, 2003) after the author's death.

ity in that world: this is the lesson an entire generation of boys and young men have learned by heart.[131]

Despite their ever-diminishing standing, white, heterosexual men nevertheless still wear the crown of thorns. They are the transgressors, through whom are justified every innocent identity—women, "people of color," and those gathered under the heading of LGBTQ. Purge white, heterosexual men and a momentous question emerges: Because identity politics involves a relationship between transgressors and innocents,[132] *can the innocents be innocent without transgressors?* Who, after the first purge, will stand in and justify the remaining innocents? White, heterosexual women, while women, are nevertheless white; "men of color," while "of color," are nevertheless men; "heterosexual women of color," while "women of color," are nevertheless heterosexual; and so on. Because of the centrality of the wound of slavery in America, white, heterosexual women are likely to take the place of white, heterosexual men as the transgressors after white, heterosexual men have been humiliated, taken their cue, and disappeared from view. Let us imagine, then, the purging of white, heterosexual women that would take place—say, after other innocent identity groups discover that under the banner of "The future is female," these women have been its disproportionate beneficiaries. Unless all women make proportionate advances, "privilege" will be the charge leveled against white, heterosexual women, and all remaining innocents will rally against them. I say this here and elsewhere: *The innocents must have their scapegoats.* It is not a stretch to see the titanic struggle that took place during the long run-up to the 2020 presidential election between the white speaker of the house, Nancy Pelosi, and the women of color deri-

131. See Warren Farrell and John Gray, *The Boy Crisis: Why Our Boys Are Struggling and What We Can Do about It* (Dallas: BenBella Books, 2019).

132. See sec. 9.

sively called "the squad"[133] over the Green New Deal and the decision to file articles of impeachment against President Trump as the first battle in the long campaign adherents of identity politics will wage to purge white women after white, heterosexual men have dutifully taken their leave. Then what? Who might the next targeted transgressor be? If the recent controversy over whether "homophobic" black American comedian Kevin Hart should have hosted the ninety-first annual Academy Awards show in February 2019 is any indicator, the formerly innocent group of black American, heterosexual men will be next in line. The standing of black Americans within identity politics warrants special attention, which I will consider in more detail in section 50. Worth remembering, for the moment, is that purveyors of identity politics take the template of the black American wound of slavery and extend it to women, people of color, and those gathered under the heading of LGBTQ. The travesty that should surprise no one who understands the inner logic of identity politics is that some portion—or all—of black America will eventually be betrayed by it. Black Lives Matter indeed. Identity politics eventually comes for everyone. The last remaining identity group will be the one that has *just enough* power to scapegoat and purge its transgressor while appearing, paradoxically, to be an innocent victim.

§42. Seeking to redeem the scapegoated innocents, identity politics itself requires a scapegoat through whom the innocents can be redeemed. For now, that scapegoat in the Democratic Party is the white, heterosexual man. He bears a toxin, "toxic masculinity," that must be purged from the body social. When he is fully humiliated and purged from society (as all scapegoats must be), a new scape-

133. This group consists of congressional representatives Alexandria Ocasio-Cortez of New York, Ilhan Omar of Minnesota, Ayanna Pressley of Massachusetts, and Rashida Tlaib of Michigan. All of these women are under fifty years old, and all came to power during the 2018 midterm elections.

goat must emerge, who will become the transgressor through whom innocence is established and proclaimed. Someone playing the part of the innocent today *will* play the part of transgressor tomorrow. Little matter who it is; the important thing is that the relationship between transgression and innocence be maintained. If that relationship collapses, the theodicy question—why is there evil in the world?—is no longer answerable. The sacrifice of former innocents on the identity politics altar will be the gruesome but necessary payment that maintains the relationship. Former innocents will be the offering that provides the answer to the theodicy question that identity politics demands. Not long ago, Christians believed that man was the transgressor; that Christ was the Innocent One; that evil could be explained by the brokenness of man; and that salvation came through this understanding of the relationship between mortal transgression and Divine innocence. In identity politics, the Innocent One, the Lamb of God, has no place. For the Democratic Party, the innocents are *here*, in a world that has been broken by the transgressors;[134] and salvation comes to those who spend their lives cleanly distinguishing between mortal transgressors and mortal innocents, and then turning their cathartic rage toward new transgressors as the old ones are purged.[135]

134. White, heterosexual man has broken the world *politically* by his invention of liberalism, *economically* by his invention of capitalism, *socially* by his patriarchal tyranny, and *environmentally* by the greed that his industrial capitalism unleashed.

135. See Aleksandr Solzhenitsyn's May 10, 1983, speech upon accepting the Templeton Foundation Prize (in "'Men Have Forgotten God': Aleksandr Solzhenitsyn's Templeton Address," *National Review*, December 11, 2018, https://www.nationalreview.com/2018/12/aleksandr-solzhenitsyn-men-have-forgotten-god-speech/): "The failings of human consciousness, deprived of its divine dimension, have been a determining factor in all the major crimes of this century. The first of these was World War I, and much of our present predicament can be traced back to it. It was a war (the memory of which seems to be fading) when Europe, burst-

I. GROUP UNITY?

§43. The need to cleanly distinguish between transgressors and innocents means that in identity politics, everyone must have an unequivocal group affiliation. My father's family emigrated from Lebanon; my mother's family emigrated from Wales, Holland, and Germany. I am Protestant, rather than Catholic. None of these descriptors—over which wars in Europe, the Mediterranean region, and America have been fought for several thousand years—matter to identity politics. Until and unless the identity category of MENA is given legal sanction by the US Government (see section 10), I am white—therefore a transgressor. Nothing more. Not one of the groups that identity politics needs in order to declare guilt and innocence are monovalent, however. White citizens with German,[136] Irish, and Italian heritage have an ample family history of harsh treatment received during the nineteenth and first half of the twentieth century at the hands of citizens who traced their ancestry to the British Isles. The category "national origin" appeared

---

ing with health and abundance, fell into a rage of self-mutilation which could not but sap its strength for a century or more, and perhaps forever. The only possible explanation for this war is a mental eclipse among the leaders of Europe due to their lost awareness of a Supreme Power above them. Only a godless embitterment could have moved ostensibly Christian states to employ poison gas, a weapon so obviously beyond the limits of humanity." Absent the Divine Innocent One, who is the Scapegoat for the entire world, European nations scapegoated one another. Europe today wishes to dissolve its nations, so that national scapegoating—read, "nationalism"—will no longer be possible. The problem is not nationalism; *the problem is group scapegoating*, which European elites continue to practice, this time around on those that do not believe in the cause of a postnational world order.

136. For a fine account of the German case, see Duncan Moench, "Anti-German Hysteria and the Making of 'Liberal Society,'" *American Political Thought* 7, no. 1 (Winter 2018), 86–123.

on the US census in 1800[137] in order to keep track of nationalities who—let's just say it—were not welcome in America, especially as the nineteenth century wore on. The term "minority" in America was initially used only for numerical calculation, without the moral overtones of national origin; it pertained to kinds of peoples from other European nations who were not yet assimilated into American culture. Only during the last half century has the term taken on the purpose it has today—which is as a means of gathering together a heretofore heterogeneous mix of whites and then distinguishing them from all nonwhites. Because "minority" is a constructed category,[138] we can be sure that a generation from now its meaning will be different.

How about religious cleavages, say, between white Protestants, Catholics, and Jews—let alone the extraordinary tensions that exist within each of these groups? Do these not indicate that whites are many rather than one? Scripture-centered Protestants have little to say to members of the dying mainline churches. Social justice Catho-

---

137. See Mike Gonzalez and Hans A. von Spakovsky, *Eliminating Identity Politics from the U.S. Census*, Heritage Foundation Backgrounder Report 3327, 3–6 (Washington, DC: Heritage Foundation, June 29, 2018), https://www.heritage.org/sites/default/files/2018-06/BG3327_0.pdf.

138. The most comprehensive account of the origin and development of the term "minority" is to be found in Philip Gleason, "Minorities (Almost) All: The Minority Concept in American Social Thought," *American Quarterly* 43, no. 3 (Sept. 1991), 392–424. A number of distinct phases can be discerned in Gleason's treatment. First, the term minority pertained without the overtones of transgression and innocence, to *kinds*. Second, minority became a euphemism for the category of "race," which, in the interwar years, was a category many Americans were uncomfortable using because they had no answers for the questions it posed. Third, as the euphemism "minority" became the synonym for race, a new term emerged to cover over American discomfort, and to allow those who were white but not white, heterosexual men to have a place in the identity politics firmament: "oppressed groups." The overall trajectory began with the physical distinctions between kinds and ended with the identity politics relationship between transgressors and innocents, between white, heterosexual men and all other groups.

---

lics are contemptuous of those Catholics who think Vatican II went too far, and vice versa. The cleavage between reformed Judaism and Hasidic Judaism is perhaps unbridgeable. Tel Aviv and Jerusalem, while both in Israel, are worlds apart.

How about class cleavages? Aspirationally, America is a classless society; therefore, our concern about class cleavage should grow as the barriers to entry into a higher class become insurmountable. Yet in their actions, white elites today largely care only about their own,[139] in conjunction with the network of primary schools, extracurricular activities, activist causes, and Ivy League colleges and universities that assure that the children of these elites, too, will become members of the privileged class. The price of admission for heretofore scapegoated innocents to join them is strict adherence to the identity politics byline. That is the central educational lesson all elites-in-the-making receive in these networks. Heaven help black Americans or other "minority" members who believe—as a vast majority do—that marriage is a fragile generative relationship between a man and a woman. Either they keep silent or they are purged. Professing the words that identity politics countenances is the linguistic prerequisite for becoming a member of the elite class in America today. If you are woke, the tree of life is yours. Woe unto you if you fall from grace, for then the flaming sword will bar your return to the Edenic world[140] that was promised; and by the sweat of your brow you will labor[141] until you die, unredeemed. Little wonder our Ivy League college students today oscillate back and forth between thinking the world is theirs for the taking and fearing that the slightest mistake will cast them

---

139. See David Brooks, "How We Are Ruining America," *New York Times*, July 11, 2017, https://www.nytimes.com/2017/07/11/opinion/how-we-are-ruining-america.html.

140. See Gen. 3:24: "So he drove out the man; and he placed at the east of the garden of Eden Cherubim, and a flaming sword which turned every way, to keep the way of the tree of life."

141. See Gen. 3:19.

into outer darkness—the outer darkness of dwelling among the "deplor-ables," who can never rise. "Yale or jail"; "Harvard or homeless."[142] Iden-tity politics is the fig leaf that hides the sin of class privilege among many white elites in America today.[143] On the measure of class, white people divide into two antithetical political and class clusters: the right kind of white person who espouses identity politics and the wrong kind of white person who does not. By definition, white members of this latter, lesser class are considered racists, misogynists, homophobes, Islamophobes, fascists, Nazis, haters, deniers, and so on in the eyes of white elites. So much for the supposed unity of whites in classless America.

§44. Perhaps if whites are not a single monovalent group, we can find the group unity we seek by looking to women. Are women one or are they many? Feminist rhetoric about the solidarity of all women suggests a common "women's experience," yet nothing could be further from the truth. Elite white woman aspire to successful careers, defer having chil-dren until a time of their own choosing, sometimes pay women of color to care for their children while they work since they are unable to afford the time off themselves, and defend no-fault divorce. The obstacles they perceive to achieving equality are the glass ceiling above them and the prospect that they may be constrained by law from doing with their bod-ies whatever they choose should pregnancy befall them. Colleges and universities dutifully train the young men in attendance to believe these things as well, as the precondition of marrying and forming households with these soon-to-be career women. The combined income of these

142. Revered by several generations of Americans, Robert Frost's 1916 poem "A Road Not Taken" invites the reader to consider taking the road less trav-eled. The refrain of all too many young men and women today—"Yale or jail"; "Harvard or homeless"—countenances the well-worn path instead.

143. After Adam and Eve sinned, they hid themselves from God and pre-tended that they were innocent. See Gen. 3:7: "And the eyes of them both were opened, and they knew that they *were* naked; and they sewed fig leaves together, and made themselves aprons."

married couples will dwarf the annual earnings of the bottom 80 percent of American families. "Freedom" will be their byword in all that they do.

I am not suggesting that nothing good comes of these arrangements. Families who can afford nannies, for example, sometimes form lifelong bonds of affection with them, which redound to the benefit of all. In the democratic age, the irreconcilable tension in a woman's life between generation and personhood has afforded a few the opportunity for deep and satisfying reflections of the sort that would not have been possible in an earlier age. I *am* suggesting, however, that these important and sometimes precious developments are the purview of a narrower group of women than the beneficiaries of these developments imagine.

What of the unfree "sisters" of these women? A chasm Achilles himself would not leap often separates them. A woman is vulnerable in the way a man never will be: She has children. Not all do; but if not enough do, civilization perishes. Pregnancy is exhausting; childbirth, nursing, infancy, the long labor of civilizing sons and daughters—these all require an inward-looking disposition that women far more often than not have, and in full measure. This leaves them vulnerable to the chaos, threats, and demands that come at them from outside the home. No one can look both ways, inward and outward, at the same time, with equal concentration. In this, the age of freedom, every working mother knows this agonizing and unresolvable truth.[144] Protection against their vulnerability can be provided by the state,[145] can be purchased by wealthy married couples or wealthy single mothers, or can be provided by a hus-

---

144. See Elizabeth C. Corey, "No Happy Harmony: Career and Motherhood Will Always Tragically Conflict," *First Things*, October 2013, https://www.firstthings.com/article/2013/10/no-happy-harmony.

145. The greater the state welfare available, the lower the rates of marriage will be. Women will have children under this arrangement—but not too many, because while the state can provide the cash payments and modest services needed to raise one or two of them, it cannot provide enough in the way of the daily array of protections needed against the outside world to justify having more.

band, who promises his vulnerable wife and the mother of his children to attend dutifully to the outward world on her behalf. For unfree sisters, no-fault divorce has not meant the chance to start over with someone more "compatible"; it has meant the proliferation of single-mother households situated at or below the poverty line, with children whose prospects are dim, and whose cost to society is staggering. When the solemnity of the marriage vow is a relic without meaning, and when the state, or the church, ceases to enforce marriage or impose a high cost for reckless exit, some women are liberated while others are condemned to penury. Elite woman buy their protection against vulnerability. Daily and unremittingly, their unfree sisters are exposed to it. The unfree sisters do not dream of shattering glass ceilings and overthrowing the patriarchal order; those who wish to marry or those who stay married ponder the iron manhole covers, the dirty jobs in America held twenty-to-one by men, and wonder if the wages earned by their husbands in those jobs will be enough to pay next month's bills. Women in America are not one.[146] Feminism may claim to speak for all women but, like so many other "isms"—communism, environmentalism, capitalism,[147] and the like—it never does. A few win; many lose. Women in America are not monovalent. No one group of women speaks for the whole.

§45. How about black Americans? Are they one group or many? The slavery to which all but the free-born were subject destroyed fami-

146. For an account of how women in America are divided in their assessment of President Trump, see Joshua Mitchell, "Sex and Sin in Protestant America," *First Things*, October 25, 2016, https://www.firstthings.com/web-exclusives/2016/10/sex-and-sin-in-protestant-america.

147. Marx uses this term; Adam Smith never does. In Smith's estimation, market commerce is not a comprehensive system. If Marx is correct that capitalism is a system with an internal logic that must unfold in the way he describes, then a few win and many lose. If Smith is correct that market commerce and its necessary institutional correlates can undergird a healthy middle-class commercial republic, then the arrangement Marx suggested is inevitable need not develop. For conceptual clarity, it is important not to equate Smith with capitalism.

lies from forming in the first place, and authorized sexual dominion over enslaved women, who had neither the legal nor the moral right to their own bodies. So prevalent was such sexual predation by slave masters that the organizers of the 1850 US census thought it necessary to establish the categories "black slaves" and "mulatto slaves."[148] The 1890 US census contained the categories "black," "mulatto," "quadroon," and "octoroon"—distinctions thrown out in the 1900 US census on the recommendation of the former census superintendent Robert Porter, who argued that the differentiations had become so complex and cumbersome that they yielded little usable information. It helped considerably that a number of prominent black leaders had argued for the collapse of those categories into one as well.[149] That determination allowed the biracial President Obama to become our first black American president. If, as W. E. B. Dubois argued, a single drop of black blood stained blacks, so much so that no amount of white blood within them could wash them clean in the

---

148. A timeline of the categories employed by the US census from 1790 to the 2010 can be found at: "What Census Calls Us," Pew Research Center, February 6, 2020, http://www.pewsocialtrends.org/interactives/multiracial-timeline/.

149. See Jennifer L. Hochschild and Brenna M. Powell, "Racial Reorganization and the United States Census 1850-1930: Mulattoes, Half-Breeds, Mixed Parentage, Hindoos, and the Mexican Race," *Studies in American Political Development* 22, no. 1 (Spring 2008), https://scholar.harvard.edu/jlhochschild/publications/racial-reorganization-and-united-states-census-1850-1930-mulattoes-half-br: "Blacks were also increasingly committed to a move from blurred to rigid boundaries, albeit for different reasons. Although a significant segment of light-skinned blacks continued to affirm the distinctive classification of mulatto, many black leaders had long claimed that distinguishing blacks from mulattoes was conceptually mistaken and destructive of solidarity. W. E. B. Du Bois, for example, had urged census officials in 1900 to 'class those of African descent together,' and to accept an expert advisory panel that included Booker T. Washington and Kelly Miller, a prominent black sociologist. Du Bois chose his list of experts carefully; both Washington and Miller advocated black unity and erasure of the line between blacks and mulattoes."

eyes of whites,[150] is an external imputation by whites such as this one enough to make all black Americans one rather than many? What of their differing inheritances? In the illuminating 1979 essay "Ethnicity: Three Black Histories," Thomas Sowell suggested that black America is not one, but rather three: descendants of "free persons of color," whose numbers had reached 488,000[151] by 1860; descendants of American slaves, the largest portion of black Americans; and descendants of West Indian slaves, the smallest but most successful of the three groups.[152] Relatively intact families, property holdings, and education—each being a prerequisite of liberal citizenship—explain the relative success of the latter group. Tensions among these three groups exist to this day. The groups differ, as well, in the extent to which each has benefitted from the Great Society programs President Johnson called forth in his University of Michigan commencement speech of 1964.[153]

The supposed imputation by whites who see a *stain* in one drop of black American blood gives the false appearance of unity. Dif-

---

150. See W. E. B. Dubois, chap. 2 in *Darkwater: Voices from Within the Veil* (Atlanta: Two Horizons Press, 2011), 38: "But let the murderer be black or the thief brown or violator of womanhood have a drop of Negro blood, and the righteousness of the indignation sweeps the world."

151. According to the US census, the slave population in 1860 was 3,953,760. One of every nine black Americans in the United States at that time was a "free person of color."

152. See Thomas Sowell, "Ethnicity: Three Black Histories," *Wilson Quarterly* 3, no. 1 (Winter 1979), 96–106.

153. In the world identity politics constructs, governmental programs offer compensation for the innocents. President Johnson had something else in mind. Through such programs, disadvantaged citizens would be helped, so that they, too, could develop competence and build a world together. In his words, "But most of all, the Great Society is not a safe harbor, a resting place, a final objective, a finished work. It is a challenge constantly renewed, beckoning us toward a destiny where the meaning of our lives matches *the marvelous products of our labor*" (Lyndon Johnson, "President Johnson's Speech on the 'Great Society'" [speech, University of Michigan, May 22, 1964; emphasis added], https://www.pbs.org/ladybird/epicenter/epicenter_doc_society.html).

fering inheritances reveal durable cleavages among black Americans. What of those cleavages that, as Tocqueville put it, exist by virtue of the fact that whites and black Americans mix but do not yet combine?[154] The history of black American political thought is the response to this ambiguous position—neither quite in nor out—which takes the form of arguments to *exit*; arguments to *voice* political opposition; and, notwithstanding its problems, arguments for *loyalty* to the American regime.[155] The works of Malcolm X, W. E. B. Dubois, and Booker T. Washington, respectively, are emblematic of these arguments. On this reading, the division among black Americans today derives not from differing inheritances but rather from the agonizing ambiguity of the standing of black Americans in America. Division along these lines gets electrically supercharged by a universal fact about all communities: They will have their scapegoats. In section 39, I noted that white brokers scapegoat other whites in order to have their standing as transgressors covered over. Transgressors, too, need scapegoats—to deceive themselves, if not the innocents, that they are pure. In the case of black Americans, the universal fact of scapegoating within a community is supercharged by the historical legacy of slavery in America and the standing of innocence it announces. Unlike whites, who in the world identity politics constructs are forever stained, black Americans confront the momentous question, If because of slavery we are innocent, who among us is to be the scapegoat? One answer is that the scapegoat is the black American who refuses to believe that any salubrious benefit derives from declaring black

154. See Tocqueville, pt. 2, chap. 10 in *Democracy in America*, vol. 1, 340: "The Indians die as they have lived, in isolation; but the fate of the Negroes is in a sense linked with that of the Europeans. The two races are bound one to the other without mingling; it is equally difficult for them to separate completely or to unite."

155. See Albert O. Hirschman, *Exit, Voice, and Loyalty: Responses to Decline in Firms, Organizations, and States* (Cambridge, MA: Harvard University Press, 1970).

American innocence. To put the matter more starkly, the scapegoat is the black American who has seen enough of purported innocence that justifies debilitating self-satisfaction, and that precludes building a world of the sort liberal citizens envision. Here are the "conservative" black Americans who have been a scandal for their fellow black Americans, and for whites who, wishing to cover over their own transgressions, fix their attention on innocence rather than competence (see sections 22–23). In the last quarter century, a modest list of prominent black American conservatives include Ben Carson, Herman Cain, Alveda King, Glenn Lowry, William Raspberry, Condoleezza Rice, Shelby Steele, Thomas Sowell, Carol Swain, Clarence Thomas, Walter Williams, David Webb, and Robert Woodson Jr. Within identity politics, they are not black Americans; they are betrayers and adversaries, whom everyone else must denounce.[156] The relative standing of Booker T. Washington and W. E. B. Dubois, two towering figures in early twentieth-century black American thought, illustrates the issue: The former is today scapegoated; the latter is a saint among the innocents. Every community needs its scapegoats.

§46. What of Hispanics? Are they one or many? Long before "Hispanic" first became an umbrella political category in the 1970 US census, it was a literary genre, pertaining to Spanish-speaking authors from Latin America, the Caribbean, and the Iberian Peninsula. What gathers these regions together is the sea on which sailed Spanish galleons, searching for gold and silver during the mercantile period.[157] Like all colonizers, the Spaniards ruled by cutting deals with

---

156. See "Different Rules—Created Equal: Clarence Thomas in His Own Words," YouTube video, 0:58, posted by ManifoldProductions, October 25, 2019, https://youtu.be/LCYERqQDjQg.

157. Adam Smith's 1776 masterpiece, *The Wealth of Nations*, was among the first to argue that wealth is not measured by the amount of gold and silver in the national treasury but by the labor of its citizens. The Spanish con-

PART ONE: IDENTITY POLITICS

local elites across the ocean, who then mediated between oppressor and oppressed. Were these mediators, many of whose heirs today fall under the category of Hispanic, transgressors or innocents? What of the never-ending wars prior to the arrival of the Spaniards between the ancestors of those currently labeled Hispanic? Did the victor-transgressors of those wars suddenly become innocents after the Spaniards conquered them? We may ask this question of the African theater as well: Did the African warriors who conquered weaker tribes and sold their conquest to white slave traders suddenly become innocent when European colonialists took control and subdued them? What of those African warriors whose tribes once conquered others and then themselves were conquered and sold into slavery? Are they innocents? What, too, shall we make of the American Indian tribes—the Cherokee, Creek, Choctaw, and Seminole—who owned black slaves? Are they transgressors or innocents? When identity politics fixates on white, heterosexual men, the stain of the transgression is indelible. What, then, is the status of black Americans, Hispanics, and American Indians whose ancestors were transgressors? If they were once transgressors, are they not always transgressors? What of white, heterosexual women whose ancestors managed households in which slaves labored? In the American Southwest, where Native American Indian tribes were decimated by Spanish conquest long before whites arrived, are the Hispanics now living there transgressors or innocents? If some Hispanics living there were transgressors, are not all of them—living everywhere—transgressors, by virtue of their common identity category?

The category Hispanic would not exist had the Spaniards not colonized the New World. The Hispanic literary genre coheres and achieves its depth and height by virtue of the renewal that miraculously followed from the transgression, suffering, and death asso-

---

quest of the New World was driven in part by the older understanding of wealth that *The Wealth of Nations* superseded.

ciated with Spanish colonialization. The history of humanity provides similar lessons. *Suffering and death are not arguments against life.*[158] If they were, not one of us would be here today. We are here by transgression. All of us. The Hispanic literary genre once recognized this. The Hispanic political category does not. That is because in identity politics, the scapegoated white, heterosexual man covers over everyone's historical transgressions, no matter how grievous and unspeakable. Before the collapse of the mainline churches in America, parishioners would have said that Christ, the Scapegoat, covers over the sins of all mankind. In identity politics, the unrelenting loathing toward the transgressor, the white, heterosexual man, is the precondition of the innocence of everyone else.

§47. What of those gathered under the heading of LGBTQ? Are they one or many? Let us admit from the outset the mystery of erotic longing.

158. See Absalom Jones, "A Thanksgiving Sermon, preached January 1, 1808, in St. Thomas's, or the African Episcopal, Church, Philadelphia: On Account of the Abolition of the African Slave Trade, on That Day, by the Congress of the United States," in *American Sermons* (New York: Library of America, 1999), 543: "It has always been a mystery, why the impartial Father of the human race should have permitted the transportation of so many millions of our fellow creatures to this country, to endure all the miseries of slavery. Perhaps his design was, that a knowledge of the Gospel might be acquired by some of their descendants, in order that they might become qualified to be the messengers of it, to the land of their fathers. Let this thought animate us, when we are teaching our children to love and adore the name of our Redeemer. Who knows but that a Joseph may rise up among them, who shall be the instrument of feeding the African nations with the bread of life, and of saving them, not from earthly bondage, but from the more galling yoke of sin and Satan."
Suffering is only the final word if redemption is unavailable. The suffering of slavery, to which the sermon fully attests, has a meaning: God gave to His suffering servants the keys to His eternal kingdom so that they might return to their transgressors in Africa and invite them into the eternal kingdom. Remove the vindication of suffering in the spiritual economy, and direct payment alone must compensate for it. Identity politics demands such payment—not yet as reparations but as victim debt points to be accumulated.

What, really, does it mean and portend? Plato long ago suggested that we deceive ourselves when we opine that in *having* another, we find what we are truly looking for.[159] Erotic love is a Divine summons. We misunderstand its directive if active possession is all we hope to gain through it. Erotic love is an invitation to the Good, the True, and the Beautiful; these, man cannot possess but only behold and passively receive, like warm sunlight on a cold day.[160] The contemporary debate about "sexual orientation" rests on the hobbling illusion that genuine satisfaction comes through active possession. Who today is prepared to declare that erotic longing that ends in possession cannot fill the emptiness in our soul? Because we are a sex-obsessed society, the political parties that have gathered around this question have already rejected this sublime answer; they disagree only about *who* may rightly possess and be possessed.

However inadequate all active possession may be from the philosopher's vantage, there is nevertheless a basis for distinguishing between different sorts of erotic longing, one that hinges on the uncontestable fact that regeneration of life cannot happen without active possession,[161] and the institution of generative marriage that

159. See Plato, 210a–212a in *Symposium*, trans. and intro. Alexander Nehamas and Paul Woodruff (Indianapolis: Hackett, 1997).

160. In Plato's *Republic*, the tyrant, Thrasymachus, believes that only through possession do we "get it all" (bk. 1, 343c). This understanding is contrasted with that of the philosopher who "gets it all" (bk. 5, 476a–c) by seeing the whole of which particular things are but partial manifestations.

161. The opening scene of Plato's *Republic* has Socrates "coming down" (bk. 1, 327a in *The Republic*) to the Piraeus from Athens. This locution has its counterpart in the "Allegory of the Cave." There, Plato tells his interlocutors that once the philosopher has seen the light of the Good, he must "go down" (bk. 7, 520c in ibid.) and dwell with those who are still enchained in the shadowy world of coming-into-being-and-passing-away—that is, in the place where death is always a worry. That is why Plato has the Athenians worshipping the goddess Bendis, the goddess of fertility, in the opening passage of *The Republic*. Through Bendis, the worshippers hope to increase their fecundity, so that through the regeneration that her blessing bestows, the Athenians may keep their family name alive and keep death at bay.

ensconces it. Contemporary romantics wish generative marriage to be a lofty thing, unburdened by possession.[162] Never can that be entirely so—a fact confirmed when marriages founded on the romantic view crash to earth and end in divorce court, haggling over who owns what.

Marriage based on the *having and holding* of possession is not the lone institution subject to this romantic embarrassment. So, too, is private property. Through property ownership, we secure our households and regenerate our society. Because death is always near, for everyone and for every civilization, possession is the prerequisite to the regeneration that keeps death at bay. Family and market commerce based on private property demand this.

Identity politics does not declare, as liberal thought might, that erotic longing institutionalized in generative marriage must have a higher stature in society than other sorts of erotic longing; and

---

162. See Friedrich Nietzsche, sec. 39 in *Twilight of the Idols* and *the Antichrist*, trans. R. J. Hollingdale (New York: Penguin Classics, 1990), 105–6: "The decadence in the valuing instinct of our politicians, our political parties, goes so deep that *they instinctively prefer* that which hastens the end. . . . Witness modern marriage. It is obvious that all sense has gone out of modern marriage: which is, however, no objection to marriage but to modernity. The rationale for marriage lay in the legal sole responsibility of the man: marriage thereby had a center of gravity, whereas now it limps with both legs. The rationale for marriage lay in its indissolubility in principle: it thereby acquired an accent that could *make itself heard* against the accidents of feeling, passion and the moment. It lay likewise in the responsibility of the families for the selection of mates. With the increasing indulgence of love matches, one has simply eliminated the foundation of marriage, which alone *makes* it an institution. One never establishes an institution on the basis of an idiosyncrasy, one does *not*, as aforesaid, establish marriage on the basis of 'love'—one establishes it on the basis of the sexual drive, the drive to own property (wife and child considered as property), the *drive to dominate* which continually organizes the smallest type of domain, the family, which *needs* children and heirs so as to retain, in the physiological sense as well, an achieved measure of power" (emphasis in original).

that some other sorts of longing, which history confirms have always been with us, can also be accommodated. Identity politics declares that conventional generative marriage is not "inclusive," and, as such, is a prejudice that must be ousted. Only members of a civilization that has cheated death, through technology or through the one-sided expropriation of life-giving resources from other civilizations (often to their detriment), can ignore the need to elevate conventional generative marriage above other sorts of erotic longing. Identity politics operates from a viewpoint made possible by our privileged civilization. As such, its beneficiaries are blind to the way in which their privilege serves themselves and harms others. Yet for identity politics to work, this privileged viewpoint must be maintained. Without the indictment leveled at the white, heterosexual man who is involved in conventional generative marriage, there can be no transgressor through whom all Ls, Gs, Bs, Ts, and Qs gather together and achieve their innocence. The innocent unity announced by the term "LGBTQ community" *is* a unity only insofar as there is a transgressor to scapegoat. Without the white, heterosexual male transgressor who provides the fig leaf that conceals the differences between them, there are only Ls, Gs, Bs, Ts, and Qs who are, or will eventually be, at odds with one another. On this point, the reader should be clear, in light of my earlier remarks about the mysterious nature of erotic longing, that these remarks are made with a view to calling out what I take to be a rather poor basis of achieving unity, and nothing more. A unity achieved by scapegoating another person or group is a cheap imitation of the genuine communion for which we long. Identity politics chooses the cheap imitation as a shortcut to the real thing. Always.

What are some of the concealed differences between Ls, Gs, Bs, Ts, and Qs that belie the claim of unity? Mainstream media silence about this matter notwithstanding, gay men are not univocal in their political views. Gay conservatives have long argued against identity politics.[163] Like their fellow liberal citizens, they wish to build a world around competence rather than innocence. These gay men have no place in the world identity politics constructs; they are a category that cannot exist. Lumped together with conservative women and conservative black Americans, gay men who find identity politics pernicious, who refuse the abridgement "innocent victim," are invisible men. The professed longing of identity politics is that the voiceless be heard. The ugly truth is that identity politics silences a vast swath of humanity in order to accomplish its aim. With each extension into uncharted territory, the warriors of "inclusion" purchase their purity by besmirching a growing pool of others. In the 1970s, we should remember, feminists insisted they be referred to as "womyn" rather than as "women," in order to *elevate and distinguish* themselves from men and the designation

---

163. Before founding the Log Cabin Republicans in 1993, Richard Tafel received a stern rebuke from his Harvard Divinity School classmates for his politically incorrect views. In a prescient brief essay in the July/August 1991 issue of *Harvard Magazine*, which anticipated the logic of identity politics, he wrote: "To play the Game [at Harvard], you had to know card values; straight white male was worth least—the joker. Straight white female next, gay white male next, gay white female next. The most powerful card was the one considered most oppressed. If your oppression status was worse than the person with whom you were arguing, perceived victim status conferred academic and moral authority. To play the game right, one had to speak the lingo. Failure to use the right words could cost you. Calling a 'person of color' a 'colored person' would set you way back. Calling a person 'handicapped' was an equal disaster. The name for 'handicapped person' kept evolving: from 'specially challenged' to 'differently abled' to 'differently gifted' to 'bodily challenged.' When writing the word "women," one gained points if he spelled it with a *y* instead of an *e*. But I would have lost points, as you might have noted—because I used "he" in the last sentence. Linguistic points mattered more than intellectual points. I believe the PC movement is having the same chilling effect on our universities that McCarthyism had on the entertainment industry. When—for all the best reasons—our academic institutions start acting as thought police, stifling the marketplace of ideas, we begin to erode the foundation of scholarship and American society, which is free thought and free speech." Richard L. Tafel, "And from My Lips Will Come What Is Right," *Harvard Magazine* (July/Aug. 1991), 12.

PART ONE: IDENTITY POLITICS

they had imposed for millennia. Today a war is being waged on feminists who wish to retain their distinction by those—largely *T*s and *Q*s—who now seek to erase the feminist designation womyn and replace it with "womxn."[164] Facing the dysphoria of life that occasionally enshrouds every questioning being, many *T*s and *Q*s have settled upon the conclusion that birth sex is the source of their generalized dissatisfaction, and that the designation womyn is actually a poison rather than an antidote to their suffering. For them to feel *included*, feminists—many of whom believed in generative marriage, just on unconventional terms—must now be *excluded*. That this former group has reached this conclusion should not surprise us in light of the growing consensus among our young men and women that their sexed bodies are archaic, burdensome, unjustifiable relics of a generative civilization they now must renounce. I noted the irony earlier: Only a privileged hegemonic civilization that has cheated death dare dream that it has no duty to reproduce itself. False humility always rests on monstrous pride.

The *strangeness* of our embodiment and the death it portends have long fascinated our greatest minds.[165] What is remarkable today is the narrowness of the range of reflections on the meaning of that strangeness. Pondering the human condition, Tocqueville wrote:

> The short space of sixty years can never shut in the whole of man's imagination; the incomplete joys of this world will never satisfy his

164. See Luis Miguel, "WOMXN: The Latest LGBTQ Newspeak Aimed at Destroying Womanhood," *New American*, December 31, 2019, https://www. thenewamerican.com/culture/family/item/34479-womxn-the-latest-lgbtq-newspeak-aimed-at-destroying-womanhood.

165. In the "Allegory of the Cave" (bk. 7, 514a–520d in *The Republic*, 209–14), Plato suggests that the seemingly familiar world of the prisoners is a *strange* world for those who have eyes to see the Truth. Pressing contemporary terminology into service, the shadowy world of the cave is the *cis*-world, in which most feel at home. The philosopher, however, knows his home is elsewhere. See bk. 4, 592b in ibid.

heart. Alone among created beings, man shows a natural disgust for existence and an immense longing to exist; he scorns life and fears annihilation.[166]

Tocqueville and so many others before and after him concluded that dysphoria arises from the collision between the intimation that our souls are eternal and the wretched fact that death is the fate of all embodied life. Taking on a *different* embodied form does not halt the collision; it only delays it. Just as the redemption *of* the world cannot happen from *within* the world, so, too, the redemption of our embodied form cannot happen from within *another* embodied form. As such, we may wonder why, today, a number of people believe that the release from their birth sex will offer salvation for their dysphoria. The epithet "cisgender," leveled as a critique of those men and women who are at home with their birth sex, does have a ring of truth to it. As death comes near, the bodies in which we have been at home will betray us, and reveal to us as we approach the threshold that if we are to have a home, we will not find it in our once trusty companion. Christianity, too, tells us that the body that has been our home in "the short space of sixty years" is not enough. Redemption is the ecstatic release from mortal embodiment and the homelessness of sin that attends it. Today, when in the lives of so many people God is either distant or absent, the *ecstasis* of release from our birth sex has become, for some, a surrogate for the redemptive *ecstasis* God once offered. Identity politics sanctions this surrogate—as the deepest expression yet of the liberation from the heterosexual transgressor. Insofar as *L*s, *G*s, *B*s, *T*s, and *Q*s are all not heterosexual, they are a unity by virtue of the distinction they have in common. However, insofar as many of them are, like so many heterosexuals, at home in their birth sex, and perhaps even believe that there are natural differences between men and women,[167] while others are

166. Tocqueville, pt. 2, chap. 9 in *Democracy in America*, vol. 1, 296.
167. See Andrew Sullivan, "The Nature of Sex," *New York*, "Intelligencer,"

not, *L*s, *G*s, *B*s, *T*s, and *Q*s are not a unity. Only by scapegoating the transgressive heterosexual can the appearance of unanimity among them be maintained. The uncovering of the substantive differences between them will take the form of one innocent among them scapegoating another. This has already begun to happen.[168]

§48. In the world identity politics constructs, everyone has a monovalent group affiliation. They may have more than one monovalent affiliation, as the growing "intersectionality" literature now stresses,[169] but the aggregated identities whose synergy is greater than the sum of the parts[170] are nevertheless comprised of monovalent unities. On the question of whether and how such unities exist hangs the fate

---

February 1, 2019, http://nymag.com/intelligencer/2019/02/andrew-sullivan-the-nature-of-sex.html: "We have to abandon the faddish notion that sex is socially constructed or entirely in the brain, that sex and gender are unconnected, that biology is irrelevant, and that there is something called an LGBTQ identity, when, in fact, the acronym contains extreme internal tensions and even outright contradictions. And we can allow this conversation to unfold civilly, with nuance and care, in order to maximize human dignity without erasing human difference."

168. See Sky Gilbert, "Homophobia and the Modern Trans Movement," *Quillette*, January 31, 2019, https://quillette.com/2019/01/31/homophobia-and-the-modern-trans-movement/.

169. The origin of the term is attributed to Kimberle Crenshaw, "Demarginalizing the Intersection of Race and Sex: A Black Feminist Critique of Antidiscrimination Doctrine, Feminist Theory and Antiracist Politics," *University of Chicago Legal Forum* 1989, no. 1, art. 8, 139–67.

170. See ibid., 140: "I argue that Black women are sometimes excluded from feminist theory and antiracist policy discourse because both are predicated on a discrete set of experiences that often does not accurately reflect the interaction of race and gender. These problems of exclusion cannot be solved simply by including Black women within an already established analytical structure. Because the intersectional experience is greater than the sum of racism and sexism, any analysis that does not take intersectionality into account cannot sufficiently address the particular manner in which Black women are subordinated."

of identity politics and the intersectionality that exponentially multiplies the universe of possible innocents. In the categories we have briefly considered—white people, women, black Americans, Hispanics, and those gathered under the heading of LGBTQ—the empirical facts of division and disunity are controverted and covered over by the unity of the transgressor, who confers innocence and unity on all who stand in relationship to him.[171] This is not the immediate face-to-face relationship that liberal citizens understand, in which the parties to the relationship *discover* who they are through their ongoing conversations and arguments, and through what they build together. It is a relationship mediated by the monovalent (or intersectional) identities each person unalterably stands for and represents. In this latter sort of relationship, there is nothing to argue about, nothing to build.

J. THE TWO MINUTE HATE

§49. I distinguished two vastly different understandings of citizenship in sections 12–23: Liberal citizens are concerned with competence; identity politics is concerned with innocent victimhood. Liberal citizens cannot dwell on innocent victimhood, because the purportedly unalterable identities that justify such a status do not help liberal citizens build a world of competence together. When citizens no longer need to associate with one another in their everyday lives, there will be scant evidence that their fellow citizens are not monovalent representatives of this or that group identity. When citizens no longer need to build a world to-

171. See Andrew Sullivan, "We All Live on Campus Now," *New York*, "Intelligencer," February 9, 2018, https://nymag.com/intelligencer/2018/02/we-all-live-on-campus-now.html: "The goal of our culture now is not the emancipation of the individual from the group, but the permanent definition of the individual by the group. We used to call this bigotry. Now we call it being woke. You see: We are all on campus now."

gether, they can be seduced into looking at one another in the way identity politics proposes.

Tocqueville did not anticipate identity politics, but he did anticipate the isolation of citizens, one from another, that would be its prerequisite. He praised the Americans for building a world together, foresaw a distant future where they would turn away from face-to-face horizontal relations with their fellow citizens, and predicted that unless stronger motives deterred them, they would come to depend only on their vertical relationship with the state.

> I am trying to imagine under what novel features despotism may appear in the world. In the first place, I see an innumerable multitude of men, alike and equal, constantly circling around in the pursuit of petty and banal pleasures with which they glut their souls. Each man, withdrawn into himself, is almost unaware of the fate of the rest. . . . Mankind, for him, consists of his children and his personal friends. The rest of his fellow citizens are near enough, but he does not notice them. He exists in and for himself. . . . Over this kind of man stands an immense, protective power, which alone is responsible for securing their enjoyment and watching over their fate. That power is absolute, thoughtful in detail, orderly, provident, and gentle. It would resemble paternal authority if, father-like, it tried to prepare its charges for a man's life, but on the contrary, it only tries to keep them in perpetual childhood. It likes to see citizens enjoy themselves, provided that they think of nothing but enjoyment.[172]

Chilling and prescient as Tocqueville's 1840 prophecy about the disappearance of liberal competence is, he thought citizen competence would be supplanted by state competence, not by the politics of innocence that identity politics foments. Another way of putting this would be that Tocqueville anticipated progressivism but not identity politics. To move

172. Tocqueville, pt. 4, chap. 6 in *Democracy in America*, vol. 2, 691–92.

from Tocqueville's prophecy to the catastrophe of identity politics, the categories of transgression and innocence have to migrate from religion into politics, something I briefly considered in section 23. To his credit, Tocqueville saw that this *could* happen but did not think the Americans would succumb because "religion [remained] free and powerful within its own sphere and content with the position reserved for it."[173]

Tocqueville is not our only guide to what has befallen us, however. On the other side of the Atlantic a century later in 1949, after two world wars left Europe without faith in itself or in God, George Orwell described a tyrannical future, like Tocqueville's, inhabited by citizens who were isolated from one another—but unlike Tocqueville's, this tyrannical future was held together by scapegoating a transgressor rather than by state competence. In what is perhaps the most memorable passage of Orwell's novel *1984*, isolated citizens of Oceania gather daily for a "Two Minute Hate" directed toward Emmanuel Goldstein. Without this scapegoat, Oceania's own blemishes would become visible. Through Emmanuel Goldstein—a man whose last name indicates he is Jewish,[174] and whose first name is the name of Christ,[175] "the Lamb

173. Tocqueville, pt. 1, chap. 2 in *Democracy in America*, vol. 1, 47.

174. The long history of the scapegoating of Jews within Christianity and, therefore, in the West shows no sign of abating. St. Augustine's *City of God* (bk. 4, chap. 34, 178) contains among the first articulations of it. Martin Luther's 1520 essay "On the Freedom of a Christian" (in *Luther's Works*, vol. 31, 329–77) establishes the trope of "dialectical history," which became the forum through which Jews were later scapegoated in the nineteenth-century works of Hegel and Marx. Under the unassuming heading of "the narcissism of minor differences," Freud suggested in 1930 that the scapegoating of the Jews was the "means [by] which cohesion between the members of the [larger] community is made easier. In this respect the Jewish people, scattered everywhere, have rendered most useful services to the civilizations of the countries that have been their hosts." Freud, chap. 5 in *Civilization and Its Discontents*, 72.

175. See Matt. 1:23: "Behold, a virgin shall be with child, and shall bring forth a son, and they shall call his name Emmanuel, which being interpreted is, God with us."

of God who takes away the sins of the world"[176]—Oceania washes itself clean and restores its purity.

> Before the Hate had proceeded for thirty seconds, uncontrollable exclamations of rage were breaking out from half the people in the room. . . . In its second moment, the Hate rose to a frenzy. People were leaping up and down in their places and shouting at the tops of their voices in an effort to drown the maddening bleating [lamb-like] voice that came from the screen. . . . The horrible thing about the Two Minute Hate was not that one was obliged to act a part, but that it was impossible to avoid joining in. Within thirty seconds, any pretense was always unnecessary. A hideous ecstasy of fear and vindictiveness, a desire to kill, to torture, to smash faces with a hammer, seemed to flow through the whole group of people like an electric current, turning one even against one's will into a grimacing, screaming lunatic.[177]

However disturbing this dystopia may be, bound together as it is by a sacrificial scapegoat who may not even exist, Orwell's *1984* doesn't come close to anticipating the fever of identity politics in America today. First, although citizens of Oceania are isolated, they are not proxies for monovalent group identities that bear the mark of either transgressors or innocents. Citizens of Oceania may be unable to love and forgive one another's foibles and betrayals,[178] but one group's stain is not the precondition of another group's purity. No

176. See John 1:29: "The next day John seeth Jesus coming unto him, and saith, Behold, the Lamb of God, who takes away the sin of the world."

177. George Orwell, pt. 1, sec. 1 in *1984* (New York: Harcourt Brace Jovanovich, 1949), 15–16.

178. See pt. 3, sec. 7 in ibid., 240. Tyranny in the democratic age, both Tocqueville and Orwell understood, would be possible only if the links between citizens were dissolved. See Tocqueville, pt. 2, chap. 4 in *Democracy in America*, vol. 2, 509: "A despot will lightly forgive his subjects for not loving him, provided they do not love each other."

one group of them stands for transgressions perpetrated and, at the same time, stands in for the innocents and covers their sins. Second, in America, the ever-growing penetration of the federal government into daily life has altered the task of our congressional representatives, and contributed to a catastrophe Orwell could not have imagined. Article I, section 8 of the US Constitution enumerates the powers of Congress, and leaves to the states how daily life is to be regulated. Until the twentieth century, without the ability to levy an income tax directly, the projects of Congress were of limited scope. That changed with the ratification of the Sixteenth Amendment, in 1913, which effectively turned congressional representatives into patronage brokers who measure success by the metric of funds returned to their congressional districts from the income tax–enriched federal treasury. The political configuration of Orwell's *1984* includes the ministries of truth, love, peace, and plenty, presided over by Big Brother. Elected representatives play no part. Not so in America. Therein lies the problem. In my earlier discussion of the distinction between brokers and innocents in sections 39–40, I noted that by its own internal logic, identity politics cannot countenance the representation of innocents by white transgressor-brokers. The innocents must speak for themselves.[179] There, I did not consider the fact that in our post-1913 republic, all congressional members, innocents or otherwise, are patronage brokers. The metric of funds returned to their congressional district invites these patronage brokers to declare that citizens in their district are innocent victims, incapable

179. "Cultural appropriation" involves taking on the trappings of an innocent identity without asking the permission to do so from those who are of that identity. Technically, transgressor-brokers who are the congressional representatives of innocents have received such permission—not so much to speak like them or dress like them, but to speak on their behalf in public—by virtue of having been elected by them. It is unclear on what grounds they would be justified in doing the latter, if they are not justified in doing the former. Moreover, if consent is required, would it not have to be unanimous to count?

of solving their own problems without massive federal assistance, which they will oversee.

To their discredit, both political parties are content with this patronage-broker model of congressional representation. The Republican Party has generally done this on behalf of wealth. The current Democratic Party's unwavering embrace of identity politics has sent it searching in every corner of America for indebted innocents it can purportedly represent—most recently, transsexuals. We can be sure there will be more—currently undreamed of—innocents in the future. What this means is that unlike the arrangement Orwell describes, in which politics remains independent of the Two Minute Hate that purges the community, in the Democratic Party political activity is concerned with the ever-expanding search for new innocents through whom the sins of the transgressor-scapegoat can be revealed and the rage against him can increase.

The frenzy of identity politics in America and in the Democratic Party cannot die down after it reveals and certifies a new group, however. Because little holds the Democratic Party together today besides the white, heterosexual male transgressor who, unlike Emmanuel Goldstein, is without luster or charisma, current innocents within the party machinery must continually discover new groups of innocents who have suffered at his hands. Together they then gather in incredulity and wonder aloud why they did not recognize beforehand just how sinister their common transgressor really was. Orwell's Two Minute Hate would not be enough today. In *1984*, Big Brother offered up Emmanuel Goldstein as the one sufficient sacrifice, who allowed Oceania's citizens to go back to their grim everyday lives without sacrificing one another.[180] The fever of identity politics offers so much more than a return to grim lives. Because this is America, the land of the Puritan

---

180. For Christians, Christ is the one sufficient Divine sacrifice, who puts an end to the sacrifice of living creatures. See St. Augustine, bk. 9, chap. 15 in *City of God*, 359–61.

fixation on stain and perpetual novelty, identity politics—being thoroughly American, in spite of appearances to the contrary—also offers us both. In every waking moment, we rummage through our personal and national memories to expose past and present transgressions to the light of day; and we perpetually seek out novel groups whose innocence confirms the depravity of the transgressors. Such is the character of our American Awakening without God and without forgiveness.

K. BLACK AMERICANS BETRAYED

§50. No American citizens have been betrayed more by identity politics than black Americans, whose special standing bestowed on them by the deep wound of slavery in America has been used unabashedly as a template for all other supposed innocents to make their own claims. Civil rights, women's rights, gay rights, transsexual rights: are these not all fungible variants on the same theme of transgression and innocence? Asked to step back while new franchise-expanding innocents are invited to figuratively occupy the front seats of the Democratic Party bus, black Americans are expected to sit tight and not complain about where the bus is headed or how much it is costing them—or at least costing a large number of them. Identity politics *needs* to render black Americans not as struggling, albeit competent, liberal citizens whose history evinces extraordinary, and reproducible, models of success but instead as perennially innocent victims. For that reason, the history of their successes against formidable odds must be erased, without regard for those black Americans most harmed by that erasure. In its stead has been placed a new history and a new formula for benefiting not all black Americans but only a small group among them whose fortune and hard work have prepared them to take full advantage of the configured opportunities that now come their way. Along the way, the tacit understanding is that they will adhere to the account of their plight that identity politics promulgates. In Robert Woodson's words:

The Guardians of Grievance, the cohort of advisors that are today's version of W.E.B. Dubois' "talented tenth" . . . [have revised history to focus] almost exclusively on the degradation whites have imposed on blacks and the accomplishments of the civil rights leadership's efforts since the sixties. Conveniently airbrushed from the portrait of black America are the remarkable models of self-help—accomplishments of black entrepreneurs and mutual aid societies during eras of the most brutal racial repression and slavery. Lost is the legacy of personal responsibility and principle-based entrepreneurship that could provide today's youth with a pride in their heritage and an adaptable model that could guide their futures. The selective history that is transmitted to our young people is, simply put, that blacks came to this country on slave ships; from there they went to plantations and slavery; from the plantations to the ghetto, and, finally, to welfare.[181]

In the world identity politics constructs, oppressive social forces loom large and human freedom looms small.[182] Have not the transgressors systematically scapegoated the innocents and kept them from sharing in the bounty of America? The history of slavery and its after-

181. Woodson, chap. 3 in *Triumphs of Joseph*, 51–52. See also Robert L. Woodson Sr., "A Betrayal of Martin Luther King," *Hill*, January 20, 2019, https://thehill.com/opinion/civil-rights/426017-a-betrayal-of-martin-luther-king: "The surest way to sabotage the prospects of blacks is to convince them that they have no agency and, therefore, no responsibility and no hope. This is insulting to the memory of Dr. King and immoral in its continued intellectual incarceration of people into a mindset of victimhood, rather than one of achievement."

182. Tocqueville thought that as citizens in the democratic age become more lonely and isolated, they would be enticed by histories that inform them that they are caught up among vast social forces that they are powerless to alter. See Tocqueville, pt. 1, chap. 20 in *Democracy in America*, vol. 2, 496: "Classical historians taught men how to command; those of our own time teach next to nothing but how to obey [social forces]. In their writings, the author often figures large, but humanity is always tiny." Marx's theory of the necessary historical development of communism is a fine example of the sort of history Tocqueville criticizes.

math confirms this wretched fact. "Systemic racism" is the cause of the disproportion.[183] The attainment of proportional representation of innocents in every field of endeavor will overcome this hovering, shameful legacy. White privilege is the stumbling block; identity politics is the Gospel's good news.

There is something to these claims—though not what proponents believe. The grim wounds from our nation's history have not entirely healed.[184] No one knows the path to conciliation we must take—dare

---

183. What, then, are we to make of certain minorities—Asian and East Indian Americans—who are *over-represented* in many fields of endeavor? Should the logic of identity politics be applied to them as well, which would require quotas that work *against* their success? Harvard University, the city on the hill for identity politics, is under legal scrutiny for doing just that for decades. See Anemona Hartocollis, "Asian-Americans Suing Harvard Say Admissions Files Show Discrimination," *New York Times*, April 4, 2018, https://www.nytimes.com/2018/04/04/us/harvard-asian-admission.html.

184. The portions of Tocqueville's *Democracy in America* that are most difficult to read and to teach are the portions about slavery (vol. 1, pt. 2, chap. 10, 316–20, 341–363). Rejecting the racialist arguments of his day, Tocqueville thought through slavery, using as his model the Egyptian captivity of the Israelites. His reference to the slave's satisfaction with "his master's hearth" (vol. 1, pt. 2, chap. 10, 317) harkens back to the Hebrew Bible's account of the longing of the Israelites wandering in the desert to return and sit "by the flesh pots . . . when we did eat bread to the full" (Exod. 16:3). Later, Tocqueville noted that "the Negroes will be unlucky *remnants*, a poor *wandering tribe* lost amid the huge nation that is master of the land" (vol. 2, pt. 1, chap. 10, 351, emphasis added)—which is an allusion to Josh. 14:10; Ps. 107:4; Isa. 16:8; and Ezek. 34:6. Tocqueville's insight is that slavery and mastery are habits, which altering legal arrangements will not immediately erase. That is why the wound of slavery has taken so long to heal in America. After the Israelites were released from Egyptian bondage, their habits did not immediately change. The Hebrew account is that only God, mediated through Moses, can fully release man from slavery, and bring him to the promised land—a theme echoed from the black American pulpit right from the beginning. When Martin Luther King Jr. said, on the steps of the Lincoln memorial, "I may not get there with you," he was alerting his listener-parishioners to this biblical account, and reminding them that Moses

I say—to fulfill our national covenant. The self-certain path identity politics insists we tread assuages white liberal guilt without prompting whites to any action other than voting for more government programs, empowers innocent patronage brokers who themselves claim to speak for the innocents,[185] and showers some black Americans with enviable opportunities, while leaving an embarrassingly large number of them behind. Every community needs to provide exemplars for the next generation, whose members will dutifully superimpose what they have gleaned upon an uncertain future, so that their world becomes just familiar enough to live in and build up. With a view to providing new life-giving exemplars, identity politics introduces black Americans into domains of society they have yet to occupy in appreciable numbers. A liberal who is committed to robust pluralism can hardly object. That same liberal should then ask, Is there no recognition of the paradox at the very heart of the justification identity politics offers for doing this? *Because* black Americans are innocents, without a proud historical record of competence that provides them with exemplars with which to build a world, intercession is necessary in every societal domain to achieve proportionality. Why, the liberal asks, should this be assumed? Who gains from this incredulous claim, and what are its perverse consequences? First, set aside the wrenching collateral damage some black Americans suffer because they do not have the requisite habits and academic preparation needed to succeed in

---

himself did not cross over into the promised land (see Deut. 34:5). King's "I Have a Dream" speech of August 28, 1963, is the high watermark of American covenantal theology in the twentieth century.

185. There is no mention of a national census in Orwell's *1984*. The scapegoating of Emmanuel Goldstein does not require it. Identity politics requires that Americans understand themselves as transgressors or innocents. That is why efforts to eliminate those identity politics categories on the US census have been denounced by the Democratic Party. The innocents must know who they are—and vote for innocent brokers who will do their patronage bidding as their congressional representatives.

these new domains[186]—or worse, suffer because they *do* have them, but do not have the financial wherewithal to finish their academic programs or pay for them later? Second, how can the large numbers of black Americans who remain after this painful winnowing, who will *never* be privy to the intercession identity politics promises, build a world together, sometimes in broken neighborhoods they may never leave? The history of the black American exemplars they most need to build their world—*a history that exemplifies competence and pride*—is inadmissible. The goal of identity politics is to provide new exemplars for innocents to benefit from. To become competent liberal citizens rather than custodians of the state, those who cannot meet the eligibility requirements need the old exemplars whom identity politics erases. Therein lies the difficult paradox. Identity politics must erase the old exemplars in order to justify creating new ones. It thereby sacrifices the prospects of the least among us for the benefit of others, many of whom would now rise without extra assistance. An America committed by law and sentiment to the idea that one group should prosper at the permanent expense of another was renounced in 1865, at the close of the Civil War. A century and a half later, the old slavery of chains has been replaced by a less obvious servitude that holds a smaller portion of black America in thrall, *and will not let them go*. This, too, is a national embarrassment, which is in no way mitigated by ceaselessly fixating on the first national embarrassment that ended in 1865.

Surely, there is a better way to heal our national wound. Much good has come from constructively opening different domains of experience to black Americans. Robust pluralism requires nothing less. If, however, the consequence of the way we are currently achieving this result is the penury of other black Americans who become permanent custodians of the state—*to be pointed to as proof of the innocent*

---

186. See Richard H. Sander and Stuart Taylor Jr., *Mismatch: How Affirmative Action Hurts Students It's Intended to Help, and Why Universities Won't Admit It* (New York: Basic Books, 2012).

victim status that justifies identity politics policies in the first place—then we have not healed the wound, we have poured salt into it. Without encouraging liberal competence among all our citizens, this wound will never heal. As William Raspberry once put the matter:

> The inner-city poor furnish the statistical base for the proposals [for racial proportionality], but the benefits go primarily to the already well-off. Black executives who already hold good jobs get promoted to better ones; blacks who already sit on important corporate boards get another directorship. And the people who provide the statistical base get nothing.[187]

§51. The Democratic Party today purports to defend the innocents against the transgressors. In the black American case, identity politics' policies of racial proportionality have elevated some while holding many others fast. How can those who are considered ineligible rise when the satisfaction of their every need requires not the development of trust with their neighbor, but a meeting with government agents, which, in reality, usually only serves to circumscribe in advance the courses of action available to them and to crush their civic spirit? Identity politics does not elevate all the innocents, only the more well-off among them. I have focused on black America because its fragility most reveals the division identity politics produces. This is not a problem for black Americans alone, however. Identity politics purports to liberate entire groups. The truth is that it advances only a numerical minority of the group members it claims to defend, and only as long as they wave its banner. Women are among the innocents! Why, then, are their unfree sisters[188] left behind, ignored, and castigated? Hispanics are among the innocents! Why, then, are people from nations within the Hispanic literary orb who want nothing to do with the politi-

187. William Raspberry, quoted in Woodson, chap. 2 in *Triumphs of Joseph*, 21.

188. See sec. 44.

cal category Hispanic bludgeoned with the term, and told they only count if they identify as a member of this group?[189] Whether white, black American, woman, Hispanic, or otherwise, your voice will be heard only if you confess the creed of transgression and innocence. Oppose or dare to doubt it, and through the mystery of social transubstantiation you will suddenly be the scapegoat that the innocents need to hold together their world. The Salem witch trials of 1692–93 have nothing on identity politics. Puritan America: ever involved in casting out the impure and the doubting. A Democratic Party that once defended the laboring middle class, that once recognized the singular plight of black Americans, and that once recognized the need to defend the nation from foreign threats at home and abroad—this party now singularly focuses on innocence, by which criteria it judges all policies and all people.

L. THE ALT-RIGHT COMETH:
BEYOND TRANSGRESSION AND INNOCENCE

§52. Identity politics is not the cause of the emergence of the Alt-Right, but the steadfast claim of identity politics that transgressors are permanently marked sends many who are so marked scurrying about looking for ways to respond to their indictment. Some respond by directing their wrath toward others in their identity group, in order to say to the innocents: "See, even though I wear wolf's clothing, I am a sheep. Like you, I belong among the innocent." White liberal guilt in its various fawning and disingenuous guises sits here. Others respond not by scapegoating

189. On campuses across America today, there is a call for diversity among the faculty, students, and staff. But propose that a conservative woman, black American, Hispanic, gay, or lesbian be hired, and quickly there will be pushback. Real diversity is not wanted; what is wanted is visibly different group identities, all sharing the same ideas. Members of those groups that do not believe in identity politics are marginalized.

their own, so to speak, but by declaring, "I, too, have been victimized. I am a sheep in sheep's clothing." The "men's Me Too movement," as I called it earlier,[190] sits here. So, too, does climate change–ism, at least insofar as otherwise privileged transgressors declare that they are being victimized by increasing levels of carbon dioxide in the atmosphere.[191] Here, also, sits woke capitalism. If you are a white, heterosexual man, not even the wealth of King Midas can redeem you. Dedicate the fortunes of your corporate enterprise to social justice, however, and your stain is covered over. These declarations echo Adam's response to God when He called out Adam's transgression: "I did not do it; it was Eve's fault."[192] Here, transgression is covered over through redirection.

Still, within the constellation of possible responses to transgression through redirection is the Christian response to which I have alluded on many occasions: the Innocent One, the Lamb of God, takes upon Himself the sins of the world. Man's transgression is covered over through the sacrifice of Christ, the Innocent Scapegoat, who redeems the broken world and makes it new. The impossibility of self-redemption from transgression—affirmed by both identity politics and Christianity—is, in the Christian instance, overcome by God's intervention, which alone saves the transgressor from the condemnation and death his transgression rightly invites.

The Alt-Right takes none of these paths. Its breathtaking claim is not that white, heterosexual males are innocent; rather, its claim is that *the entire configuration of transgression and innocence is responsible for the decay we witness in the West.* Civilizational renewal will only come when we altogether leave behind the relationship between trans-

---

190. See part 1, n. 19.

191. See Stanley Kurtz, "The Wannabe Oppressed," *National Review*, October 16, 2013, https://www.nationalreview.com/education-week/wannabe-oppressed-stanley-kurtz/.

192. Gen. 3:12–13. Eve is silent until the blame is shifted to her—at which point she redirects the blame to the serpent.

gression and innocence,[193] along with the scapegoating that makes that relationship possible and necessary.

§53. I will consider the meaning and implications of this idea shortly, but first I will pause to say a few words about the purported link between the Alt-Right and conservatism. The political distinction between the Left and the Right dates to postrevolutionary France in 1793. Those on the right who fix on the inheritance of tradition have been a healthy corrective to the Left since Burke first articulated the conservative position in his *Reflections on the Revolution in France* in 1790. In addition to this sort of defense of inheritance, there are those who by virtue of their focus on inheritance are also placed on the right, but whose understanding of inheritance must be distinguished from those who focus on tradition. Perhaps the most important thing to say about them is that they seem little interested in preserving the fragile prudential knowledge developed by living inside a tradition, which is handed down through the generations, in a distinct place, and more interested in reified external markers based on the physiognomy of different groups. This latter sort of defense of inheritance is rising around us everywhere. Many who claim to be members of the Alt-Right see the world in this way. They are not concerned with the difficult trade-offs that all those who dwell within a living tradition recognize, but rather with imagined physiognomic distinctions that invest inheritance with mystical importance. Conservatives and members of the Alt-Right are both concerned with inheritance; their understanding of it is quite different, however.

193. The attentive reader will hear in this formulation the echo of Friedrich Nietzsche's *Beyond Good and Evil*, a book intended to diagnose the long-developing pathology of Judaism and Christianity in the West and to guide noble souls beyond the ethic of resentment on which these religions were founded. Of special importance are the passages that distinguish between master morality and slave morality (pt. 9, secs. 260–61, 204–9). Judaism, in Nietzsche's estimation, invented slave morality; Christianity brought it to the whole world. See Friedrich Nietzsche's *Beyond Good and Evil*, trans. Walter Kaufman (New York: Random House, 1966).

There is an additional confusion. Many who purport to be among the Alt-Right have no idea what it really means or portends. Richard Spencer's "The Charlottesville Statement"[194] is taken to be emblematic of the Alt-Right, yet we can be sure that its invocation of the term "identity" and its need to scapegoat Jews, black Americans, and others means that it is a predictable species *of* identity politics, rather than an attack on it. The standings of the groups may be reversed, but the logic and the categories are the same. "The Charlottesville Statement" defends the identity politics transgressor, and claims that identity politics innocents are the proper scapegoats. This is reverse identity politics. Its further development is to be feared and watched. Like the Ku Klux Klan, it has been an ugly aspect of American history for a very long time. Although identity politics did not cause it, identity politics now inflames it.[195] Many who hold identity politics dear *want* this to be the full extent and amplitude of the Alt-Right, because it confirms that white, heterosexual men *really are* the transgressors identity politics says they are. To rest there, with that understanding, is a serious mistake, however. The emerging Alt-Right is far more menacing and destructive than reverse identity politics. It has deep and well thought-out intellectual roots.[196] If it conquers identity politics—if, that is, it puts an end to the relationship

194. See Richard Spencer, "What It Means to Be Alt-Right," AltRight.com, August 11, 2017, https://www.altright.com/2017/08/11/what-it-means-to-be-alt-right/.

195. For an uncanny prediction of the emergence of white identity politics, see Carol M. Swain, *The New White Nationalism in America: It's Challenge to Integration* (New York: Cambridge University Press, 2002).

196. See Matthew Rose, "The Anti-Christian Alt-Right: The Perverse Thought of Right-Wing Identity Politics," *First Things*, March 2018, https://www.firstthings.com/article/2018/03/the-anti-christian-alt-right. Rose traces the Alt-Right in the twentieth century to Oswald Spengler's *The Decline of the West* (1918), Julius Evola's *Revolt against the Modern World* (1934), and Alain de Benoist's *On Being a Pagan* (1981). All three writers were critical of Judaism and Christianity, which is why many conservatives in America are opposed to the Alt-Right. The nineteenth-century figure on whom these three authors based their claims is Friedrich Nietzsche.

between transgression and innocence—the reverse identity politics of "The Charlottesville Statement" will seem pathetic and quaint in comparison to what is to come. Pointing out the racial and ethnic scapegoating that that statement endorses will not get us very far if we wish to understand the Alt-Right. Nor will claiming the Alt-Right is conservative. The Alt-Right is so revolutionary that it puts an end to the political distinction between the Left and the Right, as we have received it from the French Revolution, in that it opens a new post-French Revolutionary stage of history. The French Revolution, Tocqueville reminds us, was less of an entirely new beginning than a realization of political form of the moral sentiment of equality that derived from Christianity.[197] Just as the French Revolution was the death knell of medieval Europe, the Alt-Right promises to put an end to the relationship between transgression and innocence, without which the equality that justified the French Revolution would have been unjustifiable. Christianity gave us the visibility of the voiceless innocent, the paradigmatic case for which is Christ, standing mute before his accuser Pontius Pilate.[198] That is the true font of the equality that is so loved today, an equality that destroyed the "pathos of distance," as Nietzsche called it, which once separated aristocrats from those they ruled. Equality, dignity, rights, compassion, and recognition—in short, the entire constellation of concepts that undergird democracy—could never have emerged if the pathos of distance that Christianity destroyed had remained intact. In Nietzsche's words:

> Every enhancement of the type "man" has so far been the work of
> an aristocratic society—and it will be so again and again—a society

197. See Alexis de Tocqueville, *The Old Regime and the French Revolution*, trans. Alan S. Kahan (Chicago: University of Chicago Press, 1998).

198. See Mark 15:2–5. Nowhere has Christ's silence in the face of accusation been more deeply explored than in "The Grand Inquisitor" chapter of Fyodor Dostoyevsky's *The Brothers Karamazov*. See Fyodor Dostoyevsky, pt. 2, bk. 5, chap. 5 in *The Brothers Karamazov*, trans. Constance Garrett (New York: W. W. Norton, 2011), 213–30.

that believes in the long ladder of an order of rank and differences in value between man and man, and that needs slavery in some sense or other. Without that *pathos of distance* which grows out of the ingrained difference between strata—when the ruling caste constantly looks afar and looks down upon subjects and instruments and just as constantly practices obedience and command, keeping down and keeping at a distance—that other, more mysterious pathos could not have grown up either—the craving for every higher, rarer, more remote, further-stretching, more comprehensive states—in brief, simply the enhancement of the type "man," the continual "self-overcoming of man," to use a moral formula in a supra-moral sense.[199]

The Alt-Right seeks nothing less than to return man to an aristocratic world, which is to say, a *non-Christian* world.

§54. We can illuminate the Alt-Right assessment of the crisis of the West, in which identity politics today plays its predicted central part, by pondering a section from Nietzsche's *Thus Spoke Zarathustra* (1883) entitled "The Three Metamorphoses."[200] Here, the camel must transform into the lion. The lion, in turn, must transform into the child for civilizational renewal to occur.

The camel, the beast of burden, bears much. All great things require man to bear much, require that he defy the adversity of the desert, require that he impose life and vitality on a world that he alone forms. Man: the creating animal who must bear much for his creation to prevail. Judaism and Christianity—those repudiations of aristocratic cruelty through which the common man suffered—was such a creation. In Judaism and Christianity, innocent suffering was miraculously elevated, and the aristocratic formula "Strength equals strength" invert-

199. Nietzsche, pt. 9, sec. 257 in *Beyond Good and Evil*, 201 (emphasis in original).

200. Nietzsche, pt. 1, "The Three Metamorphoses," sec. 1 in *Thus Spoke Zarathustra*, 25–28.

ed. Weakness became strength, and strength became weakness.[201] In the suffering of the innocents was found a new meaning of the world; namely, its *redemption*—from aristocratic cruelty. This fixation on suffering, which took the form of the question, Am I, or are others, at fault for the suffering I endure? deepened man and made him interesting—so much so that a god had to be invented "to do justice to the spectacle."[202] The cost of repressing man's strength, and of ruling out the cruelty that attends its expression, has been the diminution of man. Western man stands on the threshold of this great exhaustion, the result of two millennia of internalizing the "Thou shalt not" dictum against cruelty put forth by Judaism and Christianity. Western man's reactive declaration of innocence has made him afraid to act, for fear that he may harm innocents. His pity for the suffering of others has brought him to a dead halt.[203] He has become the "Last Man,"[204]

201. See 2 Cor. 12:9–10: "My grace is sufficient for thee; for my strength is made perfect in weakness. Most gladly therefore will I rather glory in my infirmities."

202. Nietzsche, 2nd ess., sec. 16 in *On the Genealogy of Morals*, 85.

203. See Nietzsche, pt. 4, sec. 20 in *Thus Spoke Zarathustra*, 327. Here, Zarathustra realizes that pity is the last obstacle to his strength. The modern fixations of pity, fellow-feeling, and sympathy for the suffering of other sentient beings demonstrate, for Nietzsche, the twilight of the West, not its advancement. On fellow-feeling, see Adam Smith, pt. 1, sec. 1, chap. 1 in *The Theory of Moral Sentiments*, ed. D. D. Raphael and A. L. Macfie (Indianapolis: Liberty Press, 1982), 9; on sympathy for others' suffering, see Rousseau, "Discourse on the Origin, and of the Foundations of Equality among Men," in *Major Political Writings of Jean-Jacques Rousseau*, 83–85.

204. See Nietzsche, sec. 5, "Zarathustra's Prologue," in *Thus Spoke Zarathustra*, 17–18. The Last Man who is unwilling to will anew, who is satisfied with the glut of consumer goods, was famously treated in Francis Fukuyama in "The End of History and the Last Man" (in *National Interest* [Summer 1989], 1–18). Fukuyama's curious last paragraph rehearses Nietzsche's prophecy (1st ess., sec. 17 in *On the Genealogy of Morals*, 54), which states: "Must the ancient fire not some day flare up much more terribly, after much longer preparation? More: must one not desire it with all one's might? even will it? even promote it?"

who wills nothing,[205] and who no longer believes in himself or in his culture. That is why he only dare celebrate *other* cultures, through the gluttonous smorgasbord of multiculturalism, from which all return with unsated hunger.[206] Once the worm of self-contempt revealed to him the Infinite Ground of Being.[207] Now it only occasions never-ending contrition and apology for what he once said about others.[208] Once the camel bore his burden as a sign of his strength. Now he is exhausted by the burden he carries.[209] Hoping to lighten his load, he declares his incredulity that violence is the founding event of every civilization and he questions the cruel enforcements that have maintained every civilization—not the least of which are those that pertain to the sexual, *not* gendered, differences between men and women, without which there could be no regeneration of mortal life. The Last Man distances himself from such barbarism; knowing that to will is to bring forth vi-

205. See Nietzsche, preface, sec. 5 in *On the Genealogy of Morals*, 19: "It was precisely here that I saw the *great* danger to mankind, its sublimest enticement and seduction—but to what? to nothingness—it was precisely here that I saw the will turning *against* life, the tender and sorrowful signs of the ultimate illness" (emphasis in original).

206. See Friedrich Nietzsche, sec. 23 in *The Birth of Tragedy*, trans. Francis Golffing (Garden City, NY: Doubleday, 1956), 136–37: "Only a horizon ringed by myths can unify a culture. The forces of imagination and of the Apollonian dream are saved only by myth from indiscriminate rambling. . . . Over against this, let us consider abstract man stripped of myth, abstract education, abstract mores, abstract law, abstract government . . . a culture without any fixed and consecrated place of origin, condemned to exhaust all possibilities *and feed miserably and parasitically on every culture under the sun*. Here we have the present age" (emphasis added).

207. See Søren Kierkegaard, *The Sickness unto Death*, trans. Howard V. Hong (Princeton, NJ: Princeton University Press, 1980).

208. See Astead W. Herndon and Sydney Ember, "2020 Democrats Agree: They're Very, Very Sorry," *New York Times*, February 3, 2019, https://www.nytimes.com/2019/02/03/us/politics/democrats-2020-apologies.html.

209. See Andreas Lombard, "The Vanity of Guilt," *First Things*, November 2019, https://www.firstthings.com/article/2019/11/the-vanity-of-guilt.

olence and suffering, he gives himself one last hallowed act through which he pays for his crimes: the will to antinatalism, which will bring civilization to a dead halt. No more children, for the cost is too high—for the rest of humanity and to the earth herself.

§55. Either civilizations renew themselves or they perish and others replace them. What would renewal require? On Nietzsche's account, from the Enlightenment onward the West was attempting to heal itself with an antidote derived from the religious toxin that had caused its illness in the first place and, so, was getting sicker by the day. The antidote it was administering was a poison in disguise. More precisely, as I outlined earlier (see section 26), Nietzsche thought that although Westerners claimed that the Enlightenment had been the antidote that liberated them from the yoke of Christianity, they were still suffering from the poison of Christianity that the Enlightenment carried within it.[210] The metamorphosis of the camel into the lion—a merciless, calm slayer of weakened beasts—had not occurred. The second metamorphosis of the lion into the child, which would have announced the rebirth of the West, had been arrested. *For the next several centuries, the fate of the West would be to wither without renewal, poisoned not by the Christian religion it fervently opposed but by the enlightened ideas and sentiments it passionately embraced.* Christian religion had died. "Two thousand years of training in truthfulness"[211]

210. See Leo Strauss, "The Dialogue between Reason and Revelation," in *The Rebirth of Classical Political Rationalism: An Introduction to the Thought of Leo Strauss; Essays and Lectures*, selected and introduced by Thomas L. Pangle (Chicago: University of Chicago Press: 1989), 240: "Nietzsche's criticism can be reduced to one proposition: modern man has been trying to preserve biblical morality while abandoning biblical faith. That is impossible."

211. By this, Nietzsche meant that the will to truth in the question "How is my sinfulness implicated in the wreckage I witness around and in me?" sooner or later must take the form of the question "How can I, in all honesty, believe in God?" See Nietzsche, 3rd ess., sec. 27 in *On the Genealogy of Morals*, 160.

killed it. Now the enlightened West wanted equality, dignity, rights, compassion, and recognition—ideas whose coherence stands and falls with the Christian claim that God Incarnate was the scapegoated, innocent, and voiceless victim who so decisively repudiated aristocratic cruelty that the calendar of human history was reconfigured around that event. The camel *thought* he had become the lion by renouncing Christian religion—did not the French Revolutionaries propose a new calendar? He remained, however, a camel in lion's clothing—was not that new calendar abandoned? Identity politics is this camel in lion's clothing, a creature whose lion's roar against the racist, misogynist, homophobic, Islamophobic, transphobic West ushers from the camel lungs that were fashioned and given life by the central religious claim of the Christian West: the voiceless Innocent One is the Alpha and the Omega. The emergence of identity politics is the clockwork, predictable consequence of a civilization that has neither the courage nor the honesty to fully renounce its foundation and start over—or to fully return to that foundation for sustenance.

§56. We should pause here to consider what a full-on attack by the lion would really destroy. To prepare the way for a renewed world, the lion would destroy the entire Christian edifice of transgression and innocence, including the remaining portion of it that identity politics righteously proclaims. This would mean, among other things, that the lion would put an end to ever-changing identity politics bookkeeping operations, which shift persons and groups from one side of the ledger to the other willy-nilly. In early 2019, Virginia governor Ralph Northam defended third-trimester abortions and the innocents embraced him; the next day it was discovered he wore blackface decades ago. Immediately reviled as a transgressor, his innocence was rescinded.[212] In

212. See Jesse Jackson, "Governor Northam Would Be Wise to Step Down," *Chicago Sun Times*, February 4, 2019, https://chicago.suntimes.com/columnists/governor-northam-would-be-wise-to-step-down/.

late 2019, Canadian prime minister Justin Trudeau was discovered to have worn blackface on more occasions than even he could recall. His bookkeeping entry did not shift because it was not he but rather the structural forces of systematic racism and of white privilege that were said to be the causes of what he did. His defenders, unable to come to grips with what would otherwise fall under the category of racism, claim he was only "wearing make-up." Forty-nine people, a majority of them gay men, were shot dead in an Orlando nightclub and the innocents held them up as martyrs; but because they were listening to "culturally appropriated" music at the time, are their names now registered among the transgressors?[213] The ever-changing bookkeeping of identity politics guarantees that no one among the innocents is assured an indelible entry on the page that records the names of the righteous. If fifty years from now, our heirs discover that the world's ecosystems have collapsed, not from high levels of atmospheric carbon dioxide that transgressor-capitalists have spewed into the air, but from the microplastics in the water bottles from which innocents drank by the billions,[214] will those innocents, too, be marked as transgressors? Nietzsche's lion would put an end to the daily, clerk-like bookkeeping that separates the clean from the unclean. He would shred this ledger book not, as Christians claim, because *all* are unclean transgressors in the eyes of God, who can be washed clean only by the sacrifice of the One who is without blemish or stain,[215] but because the categories of transgression and innocence that once gave Western man meaning are

213. See Gilbert, "Homophobia and the Modern Trans Movement."

214. See Andrea Thompson, "Earth Has a Hidden Plastic Problem—Scientists Are Hunting It Down," *Scientific American*, August 13, 2018, https://www.scientificamerican.com/article/earth-has-a-hidden-plastic-problem-mdash-scientists-are-hunting-it-down/.

215. See 1 Pet. 1:18–19: "Forasmuch as ye know that ye were not redeemed with corruptible things, as silver and gold, from your vain conversation received by tradition from your fathers; But with the precious blood of Christ, as of a lamb without blemish and without spot."

now poisoning him. The noble souls who will someday renew Western civilization after the lion has been sated will not merely be accountants who establish their innocence by measuring the transgressions of others. Renewal will have its costs, to which they will be indifferent.
– That is not all. Destroying the entire Christian edifice of transgression and innocence would also mean destroying the many so-called secular redemptive histories invented during the Enlightenment aftermath of the death of the Christian religion—which nevertheless built from that edifice. Three German thinkers stand out. *Immanuel Kant*, for whom after long labor, seemingly senseless suffering, and innumerable wars, man would finally come to treat others not as means to be used but as ends in themselves.[216] *G. W. F. Hegel*, for whom history is the long struggle that culminates in the overcoming of human alienation, in man coming home to himself.[217] And *Karl Marx*, for whom the brutal but necessary historical suffering experienced in the capitalist stage of history would end when, after solving the problem of scarcity, we arrive at communism. In Marx's words:

> [Communism is] the genuine resolution of the conflict between man and nature and between man and man—the true resolution of the strife between existence and essence, between objectification and self-confirmation, between freedom and necessity, between the individual and the species. Communism is the riddle of history solved, and it knows itself to be this solution.[218]

216. See Kant, "What Is Enlightenment?," in *On History*, 10: "[The slow but inevitable enlightenment of man will someday produce a government that] finds it to its advantage to treat men, who are now more than machines, in accordance with their dignity."

217. See G. W. F. Hegel, pt. 8, para. 808 in *The Phenomenology of Spirit*, trans. A. V. Miller (Oxford: Oxford University Press, 1977), 492–93.

218. Karl Marx, "Economic and Philosophical Manuscripts of 1844," in *Marx-Engels Reader*, 84.

Before tossing Kant, Hegel, and Marx into the dustbin of history, we should give credit to these patient Mensheviks of the spirit,[219] these camels in lion's clothing who purported to supersede Christianity but did not. They retained just enough of the Christian spirit of suffering to invent redemptive histories that bathe man in blood,[220] and demanded that he endure suffering for millennia with nothing to show for it except a distant promise he would never live to see. Kant, Hegel, and Marx could not endure the actual Christian account of the cause and end of suffering. These good Germans nevertheless retained Christianity's patience with it.

Twentieth-century notables had no such patience. However different, and whatever our assessment of each of them might be, Margaret Sanger, John Maynard Keynes, and John Rawls all constructed their ideas on one foundation: *The patient suffering of innocents has no redemptive value*. Sanger's agonizing account of mothers who bore innumerable children and suffered through raising them even unto their own destruction[221] has given us birth control in its various forms, and the institutions around the world like Planned Parenthood that underwrite it. The periodic and painful downturns in the economic cycle, about which Keynes

---

219. The Mensheviks thought there was no historical shortcut that could whisk man directly from feudalism to communism; capitalism had to be passed through and endured. The Bolsheviks thought capitalism could be bypassed. Leon Trotsky's parting words to the Mensheviks during the Congress of Soviets in Petrograd on October 25, 1917, were, "Go to the place where you belong from now on: the dustbin of history!" Leon Trotsky, quoted in Paul Sonne, "The Dustbunnies of History," *Oxonian Review* 8, no. 9.7 (June 8, 2009), http://www.oxonianreview.org/wp/the-dustbunnies-of-history/.

220. See G. W. F. Hegel, introduction to *Philosophy of History*, trans. John Sibree (Toronto: Dover, 1956), 21: "But even regarding History as the slaughter-bench at which the happiness of peoples, the wisdom of States, and the virtue of individuals have been victimized—the question involuntarily arises—to what principle and final aim these enormous sacrifices have been offered."

221. See Margaret Sanger, *Woman and the New Race* (New York: Blue Ribbon Books, 1920).

quipped, "In the long term we are all dead,"[222] purportedly have been neutralized by the increasingly regular and massive Central Bank interventions that his writings justified. The horror and devastation of World War II broke Rawls's Episcopal faith,[223] and prompted him, in *A Theory of Justice*, to develop justifications for egalitarian social policies that have been embraced by the center-left in America and Britain during the last three decades of the twentieth century and into our own. Suffering has no redemptive meaning; therefore let us eliminate it altogether.

The two-century-long lion's labor of ending the relationship between transgression and innocence first overcame the Christian account of that relationship. Here are Kant, Hegel, and Marx, and their supposed secular histories. Next, the lion overcame the veiled historical theodicies that still expected the innocents to endure their suffering with Christian patience, and sought to build a world that minimized the suffering of the innocents. Here are Sanger, Keynes, and Rawls. Is not the third and last task of the lion—the task at hand—to put an end to the relationship between transgression and innocence altogether? Overcoming identity politics is this decisive last step.

§57. When the lion's work is finally finished, there will be no innocent sufferers to name and record in the book of righteousness, for no such book will exist. "Victim," "survivor," "marginalized," "excluded," "oppressed," and the like will be meaningless terms. Women will not be innocents; nor will black Americans, Hispanics, or those individuals gathered under the heading of LGBTQ. No one will be. There will be no further clatter about *voices* that must be heard. "Equality," "dignity," "rights," "compassion," and "recognition" will be meaningless terms because the ultimate justification for them—

222. John Maynard Keynes, chap. 3, sec. 1 in *A Tract on Monetary Reform* (London: MacMillan, 1923), 80.

223. See John Rawls, *A Brief Inquiry into the Meaning of Sin and Faith* (Cambridge, MA: Harvard University Press, 2010).

innocent suffering—will be as unbelievable as the repudiated Christian referent that underwrites them.

When the lion's work is finally finished, neither will there be transgressors. How could they exist if there are no innocents to constitute themselves in relation to them?[224] That reactive relationship behind us, there will only be the strong and weak, the noble and resentful.

When the lion's work is finally finished, the kindred relational terms "pure" and "impure," "clean" and "dirty," will be meaningless as well. There will no innocent, pure ones wanting a clean, green environment; or impure capitalist-transgressors using dirty fossil fuels, as there are today. There will be no innocent, pure ones demanding an end to the stained nation-state, or impure nationalist-transgressors defending their homeland, as there are today.

§58. Identity politics prepares the way for the lion's final assault. Kant, Hegel, and Marx gave transgressor and innocent alike a distant hope that the travails of the world would be overcome. Sanger, Keynes, and Rawls gave transgressor and innocent alike an immediate hope that their travails in the world could be overcome by a bit of planning and institutional tinkering. Identity politics gives no hope to either transgressor or innocent. Daily, the hollow satisfaction of the innocents involves reminding transgressors that there is no atoning for their sins; daily, the transgressor's penance involves the never-ending humiliation that he cannot repent.[225] Then, concluding that this penance is of no avail, the transgressor abandons repentance altogether, lifts the millstone of transgression from his shoulders, and casts it away from him *by forgetting*, so that a tomorrow is possible. In Nietzsche's words:

224. See Nietzsche, 1st ess., sec. 10 in *On the Genealogy of Morals*, 36–37.

225. One of the finest accounts of the current inability to address the burden of transgression can be found in Wilfred M. McClay, "The Strange Persistence of Guilt," *Hedgehog Review* 19, no. 1 (Spring 2017), 40–54.

To be incapable of taking ones enemies, one's accidents, even ones misdeeds seriously for very long—that is a sign of strong full natures in whom there is an excess of power to form, to mold to recuperate and to forget.[226]

Christianity once declared that man's stain was not the last word about him. Had it been, the burden of his transgressions would have become so heavy that he would not have been able to take another step. The weight of his ever-growing debt, an inevitable consequence of all human action in history, had to be lifted from him if he were to have a future. The scapegoated Innocent Lamb took that weight from him. The mysterious transference from the transgressor to the innocent at the heart of Christianity made a tomorrow possible. Nietzsche proposed, instead, that man *forget*.

Prompted by the impossibility of hope within the world identity politics constructs, many today toy with what Nietzsche, the anti-Christian,[227] proposed. They toy with it—but go no further. Liberal citizens proclaim the importance of building a world together, through ever-developing competence. In the world identity politics has constructed, innocence alone matters. After decades of telling liberal citizens that only those who have an identity count, defenders of identity politics have awakened to discover that vast swathes of once-liberal citizens have decided that *they, too, have an identity*. Wanting to be heard, some of these once-liberal citizens who have been told that they are transgressors and nothing more rise up to defend themselves—by saying "No" to the innocents, "we do not care what we have done." This is not Nietzschean forgetfulness. This lesser forgetfulness defends an imagined world, purified of the unclean and stripped of moral ambiguity and agony. However energetic this lesser forgetfulness appears, it builds nothing of the sort liber-

226. Nietzsche, 1st ess., sec. 10, *On the Genealogy of Morals*, 39.
227. See part 1, n. 194.

al citizens want, nor does it create anything of the sort Nietzsche's Übermensch[228] demands. The forgetfulness of the Nietzschean Alt-Right is far more radical than the forgetfulness many transgressors are pondering today. Whereas the Nietzschean Alt-Right would do away with the relationship between transgression and innocence altogether, many transgressors today are halfway Nietzscheans, who liberate themselves through forgetfulness, but remain captive to the relationship between transgression and innocence. This helps us understand the forces now emerging against identity politics, in America and in Europe, which *react* rather than act. These forces do not achieve the metamorphosis Nietzsche had in mind. Those associated with them still need an enemy against which to constitute themselves—women, black Americans, Hispanics, those gathered under the heading of LGBTQ, and so on. No matter how loudly they roar in defense of themselves, they remain camels burdened by the Christian categories of transgression and innocence. Horrible though these halfway movements may be, we must never forget that they operate within the world we ourselves still inhabit—the world of transgression and innocence.

The reckless outbursts of contrived forgetfulness within these halfway Alt-Right movements nevertheless illuminate the foreboding question that stands before us: Is identity politics the final ghastly and unworkable manifestation of Christianity, which poisons us because Christianity itself is a poison; or is identity politics a pernicious defection from Christianity, whose incoherence and destructiveness can only be remedied by returning the categories of transgression and innocence to their Christian framework—and to their Hebrew context, too? What, we must ask, is the greater danger: the Christian invitation to attend firmly to our own transgressions,

228. See Nietzsche, prologue, sec. 4 in *Thus Spoke Zarathustra*, 15: "What is great in man is that he is a bridge and not an end; what can be loved in man is that he is an *overture* and a *going under*" (emphasis in original).

in the knowledge that there is no earthly remedy for them; or is it the Nietzschean Alt-Right demand that we cease to take our transgressions seriously? *How, we must ask, is a tomorrow possible—through a mysterious Divine remedy or through forgetting?* That is the staggering question before us today. I suspect it will take another century or more before we have our answer.

M. THE DEAD END OF GROUP SCAPEGOATING

§59. Will we achieve justice by innocent identity groups scapegoating a transgressor group or by putting an end to group scapegoating altogether? The Nietzschean Alt-Right proposes the latter. The answer identity politics gives is that one group must scapegoat another group to find justice. This has generated a politics concerned with little more than recording who, in the book of righteousness, is stained and who is pure, a politics in which those who are innocents one day become transgressors the next—but rarely the reverse. I have noted that after the first group of transgressors—heterosexual, white men—has been purged, a new group of innocents must step in to take its place; and that the purging sequence will probably fix on white, heterosexual women next, and black, heterosexual men after that. With only a little imagination, we can anticipate what the last indictment will be: the indictment of man himself, for which the resolution will be either the embrace of transhumanism or the eradication of man altogether. In some quarters, these alternatives are already being given serious consideration. How petty our current identity politics scuffles must look from those quarters: while we argue about who among us is righteous, they know that all traces of man as we actually know him today must be purged.[229] Echoing the Christian

---

229. See Pascal Bruckner, *The Fanaticism of the Apocalypse: Save the Earth, Punish Human Beings*, trans. Steven Rendall (Cambridge, UK: Polity, 2013).

claim that I have noted is the font of identity politics, they know that either the soul of man conquers death or it suffers "the wages of sin," which is death.[230] Christianity once offered redemption or damnation to Adam's heirs. The final revelation of identity politics gives us transhumanism or human extinction; the one clears away Adam's transgressive inheritance so that he may finally—literally—be "without blemish or spot,"[231] and the other restores nature's innocence by killing off the heirs of Adam altogether.

But wait! Perhaps to wipe the stain away entirely, we need to go further. Maybe homo sapiens as a species are only the surface manifestation of a deeper blemish. The Hominidae family and the primate order may not go deep enough, either. Perhaps the class Mammalia gets us where we need to go. Look at the polar bear (a mammal); is *he* not the poster child for climate change? Mammals! They always have one another's back. Perhaps the current era of mammalian dominance, which began after the Chicxulub asteroid wiped out the dinosaurs sixty-six million years ago, *should* come to an end. If man alone is purged, other mammals carrying the stain man has exhibited will arise. By eradicating man, we will not have eliminated the stain. The good news, we must now acknowledge, is that radical climate change could wipe out all mammals, after which a new class within the phylum Chordata will emerge—perhaps it will be reptiles. But here, too, we should be weary: What if all members of the Chordata are also implicated? Creatures with backbones are not to be trusted. Eventually they grow upright and full of themselves. Nietzsche thought that all life involved the will to power. Perhaps he was right.

This odd thought experiment has not been in jest. To what lengths must we go, in all honesty, before the stain of man is cleansed? That is the searing question of our times. What the two seemingly antithet-

230. See Rom. 6:23: "For the wages of sin is death."
231. See Thompson, "Earth Has a Hidden Plastic Problem."

ical longings for redemption through transhumanism and innocence through human extinction have in common is the need for purity, and the need to find a mortal group to scapegoat in order to achieve it. That is the dead end into which identity politics takes us.

Liberal citizens grant man no such purity. The much maligned John Locke, by many accounts the father of liberal thought, built his defense of property, of limited government, and of toleration on the basis of what happened to Adam *after* his ejection from Edenic innocence. Most scholars today see Locke's invocation of Adam as a quaint device through which he developed a purportedly secular liberal account of man. This is a grievous mistake, which must be rethought in light of *our* problem; namely, the prospective eclipse of the politics of competence by the politics of innocence. It was Locke who first articulated the liberal politics of competence, as I have called it here, in which citizens build a world together through their labors, and ask government to stand by and protect those labors. Locke was not oblivious to the categories of transgression and innocence on which identity politics depends; on the contrary, he thought that Christianity had *already resolved* the issue of transgression and innocence. Locke's liberal politics was possible only because Christianity already had done this. As he put it:

> I have set down all these texts out of St. Paul, that in them might be seen his own explication of what he says here, viz. that our Saviour, by his death, atoned for our sins, and so we were innocent, and thereby freed from the punishment due to sin.[232]

The liberal politics of competence, unlike the identity politics of innocence, presumes a Divine resolution to the problem of transgression, not a mortal one. Not by specifying a mortal group to

232. John Locke, "Essays and Notes on St. Paul's Epistles," in *The Works of John Locke*, vol. 7 (London: Rivington, 1824), 285.

scapegoat, through whom he establishes his innocence, does man resolve the problem of his stain.[233]

§60. Nor does scapegoating a specific mortal group help establish the publicly stated goal of identity politics—namely, to achieve equality. Identity politics purges and humiliates.[234] It does not make room for the innocents *among* the transgressors; rather, it purges the transgressors through cathartic rage, and then requires another group of innocents to step in and take their place. Equality cannot be achieved in this way. Equality can only be achieved on the basis of the radical asymmetry between God and man. Only if the scapegoat is Divine[235] can citizens be relieved of the need to scapegoat other mortal groups, look

233. Eric Voegelin famously wrote that Marxism "immanentized the eschaton." Eric Voegelin, chap. 4, sec. 4 in *The New Science of Politics* (Chicago: University of Chicago Press, 1952), 124–25. Identity politics immanentizes the scapegoat. Late in his life, in 1894, after five decades of struggling to make sense of the wound of slavery, and concerned about this impulse to scapegoat groups, Frederick Douglass wrote: "Since emancipation we hear much said of our modern colored leaders in commendation of race pride, race love, race effort, race superiority, race men and the like. . . . In all this talk of race, the motive may be good, but the method is bad. It is an effort to cast out Satan by Beelzebub. The evils which are now crushing the Negro to earth have their root and sap, their force and mainspring, in this narrow spirit of race and color and the Negro has no more right to excuse or to foster it than men of any other race. . . . Not as Ethiopians, not as Caucasians, not as Mongolians, not as Afro-Americans, or Anglo-Americans are we addressed but as men. God and nature speak to our manhood and manhood alone." Frederick Douglass, "The Blessings of Liberty and Education," in *The Frederick Douglass Papers: Series One*, vol. 5, ed. John W. Blassingame and John R. McKivigan (New Haven, CT: Yale University Press, 1979–1992), 625.

234. The purpose of Roman crucifixion was to humiliate the victim. In Christian theology, Christ moves from humiliation to exultation, from Good Friday to Easter Sunday. In identity politics, there is no exultation for the scapegoat, only humiliation; the transgressor lives forever on Good Friday, without hope of seeing Easter Sunday.

235. Alternatively, the scapegoat can be an animal. See part 1, n. 13 and Lev. 16:1–34.

upon one another as equals,[236] and thereafter build a world together. Locke understood this. In such a radically asymmetrical relationship, all mortals are broken, all mortals stained, and none can be redeemed by scapegoating another kind. Within this radically asymmetrical relationship, the problem of man is not a group problem. Man's transgression, inherited from Adam, runs deeper than the inheritance of kind that his father and mother bequeath to him. Not incidentally does the New Testament proclaim that the follower of Christ must leave his father and mother,[237] or that kinds are overcome entirely in Christ,[238] or that disciples are to "go therefore and make disciples of all nations."[239] No Divine Scapegoat, no mortal equality. Tocqueville saw this clearly a century and a half later in *Democracy in America*:

> The profoundest and most wide-seeing minds of Greece and Rome never managed to grasp the very general but very simple conception of the likeness of all men and of the equal right of all at birth to liberty. . . . All the great writers of antiquity were either members of the aristocracy of masters or, at the least, saw that aristocracy in undisputed possession before their eyes. Their minds roamed free but were blinkered there. Jesus Christ had to come down to earth to make all members of the human race understand that they were naturally similar and equal.[240]

236. Might money provide the basis for equality? Money *promises* to do this, as Voltaire noted long ago (see part 1, n. 24); but when money becomes the measure of all things, it produces pernicious inequalities, as writers from Plato (see bk. 4, 423a in *The Republic*) to Marx (see "Manifesto of the Communist Party," 475–76) have noted.

237. See Matt. 19:29; Mark 10:29; and Luke 18:29.

238. See Gal. 3:28: "There is neither Jew nor Greek, there is neither bond nor free, there is neither male not female; for ye are all on in Christ Jesus."

239. Matt. 28:18–19.

240. Tocqueville, pt. 1, chap. 3 in *Democracy in America*, vol. 2, 439.

In 1887, Nietzsche abhorred what the scapegoated God, Christ, had turned man into; but he, too, understood the indissoluble link between Christ and equality. In his words:

> The 'redemption' of the human race (from 'the masters,' that is) is going forward; everything is visibly becoming Judaized, Christianized, mob-ized (what do the words matter!).[241]

§61. Let us go further. The radical asymmetry between God and man—*which in making distinctions between kinds irrelevant, makes equality possible*—is also the real basis of the much criticized "individualism" in Locke's thought. Locke's individual should not be set against an ephemeral communitarian alternative, as so many dreamy scholars believe today. He should be set against that *other* solution by which the transgressor's stain is transferred onto a scapegoat; namely, the identification of a specific mortal group onto which will be transferred "the sin of the world." The individual emerges in the formulation of the radical asymmetry that Christianity invents and Reformation thinkers reassert. Locke's liberal political thought begins from that foundation. *We have lost sight of the real significance of the individual in proportion to the degree to which we have lost sight of the Christian understanding of the Scapegoat.* Should this loss become complete, we would not replace much maligned individualism with wholesome communitarianism, but rather with the satisfaction that comes when one group scapegoats another group.[242] We will replace it with tribalism.

241. Nietzsche, 1st ess., sec. 9 in *On the Genealogy of Morals*, 36. The passage begs the question, Is Judaism or Christianity responsible for the equality for which Nietzsche had such disdain? In his estimation, Judaism was its source. Christianity was, in effect, Judaism in disguise (see ibid., sec. 7, 33–34). See also part 1, n. 193.

242. Donoso Cortés seemed to think that without God, you get socialism. See Donoso Cortés, "Discourse on the General Situation of Europe," sec. 2.2 in *Readings in Political Theory*, trans. Vincent McNamara and Michael

§62. We are witnesses, today, to the satisfactions of group scape-goating. They are experienced everywhere around the globe. Like the poor, they have always been with us. Identity politics *seems* to be a species of group satisfaction, because the scapegoating of white, heterosexual men accomplishes the unity and satisfaction of every group of innocents. What is actually happening is more con-voluted. Whether identity politics is the final ghastly and unwork-able manifestation of Christianity or a pernicious defection from Christianity, as I previously proposed,[243] it has not—and cannot—escape the Christian fixation on the individual. Identity politics is, consequently, a sterile hybrid, though perhaps a long-lived one.

On the one hand, in the world identity politics constructs, groups matter. We are not individual persons, born into creation and beset by unique moral challenges of the sort that no other individual in the past, present, or indefinite future will ever exactly endure. Rather, we are white, black, Hispanic, men, women, heterosexual, LGBTQ, or the like.

On the other hand, in the world identity politics constructs, the transgressive wound is not felt as a group wound; it is felt *personal-ly*. Personal fragility, in fact, is one of the hallmarks of adherents of identity politics. The calculus of transgression and innocence may pertain to groups, but it is individuals who turn out to need safe spaces, one-on-one psychological counseling, and protection from the free speech laws that expose their feelings to unnecessary inju-

---

Schwartz (Ave Maria, FL: Sapienta, 2007), 171: "If you wish to fight social-ism, it is necessary to appeal to that religion which teaches charity to the rich and patience to the poor, which teaches the poor to be resigned and the rich to be merciful." The equality to which socialism is dedicated would be impossible, however, if a vestige of the Christian understanding of the Divine Scapegoat had not survived. If it had not, tribalism, not socialism, would be the result. That socialism in Europe "worked," in the sense that the idea of equality it contained was taken for granted within socialist coun-tries, while in the Middle East tribal affiliations always obtruded, is telling.

243. See sec. 58.

ry.[244] In identity politics, the un-Christian scapegoating of one mortal group by other groups intertwines with the Christian "I am,"[245] which emerges through the radical asymmetry between God and man in which groups can have no consideration. Identity politics denies we are unique individual persons in order to mete out group judgment; yet it affirms we are unique individual persons in order that the wound from group transgression be personally felt.[246]

§63. Identity politics scapegoats the mortal scapegoat but cannot disavow its indebtedness to the Christian formulation that put an end to mortal scapegoating altogether—hence the personal turmoil

---

244. See Nadine Strossen, *Hate: Why We Should Resist It with Free Speech, Not Censorship* (Oxford: Oxford University Press, 2018).

245. See Nietzsche, 1st ess., sec. 13 in *On the Genealogy of Morals*, 44–46, for a critique of the idea of the subjective "I" that Christianity invents.

246. The legal challenges of moving from a person-based view of justice to a group-based view of justice are enormous. The US Constitution mentions "person" fifty-eight times, and never once mentions "group." Identity politics drives us in the direction of considering groups only. On the consequences of doing so, see Adarand Constructors, Inc. v. PENA, 515 U.S. 200, 299 (1995) (statement of Anton Scalia): "In my view, government can never have a 'compelling interest' in discriminating on the basis of race in order to 'make up' for past racial discrimination in the opposite direction. [See Richmond v. J. A. Croson., 488 U.S. 469, 520 (1989) (Scalia, concurring in judgment).] Individuals who have been wronged by unlawful racial discrimination should be made whole; but under our Constitution, there can be no such thing as either a creditor or a debtor race. That concept is alien to the Constitution's focus upon the individual [see Amdt. 14, sec. 1: "Nor shall any State . . . deny *to any person*" the equal protection of the laws; emphasis added] and its rejection of dispositions based on race [see Amdt. 15, sec. 1, prohibiting the abridgment of the right to vote "on account of race"], or based on blood [see Art. 3, sec. 3: "No Attainder of Treason shall work Corruption of Blood"; and Art. I, sec. 9, cl. 8: "No Title of Nobility shall be granted by the United States"]. To pursue the concept of racial entitlement—even for the most admirable and benign of purposes—is to reinforce and preserve for future mischief the way of thinking that produced race slavery, race privilege, and race hatred. In the eyes of government, we are just one race here. It is American."

it produces within its adherents. Identity politics does not think itself to be distorted Christianity, but it is. Identity politics is not alone in this confusion, however. Consider the Christians throughout history who have claimed, through the sacrifice of the Innocent Lamb, that scapegoating has ended, but who, in fact, have scapegoated groups? The perilous standing of Jews in Christian Europe is the case that primarily warrants attention.[247] On this side of the Atlantic, slavery and the scapegoating of black Americans is the most pernicious example. "Racism" is what we name any lingering scapegoating in America today, but the term has been so overused that we have lost sight of the staggering problem to which it ultimately refers—namely, claiming one thing and doing another. Consider Tocqueville's observation that "Christianity destroyed servitude; the Christians of the sixteenth century reestablished it."[248] By this he meant that Christianity put an end to scapegoating groups, and then Christians violated their central insight by doing just that.[249]

Scapegoating transgressors or those whose *kind* once contained members who were transgressors—say, by calling them racists—will not put an end to the deeper problem to which racism points, however. Christianly speaking, racism can be laid to rest only by putting an end to group scapegoating. *Reverend* Martin Luther King Jr. understood this. Today, the group scapegoating that identity politics authorizes

247. See Samuel Goldman, "The German Problem," *Modern Age* 61, no. 2 (Spring 2019), 7–15. Goldman's essay is a remarkable reflection on the ongoing agony of post–WW II Germany, which seeks redemption for scapegoating the Jews but which can return neither to pre-Christian paganism nor to Christianity to accomplish it.

248. Tocqueville, pt. 2, chap. 10 in *Democracy in America*, vol. 1, 341.

249. Nowhere is this paradox more evident than in the writings of Martin Luther. He scapegoats Jews (see "On the Jews and Their Lies," in *Luther's Works*, vol. 47, 268–377), and on the other hand lashes out at Christians who would scapegoat Jews as the cause of Christ's death (see "Meditation concerning Christ's Passion," in ibid., vol. 42).

has taken hold in the Democratic Party, in which King placed his political faith. In the interim, his title of *Reverend* has been stripped away, and he has become *Doctor* Martin Luther King Jr. to the party faithful. This is an incalculable loss. The Christian who scapegoats a group has not understood what being an adopted son[250] of God means, nor where his treasure lies. *Reverend* Martin Luther King Jr. would have had no part in this scapegoating enterprise. In polite Democratic Party company, many black Americans do not dare say it, but they believe the corruption of Christianity, of the magnitude that accommodated slavery, was so grievous, so unthinkable, that "principalities and powers"[251] must be the cause. The phrase "Whitey is the devil" sometimes expresses this belief. This makes the problem of racism mortally unsolvable—to which they will say: "Yes; principalities and powers cannot be fought by mortal means. That is why the Blood of the Cross is necessary to endure and overcome it."[252] This talk of Incarnate blood sacrifice makes the Democratic Party faithful quite nervous,[253] which is why, without a serious conversation about what might be lost, the good reverend became *Doctor* Martin Luther King Jr.—and it is why

250. See Rom. 9:8: "They which are the children of the flesh, these are not the children of God: but the children of the promise are counted for the seed." The children of the flesh are mortal *kinds*, mortal groups. They look over their shoulders at one another with suspicion. To be a child of God is to be adopted into a new home, whose head of household is God the Father. In that household, differences of kind cease to matter.

251. See Eph. 6:12: "For we wrestle not against flesh and blood, but against principalities, against powers, against the rulers of the darkness of this world, against spiritual wickedness in high places."

252. "The King's College Presents: Black History Month by Rev. Eugene F. Rivers III," YouTube video, 27:13, posted by the King's College, February 8, 2019, https://www.youtube.com/watch?v=ORaOdqLo2FQ.

253. See Peter J. Leithart, "After the End of Sacrifice," *First Things*, February 1, 2019, https://www.firstthings.com/web-exclusives/2019/02/after-the-end-of-sacrifice: "The only Protestantism that can resist the seductions and intimidations of liberalism is one committed to radical sacrifice."

black Americans became but one identity group among many in the Democratic Party. Reverend King's blood of the cross points the way to overcoming altogether the scapegoating of one group by another. Doctor King's "struggle with social injustice" is the identity politics code phrase that renders the entire world a battleground between transgressor groups and ever-proliferating groups of innocents, a battleground on which we have every reason to worry blood someday will be spilled. Reverend King's blood of the cross illuminates an America engaged in a staggering spiritual battle with principalities and powers, which invites its citizens to entertain a steely, Mosaic hope that the promised land of American redemption might someday be ours. Doctor King's "struggle with social injustice" gives us merely mortal and unredeemable transgressors, innocents whose rage must never cease, and a plan to harness the despair of both parties to the infraction for political ends.

§64. In the Hebrew Bible, we read of the death of Uzzah, son of Abinadab,[254] as King David was transporting the Ark of the Covenant to Jerusalem on an oxcart. The mood was festive, rather than appropriately somber. God had given explicit instructions about how the ark was to be transported, but they had been disregarded. King David and his entourage, after all, knew better. The oxen stumbled, and Uzzah, concerned that the ark might fall off the cart, steadied it with his hand—at which point he was struck dead by God. Uzzah no doubt thought he was helping God by steadying the ark; he was killed because mortal hands could not touch Divine things without being consumed and destroyed. Uzzah saw the ark wobble and proudly thought he would save it from falling. His arrogant reach for the ark was a desecration of it. There are some things that man is not meant to touch.

The identity politics of innocence is an Uzzah-like reach for the mortally inaccessible mystery of transgression and innocence. The

254. See 2 Sam. 6:1–7 and 1 Chron. 13:9–12.

merely mortal rendering of transgression and innocence offered by identity politics will burn all who touch it. When groups achieve their innocence by scapegoating and attempting to purge other mortal groups, it is only a question of time before a new scapegoat will be needed—*perhaps it will be them*. Then they, like the white, heterosexual men who now wear the crown of thorns, will suddenly become more than who they really are—scapegoats who take away the sins of the world, rather than mortals, like everyone else, involved in transgression and searching for redemption.

PART TWO

Bipolarity and Addiction:
Further Obstacles to the
Retrieval of Liberal Competence

N. BIPOLARITY: MANAGEMENT SOCIETY
AND SELFIE MAN

§65. Let us imagine a world freed of mortal scapegoating, a world after identity politics, in which the promissory note at the American Founding about which Reverend King spoke so eloquently can finally be cashed in by all its citizens. In his words:

> When the architects of our republic wrote the magnificent words of the Constitution and the Declaration of Independence, they were signing a promissory note to which every American was to fall heir. This note was a promise that all men, yes, black men as well as white men, would be guaranteed the "unalienable Rights" of "Life, Liberty and the pursuit of Happiness."[1]

Let us imagine, in other words, what a liberal politics of competence might involve. We must imagine it, because nothing more characterizes the current moment than that we are draining citizens of everyday competence and—often wittingly—removing the opportunities to develop and retain it. I have suggested that the world identity politics constructs is an obstacle to the return to the liberal politics of competence. That is true. In that world, what matters is not competence but our status as a transgressor or an innocent. I have also suggested, in section 49, that when citizens no longer need to build a world together, they can be seduced into looking at one another in the way identity politics proposes. That is also true. As the state grows stronger, there is less

1. Martin Luther King Jr., "I Have a Dream" (speech, Lincoln Memorial, Washington, DC, August 28, 1963), https://www.mtholyoke.edu/acad/intrel/mlkdream.htm.

need for citizens to build a world together. State competence provides for their every need. Citizen-subjects have gadgets that make possible never-ending entertainment[2] and their episodic Two Minute Hate against transgressors, which "graze[s] their skin"[3] and convinces them they are still alive in a world that no longer offers those durable connections that might otherwise tell them so. Their world is one of radical freedom, dissevered from the mediated analog world of dirt, compromise, and imperfection that would confront them if they dared face it.

§66. This curious feeling of radical freedom in an insulated world over which citizen-subjects prevail, however, is only one-half of the larger configuration that calls out for an explanation. *Juxtaposed with this feeling of radical freedom today is our intimation of insuperable forces over which citizens have no control whatsoever.* Take "globalism," for example. The prevailing sentiment is that globalism is historically necessary and that nothing can stop its advance. If the middle-class and manufactur-

2. See Mitchell, "Age of Exhaustion," 59–60: "[The distant fear for America is that citizens] will lose faith in liberty and no longer labor to maintain and defend it. Instead, they will prefer a quiet, purportedly beneficent equality in servitude, a despotism that assures them that they have security and adolescent entertainment: Facebook, Twitter, never-ending video games, and the titillation of ever more mesmerizing gadgets. This delivers them from the specter of anxiety and the burden of freedom. The democratic age ends, neither with robust Liberals *striving* in a forever imperfect world, nor with defiant anti-Liberals *striving* to perfect the world, but rather with The Great Exhaustion. Striving, uncertainty, risk, labor, suffering, insult—these become too much for our fragile constitutions to bear. Above all, in the time of The Great Exhaustion, no one wants to feel uncomfortable and, so, we conspire to organize the world so that it is without duress or hardship. The 1 percent political and commercial classes are happy to oblige."

3. Augustine, bk. 2, chap. 2 in *Confessions*, trans. R. S. Pine-Coffin (New York: Penguin Classics, 1961), 57. For St. Augustine, life without God as its center carries with it the disposition to seek poisons that yield muted, perversely enjoyable suffering. The soul lost to God finds solace in dwelling in its poisons, and only through the grace of God does that soul relinquish them.

ing sectors of America happen to be its collateral damage, then so be it; workers had better move, retool, or stand in line for a universal basic income. The intractable divide between wealth and poverty will not close.[4] The best that can be done is to mitigate the damage through increased social spending on those who are its casualties. Many global elites take this fatalistic view today, which has prompted populist outbursts and the growing sense that citizens have been betrayed by those charged with watching out for their good.[5] By many accounts, the great question of our time is whether political elites will be able to understand and address the divide between wealth and poverty, which seems to be caused by an insurmountable force beyond our control.[6]

§67. I will return shortly to how we today formulate and live out this paradox of radical freedom and utter helplessness. Let me first step back for a

4. Plato was the first to notice that a singular fixation on accumulating wealth serves to concentrate it in the hands of a few and impoverish the rest (see bk. 8, 550c–d in *The Republic*). Marx, in 1848, also saw this bifurcated pattern of wealth distribution (see "Manifesto of the Communist Party," 474: "Our epoch, the epoch of the bourgeoisie, possesses, however, this distinct feature: it has simplified class antagonisms; society as a whole is more and more splitting up into two great hostile classes directly facing each other: bourgeoisie and proletariat"). Plato and Marx, each in his own way, thought that there was an internal logic associated with the love of wealth that could not be overridden. An often overlooked book that suggests that with foresight, prudence, and planning, market commerce can contribute to human flourishing is Wilhelm Röpke, *A Human Economy: The Social Framework of the Free Market* (Wilmington, DE: ISI Books, 1998).

5. For perhaps the best late twentieth-century book on the subject, written not long after the end of the Cold War, see Christopher Lasch, *The Revolt of the Elites and the Betrayal Democracy* (New York: W. W. Norton, 1995).

6. Plato thought that no amount of tinkering by political elites could stop the revolutionary overthrow of a regime whose highest good is wealth, because the problem is the love of wealth itself, which politics cannot touch. As he put it: "[Those] who go on making and amending laws . . . do not see that they are simply cutting of the Hydra's heads" (bk. 4, 426e in *The Republic*).

minute and ask the more capacious question: How have the great minds of the past made sense of this experience of moving back and forth between feeling radically free and feeling utterly bound by the constraints all around us? What have they written about this all-too-familiar oscillation in which, at one moment, we occupy lofty heights that make us giddy and, at the next, we are lowered by the conviction that we are inert, anonymous, and without worth—that we are nothing? I indicated in section 18 of the preface that the terms "bipolarity" and "manic depression" are relatively recent accounts of this lived paradox, and that there are venerable ancient accounts that present it in a rather different light. In ancient Athens, Plato wrote that the tyrannical soul—the soul who has lost sight of the Divine light of the Good—will "always be one man's master and another man's slave."[7] Without the antidote of philosophy, the tyrant will oscillate back and forth between the two seemingly antithetical postures. Only philosophy can save us, Plato says.[8] Christian theology, too, provides an account of this lived paradox. Because the created order of which man is a part was created ex nihilo, out of nothing, his nothingness will always overshadow him. Because man is made in the image of God, he intimates what it means to be seated above the whole of creation. Man: the creature created in the image of God, who ranges *between* nothingness and eternal self-sufficiency and oscillates back and forth between these two nodal points. In St. Augustine's fifth-century terms, it might be said that when man lives without reference to God, in the City of Man, it is *inevitable* that he will suffer from bipolarity. Only when he lives in prayerful dependence and thanksgiving, in the City of God, can he find an antidote to this lived paradox.[9] Perhaps that is what St. Augustine meant to convey when he wrote, "There is no rest until I rest in Thee."[10] In the mid-

7. Bk. 9, 576a in ibid., 266.

8. See bk. 5, 473d in ibid., 165.

9. For the distinction between the City of Man and the City of God, see St. Augustine, bk. 11, chap. 1 in *City of God*, 429.

10. St. Augustine, bk. 1, chap. 1 in *Confessions*, trans. Chadwick, 3.

seventeenth century, in England, Hobbes gave an account of the state of nature in which man oscillates back and forth between the mania associated with "restless desire for power . . . that ceaseth only in death"[11] and the brooding withdrawal and despair that results when "[men use words] to grieve one another."[12] Only an awe-inspiring sovereign, a Leviathan, who lords over all citizens can ameliorate this condition and bring peace. In mid-eighteenth-century France, Rousseau wrote that "melancholy is the friend of delight."[13] He proposed that the right sort of education might provide relief from oscillating back and forth between the two. In late eighteenth-century England, Adam Smith noted that growing nations exhibit a sort of mania, while nations whose economies are shrinking are melancholic.[14] Also in the field of economics, in the early twentieth century, Keynes seemed to understand the cyclical nature of man's "animal spirits," and thought that Central Bank interventions might attenuate the amplitude of the cycle.[15] Notwithstanding the claim of microeconomics that "man is a rational animal," the most insightful economists have always understood that such an account misses the larger oscillating cycle *within which* rationality operates.

Taken together, the authors to which I have alluded provide very different accounts of how man's bipolarity (to use current terminology) can be understood and overcome. Plato thought it was a philosophical problem. St. Augustine thought it was a theological problem. Hobbes thought it was a political problem. Rousseau thought it was an educational problem. Smith and Keynes thought it was an economic problem. Of the various formulations that I have briefly considered here, only the

11. Hobbes, pt. 1, chap. 11, para. 2 in *Leviathan*, 58.

12. Pt. 1, chap. 4, para. 4, in ibid., 17.

13. Jean-Jacques Rousseau, bk. 4, *Emile*, trans. Allan Bloom (New York: BasicBooks, 1979), 229.

14. See Smith, bk. 1, chap. 8 in *Wealth of Nations*, 91.

15. See John Maynard Keynes, chap. 12, sec. 7 in *The General Theory of Employment, Interest, and Money* (New York: Harcourt, Brace & World, 2016).

one offered by Keynes has much purchase with us today. Central banks around the world operate on the basis of his theories, as we know. I suspect we will soon discover if their tacit commitment to maintaining asset *mania*, through low or negative interest rates, is sustainable.

§68. I have not yet mentioned the formulation that Tocqueville had in mind. There is a great deal we can learn from the formulations of the authors I just cited. Nevertheless, I think that Tocqueville's formulation is the most important one for us today because it is able to comprehend the phenomenon of globalism that is on everyone's mind in a way that links the fatalism that now attends it with the radical freedom that democratic man comes to experience in relation to it. Always the social theorist, Tocqueville warned in the mid-nineteenth century that *democratic social conditions* would produce this bipolar experience. He worried, in fact, that citizens would feel so small, and the constraining forces that overwhelm them seem so large in comparison, that they would renounce the idea of freedom altogether.

> I am aware that many of my contemporaries think that nations on earth are never their own masters and that they are bound to obey some insuperable and unthinking power, the product of pre-existing facts, of race, or oil, or climate. These are false and cowardly doctrines which can only produce feeble men and pusillanimous nations. Providence did not make mankind entirely free or completely enslaved. Providence has, in truth, drawn a predestined circle around each man beyond which he cannot pass; but within those vast limits, man is strong and free, and so are peoples.[16]

Life for these citizens would consist of punctuated moments of radical freedom spent with their entertaining gadgets, offset by a kind of structural fatalism—say, about "economic forces"—that would

16. Tocqueville, pt. 4, chap. 8 in *Democracy in America*, vol. 2, 705.

paralyze them. He worried, moreover, that each of these two different nodal points would contribute mightily to the draining of liberal
competence. Where they did not drain it, they would prevent it from
emerging in the first place. *Our problem today* is that citizens cannot
build a world of competence together if our challenges are so big that
we ourselves can do nothing about them, or if our radical freedom to
be entertained as we wish requires only a glass screen in our hands,
rather than friends, neighbors, and fellow citizens all around us. If we
are to find our way to liberal competence again, we must provide an account of this bipolar citizen experience, then administer an antidote.
We need not look far afield. What we are looking for is right in front
of us, and we are living it daily: the strange bipolar configuration of
management society and selfie man.

§69. Consider first management society—that arrangement in which
liberal citizens become small and insignificant and renounce their liberty. Although we might think of this as a new thing, Tocqueville saw
the phenomenon that gave rise to it already in 1840. Our understanding of management society—what, after 1989, we call globalism—is for
the most part economic and cultural. We speak of global markets; and
of the overwhelming power of Western culture, which corrodes then
dissolves local, regional, and national cultures everywhere. We take the
evermore remote management that drives us headlong into economic and cultural globalization as proof of an irreversible process, the
opposition to which is futile and parochial, and the result of which is
suffocating cultural homogeneity,[17] notwithstanding all the platitudes
we hear about diversity. The root cause of what we observe, Tocqueville thought, is not economic but rather the gradual and inevitable
breaking of links that occurs in the transition from the aristocratic to

17. See Tocqueville, pt. 3, chap. 17 in *Democracy in America*, vol. 2, 615: "Vari-
ety is disappearing from the human race; the same ways of behaving, thinking and feeling are found in every corner of the world."

the democratic age. These include the breaking of the link between man and nature, the breaking of the links between generations, and the breaking of the links within society. These delinkages, Tocqueville thought, would make society loom large and our own world become shriveled and lifeless. In his words:

> Aristocracy links everyone, from peasant to king, in one long chain. Democracy breaks the chain and frees each link . . . . Thus, not only does democracy make men forget their ancestors, but also clouds their view of their descendants and isolates them from their contemporaries. Each man is forever thrown back on himself alone, and there is danger that he may be shut up in the solitude of his own heart.[18]

How would citizens think, and what thoughts would come "naturally into [their] imagination,"[19] once those links were fully broken, Tocqueville wondered. He concluded that with respect to how citizens would think, a new philosophical method would emerge that would be impatient with the past and with any person who claimed authority over others. Its intent would be to

> escape from imposed systems, the yoke of habit, family maxims, class prejudices, and to a certain extent national prejudices as well, [to] treat tradition as valuable for information only and accept existing facts as no more than a useful sketch to show how things could be done differently and better.[20]

From this new way of thinking would arise the view that all things can be changed, improved, rationalized, and made to conform to a comprehensive system that man can devise. In the aristocratic age,

18. Pt. 3, chap. 3 in ibid., 508.
19. Pt. 4, chap. 2 in ibid., 668.
20. Pt. 1, chap. 1 in ibid., 429.

life's burdens were "ameliorated," but they could not be "changed."[21] A single coordinated world would have been conceivable only if God Himself brought it about, since by mortal effort this would have been thought impossible. The delinked world, according to Tocqueville, had however produced a new kind of man, "democratic man," who reflects a "distinct [kind] of humanity."[22] Democratic man imagines that a grand unification of the world is within his grasp—that he, not God, can save the planet, as environmentalists have declared; or that through his efforts, a globally coordinated world can be managed.

How strange this is, really. Rather than see a plurality of unique unfoldings around him that constitute emergent wagers about possible alternative futures, unknowable and unmanageable before they happen, democratic man *needs* to understand his world as a system he can manage and unify. Rather than understand liberty as an always developing response to an emergent world, he sees it as an impotent archaism in a world that must be managed. A plural, emergent future that he cannot control, about which I made preliminary remarks many pages ago (in section 18), terrifies him. Any liberal pluralism worthy of the name, evolutionary biology, and market commerce all presume an unfolding, emergent, unknowable future. Tocqueville saw already in 1840 that these sorts of political, biological, and economic accounts would frighten democratic man; and that he would become fixated, instead, on unifying systems as a way to insulate himself against the terror of a pluralistic, uncontrollable world. He wrote that in the democratic age, "unity will become an obsession."[23] Real differences—differences between men and women, between peoples, or between states—would become psychologically unbearable. Hence, in the post-1989 world, comes the *need* for men and women to be seen as interchangeable; the *need* to believe that the cultural and national inheritances that distin-

21. Pt. 1, chap. 8 in ibid., 453.

22. Tocqueville, pt. 4, chap. 8 in *Democracy in America*, vol. 1, 704.

23. Tocqueville, pt. 1, chap. 7 in *Democracy in America*, vol. 2, 451.

guish citizens are burdens to be jettisoned rather than inheritances to be honored; the *need* to institute democracy everywhere around the globe. Where are the citizens who are prepared to live, on the contrary, in a nonparsimonious world, a world that does not cohere as a manageable system—a world in which men and women know, despite all their common ground, that they will never quite understand each other; a world in which we recognize the limits of our inheritances, but understand that we must live through them rather than work around them; a world in which we accept that some (or many) nations will never have democratic government and it does not bother us? Where are the citizens who are prepared to live in a world so wondrous and unknowable that they cherish and fiercely protect the liberty that allows them to participate in its mysterious development at all levels, from the local to the national?

Although he wrote reverentially about the precious gift of liberty in the democratic age, Tocqueville understood that democratic man would find the plural world of parochial, local, and national attachments in which that liberty had to be embedded too much of an encumbrance to endure. He would wish to take flight. Having already broken free of some of the linkages that bound him to nature, to his past, and to his fellow citizens, democratic man would wish to break free from them altogether. That is why today, so many of us are "spiritual" rather than "religious"; "coparents" rather than "fathers" and "mothers"; "global citizens" rather than citizens of this or that country. Small and on our own, and always cognizant of our finitude, we imagine release from any links that remain.

This democratic impulse goes too far. Citizens are, ultimately, creatures that must have a home, a family, a locale, a nation, a religion.[24] Moreover, they cannot rescind the liberty they are to exercise in these domains. The psychological dilemma of the democratic age is that

24. See Ted V. McAllister and Bruce P. Frohnen, *Coming Home: Reclaiming American's Conservative Soul* (New York: Encounter Books, 2019).

democratic man can see beyond the immediacy of his parochial horizon, by virtue of the delinkage that characterizes the democratic age. From that vantage point, the exercise of citizens' liberty seems anachronistic. They dimly see the cosmopolitan promise that renders such an exercise superfluous. Because they are embodied creatures, however, that promise can never be fully realized—hence the heartfelt agony of romantic souls, who see in every choice a limit to the unbounded freedom they intimate is truly their own. The melancholy of man is that he cannot escape the necessity of exercising his liberty within the bounded world in which he dwells. Globalism has been the romantic attempt to overcome that melancholy.

§70. Management society—or "globalism," in post-1989 parlance—has not emerged as a singularity, however. At the same time that local and national liberty is being repudiated and our fate is being handed over to global managers, something else has emerged that we seldom connect with this arrangement—namely, a phenomenon I call "selfie man." This occurrence has insulated citizens from one another while at the same time giving them the opportunity for heretofore undreamed-of self-elevation. Why is it, we might wonder, that at the same instant when we deny that our families, neighbors, towns, regions, and states can constructively address the difficulties we face, hundreds of millions of people around the world—perhaps even billions—are monotonously taking selfies of themselves? Citizens in a globalized world acutely feel their powerlessness, *and* they are taking pictures of themselves everywhere, as if the world around them becomes important only by virtue of them recording their presence in it. Alongside this impulse to look up with resignation and declare that citizens are powerless to address "the world's problems" lies the self-aggrandizing impulse of selfie man. Together, these phenomena configure our experience in such a way that we believe we are at once powerless to act with our neighbors to solve problems together, yet also are convinced that we are so empowered that we no longer need our neighbors at all.

§71. A passage that captures the current psychic condition of American citizens can be found near the end of *Democracy in America*. Democratic citizens, Tocqueville wrote, would someday believe that they are "either greater than kings or less than men."[25] That day has arrived. Through the glass screens that we now hold in our hands, each of us is sovereign; for with the touch of a finger, we can remove from our social media kingdoms anyone who does not accede to the self-presentation we offer. We are, therefore, "greater than kings." On the other hand, with respect to the political actions necessary to build a world, we are today "less than men," and happily hand over the keys to the global managers to address our problems for us.

A liberal politics of competence is not possible if citizens are at once greater than kings and less than men. This is obviously the case when citizens feel themselves to be less than men. In handing over the keys to global managers, they renounce politics altogether. Selfie man, who feels himself to be greater than a king, also renounces politics, even if he often feels himself to be highly political. The type of episodic activism practiced by so many today should not be confused with politics because it does not entail the long-suffering labor with engaged fellow citizens over practical matters that develops competence. Politics is a face-to-face, local-to-national deliberation concerned with building a world together. It is only through the give-and-take of argumentation, compromise, trust, and forbearance that the next small step can be taken. The next small step is not what the activism of selfie man aims to achieve; rather, the goal of activism is to demonstrate wherein perfection lies, and where the world falls short. Because the world always falls short, activism is always episodic. Goaded by the imperfection of the world and the need to overcome it, selfie man rises to the level of activism, falls back into despair, and then is distracted by entertainment, because the burden is too much, until goaded anew. The liberal politics of competence

25. Tocqueville, pt. 4, chap. 6 in *Democracy in America*, vol. 2, 694.

happens in the give-and-take of everyday life, in real time. It necessarily moves from imperfection to imperfection. That is why the staunch convictions of the political activist contribute nothing to the liberal politics of competence. Animated by the belief that the task of politics is to move from imperfection to perfection, political activism is a tempting shortcut that bypasses the long-suffering labor of politics (see entry P). Only the delinked citizen, who Tocqueville thought would dominate in the democratic age, for whom unity has become an obsession, can imagine that such a task would be satisfying.

§72. The obvious renunciation of politics by dreamy citizens who defer to global managers and the less obvious renunciation of politics by citizen activists have given us a world that drains away liberal competence. The ancient Greeks had a word to describe citizens who renounced politics and withdrew into themselves: ἰδιώτης, from which derives the English word "idiot." In the world of management society and selfie man, citizen-idiots oscillate back and forth between feeling that they are greater than kings and feeling that they are less than men. In one moment, all things seem possible; in the next, nothing seems possible. Citizens cannot build a liberal politics of competence around this formula, which causes their moods and judgments to oscillate wildly. Yet this sort of oscillation has increasingly characterized the post-1989 world. The benumbed configuration of management society and selfie man has promised release and liberation from the types of parochial bonds through which liberal competence is developed. What citizens get in exchange is an interminable litany telling them that their problems are global, and that management society is equipped to deal with them. In exchange for their quiescence, citizens get gadgets to entertain themselves and the righteousness of identity politics, both of which have kept them at a mediated distance from their actual day-to-day neighbors. Citizens look *upward* to global managers. They look *inward* to their selfie-selves. This has spared them from looking *outward* to fellow citizens, many of whom they judge to be irredeemably stained, but with whom they might have nevertheless built a world of liberal competence together.

O. ADDICTION: WHEN SUPPLEMENTS BECOME SUBSTITUTES

§73. My earlier diagnosis of the pathology of the identity politics of innocence points to the need to return to the liberal politics of competence. Even if identity politics were to recede tomorrow, however, an obstacle to that return would be the configuration of management society and selfie man that has predominated since the end of the Cold War. This configuration has drained liberal competence by directing our attention away from the fellow citizens within our neighborhoods and nations with whom it would need to be developed. But there is yet another far more perilous obstacle to the return to liberal politics, the evidence for which, like the obstacle of management society and selfie man, is all around us. I will introduce it with an example that is difficult to ignore and then explore how in almost all domains of American life this obstacle arrests liberal competence.

§74. In 2016, over sixty-four thousand people in America died from opioid overdose. The following year, the *New York Times* called this "the deadliest drug crisis in American history."[26] We are in the midst of a drug overdose epidemic in America, an epidemic of addiction. The opioid crisis is not the only overdose crisis in America today, however. It is one crisis among many others in which citizens in modern America get the dosage wrong, so to speak. Opioid overdose may be the

---

26. See Maya Salam, "The Opioid Epidemic: A Crisis Years in the Making," *New York Times*, October 26, 2017, https://www.nytimes.com/2017/10/26/us/opioid-crisis-public-health-emergency.html.

most visible instance of this larger problem, but if we want to understand the greater overdose crisis in society, we need to step back and frame the larger problem in the most comprehensive way possible.

The idea that a substance can in one dose save and in another dose harm has an ancient pedigree. In Plato's *Republic*, Socrates distinguishes between two kinds of doctors—those who administer a circumscribed dose of medicine to help their patients reestablish the health they had before falling ill and those doctors whose "cure" requires their patients to take medicine indefinitely, because they say reestablishing a healthy, medicine-free condition is impossible.[27] These latter doctors misunderstand the proper use of medicine, which is as a supplement taken to cure an ailment, after which their patients regain their health, and their life. As a substitute, medicine no longer works to provide a cure, because patients must depend on a regular, and perhaps increasing, dose to stay alive. Here, medicine is a substitute, a stand-in, for their health. Patients continue to live but do not return to living, because death is always right around the corner should they stop taking their medicine. Socrates referred to such patients as living a life of "lingering death." They live between the condition of a healthy life that would require no medicine and the condition of death that would occur if they stopped taking their medicine. The proper use of medicine—as a supplement— should lead the patient back to a life without medicine; the improper use of medicine leads to lingering death. The patient living on substitutes is always living on borrowed time.

§75. Rather than use the language of dose and overdose to illuminate the problem posed for liberal competence, I will rely on the language of supplements and substitutes. Dose and overdose, on the face of it, are quantitative comparisons. But here we are considering something more nuanced than a simple Goldilocks comparison between too much, too little, and just right. A brief observation from Jean-Jacques

27. See Plato, bk. 3, 405c–406e in *The Republic*.

Rousseau makes this clear. In his "First Discourse" (1750), Rousseau compares ancient warriors, who had few weapons, with "modern scientifically trained soldiers."[28] The former, he writes, were courageous. The weapons they put on were like prostheses to supplement their courage. That is what made them truly fierce. Modern soldiers, he writes, have much more powerful weapons; but lacking courage, they do not know how to use their weapons well—and perhaps are frightened to use them at all. Modern soldiers think they are superior to ancient warriors because the power of their weapons is greater; and in a quantitative sense, that is true. Rousseau's important insight is that weapons can be supplements to courage, but in the modern case, as he avers, they have become substitutes for courage. If weapons become substitutes for courage, modern soldiers live on borrowed time. Eventually, warriors who *do* know the right use of their weapons—as supplements to their courage—will overwhelm those warriors who do not. Like Plato's doctors, warriors must understand that they cannot turn supplements into substitutes without cost.

What Plato and Rousseau understood is that the relationship between supplements and substitutes does not simply involve a question of how much the dosage should be, but that life goes very wrong when we up the dosage and turn supplements into substitutes. In our modern parlance, when the supplement becomes a substitute, we become addicted. We tend to limit the category of addiction to the use of substances, like drugs and alcohol, sex, video games, and so on. Here I will consider those sorts of addictions to be specific instances of supplements becoming substitutes, and expand the category of addiction to *all* instances of supplements becoming substitutes. This will allow us to see the full extent of the problem we face.

§76. Let's leave Plato and Rousseau behind. I have drawn from their ideas to demonstrate that thinkers have wondered about the relation-

28. Rousseau, "First Discourse," 29.

ship between supplements and substitutes for a very long time. In our day, we have lost sight of this important way of thinking about problems. To make the distinction between supplements and substitutes plainer still, and to bring it up to date, consider the everyday examples of meals and vitamins. We usually find our vitamins in the supplements section of the grocery or health food store. When we buy vitamins, we take into consideration our meals and the prosthetic amplification, so to speak, that our vitamins may provide. The meal is always the important thing, to which vitamins must refer if they are to work well.

When vitamins work as a supplement—when they make us stronger, more alert, or less fatigued—we are tempted to go further, to take more of them. We may ponder, in light of their effect, whether the source of our newfound powers is the supplement itself, independent of the meal. Why bother with the time-consuming task of becoming a good cook, making a meal, and sitting at the table when a few pills or powders will amplify our powers? In short, why bother at all with the hard-to-develop competence involved in these activities? The supplements to them, we come to convince ourselves, are the real source of our power.

At the onset of our repudiation of what I will hesitantly call the "natural order of things," we witness immediate results. We think we have miraculously bypassed the competence of making a meal. In fact, however, the wondrous results we get are only possible because our last meal is still with us, as a referent to which the supplement is oriented, even if we have lost sight of it. Rousseau's courageous warrior helps us to see this more clearly. He knew that the warrior's courage is, so to speak, the meal, and that the weapons he uses are the supplement to the meal. One day, he decides to become a more ferocious warrior and, so, dons more weaponry. He focuses on acquiring more weapons, but still has his courage within him. As long as he is still courageous, donning more weaponry will make him a better warrior. If he keeps focusing only on his weapons, however, eventually the courage that allowed him to make good use of his weapons will wither. The meal will no longer be with him. In that instant, the weapons that had been a supplement to his courage will be transformed into a substitute for his courage. Now, he is living on borrowed time.

The strange but euphoric moment after the benefits of the supplement-turned-substitute have kicked in, but before the world collapses because "man cannot live by substitutes alone," to twist a phrase,[29] is the moment of our greatest temptation. What is impossible seems miraculously possible. Lead has turned into gold. Eureka! In that moment, we fall victim to what I will call substitutism. The opioid addict, in this regard, is merely practicing a different kind of substitutism than Rousseau's modern warrior: both get high on the prospect that they have somehow cheated the natural order of things, and avoided the fixed law that when supplements are turned into substitutes, an immense price must be paid. My thesis, in fact, is that substitutism is a debilitating pathology in American life, and that any number of interesting developments, intractable problems, and even sources of great pride, many of which seem quite unrelated, fall within its purview and under its spell. Nearly everywhere we look, we are living an unsustainable high, on borrowed time, at the expense of developing the nourishing, hard-to-develop competence that would keep the supplement from becoming a substitute. We dimly understand this but cannot figure out how to name our malady, let alone diagnose it. That malady is substitutism. It subverts liberal competence.

§77. Consider the phenomena I lay out in the following sections, which catch our attention as curiosities, strike us as serious problems, or bring us inordinate joy. I will comment briefly on each. They range widely, and do not seem to go together under a recognizable heading. In each case, a supplement has been turned into a substitute. As such, the phenomenon is living on borrowed time, as all instances of substitutism necessarily are. How long the strange and euphoric high can last, no one can say. What we can say is that the substitute

29. See Matt. 4:4.

must eventually change from gold back to lead, must return to being a mere supplement. Moreover, the sober act of reverse alchemy that must be undertaken can only happen when we first remember, and then return to, the competence associated with the meal for which the supplement was able to emerge in the first place.

§78. *We will consume five hundred billion plastic bottles of water per year by 2021.* And the number of bottles of water we drink per year after that will probably only rise. Most of those bottles will end up in landfills, burn in incinerators (if not in smoldering garbage piles), or float in our oceans for generations. Before bottled water, most of us got our water from the faucets in our homes, without beverage companies monetizing it. Home was where we lived and developed our many competences; our water, so necessary for life, flowed from our tap. Where your water is, your home is, and vice versa. We left our homes on errands and trips, of course; and when we did, we occasionally brought along a thermos of tap water as a supplement, knowing that our steady water supply—the meal, so to speak—would be waiting for us, again, on tap when we got home. For some time, beverage companies have wanted us to get all the water we need from them in bottled form. Why turn on the tap, when you can unscrew the cap of a plastic water bottle? This goal would have been unachievable unless the temptation to turn supplements into substitutes was already in us, so the beverage companies are not entirely at fault. Consider, though, the consequences of their success.

First, we no longer learn the basic competence of turning on the tap for the water we need and then turning it off when we are done. This sounds trite, but it is not. Nearly every public restroom in America now has faucets actuated by electronic sensors, the defense for which is that citizens will leave the water running without such sensors. The competence we once expected of a five-year-old we now do not expect of adults. If you are not to be trusted to be able to turn a water faucet on and off, how can you be trusted with the responsibility of self-government? If after solemn grown-up gatherings in which we debate the grave issues facing our organizations, we go to the public restroom and are reminded by the automatic faucet that we do not yet have the competence of a teenager, what lesson about citizen competence do we take home with us at night?

Second, when we no longer turn to our faucet for the water we need, but instead buy it in bottles from a store, we lose sight of the fact that tap water comes from our local municipality, and that our home is an inseparable part of that municipality. For our tap water to be clean, our municipality must be healthy. Citizens have their part to play in making it so. Buying water in a plastic bottle not only eliminates the daily reminder that we depend on our municipality and our municipality depends on us; purchasing it by the bottle is a tacit declaration that our local municipalities are neither clean nor can be trusted. If we concede that our local environment is unclean, it is but a short step to having hand-sanitizing stations installed everywhere, on which we will rely to restore our cleanliness after we have shaken our neighbor's dirty hand. If we conclude that our local environment is not to be trusted, it is but a short step to every household purchasing a backup generator because the electrical grid, in addition to the municipal water supply, cannot be counted on. Faucets actuated by electronic sensors, ubiquitous hand-sanitizing stations, back-up generators in homes across America—these bespeak a new arrangement in which our never pure but perfectly adequate homes and their immediate municipal environments are not meal enough. Where once, equipped with a thermos of tap water as a supplement, we set forth on picnics or camping trips for adventurous and temporary escapes from our messy but adequate homes, now the ubiquitous plastic water bottle is a substitute for the messy but adequate home life associated with drinking from the tap. Through the plastic water bottle, all of life becomes an adventurous escape. Drinking water from a bottle is the substitutism befitting the homeless soul; the soul always "on the go," euphoric, and unbound; the soul who dreams of a tiny house on wheels or of van living, neither of which is ever part of a fixed, messy municipality that requires citizen involvement to work well. Plastic-water-bottle substitutism may yet give rise to the gravest natural crisis we face (see section 56). The staggering increase in the number of water bottles produced around the planet may seem like a trivial example, but it is sometimes in the trivial things that the deepest problems reveal themselves.

§79. *Fast food and our ever-fatter bodies*. Whereas plastic-water-bottle substitutism produces pollution in our world that burns and floats around, fast-food substitutism produces the pollution in our bodies that floats around inside us but does not burn. Nothing so distinctly characterizes man than that his most important moments happen around the table. Without the liturgical recapitulation of "the Lord's Supper,"[30] what would have held together the Christian churches through the ages? When tensions are high and things get serious, do we not come to the bargaining table? When we want the real scoop from our friends and family, do we not sit down for a little table talk? For family to remain the basic unit of human life, without which civilization could not survive, its members need to continue gathering for a meal around the table.

Fast food is the supplement to that meal around the table. It holds us together while we are on the go, until we return home and resume the choreography of the meal at the table—the preparation, gathering, presentation, perhaps accompanied by prayer, conversation, concluding rituals, and cleanup. This home-meal competence is the referent for fast food, without which fast food would not be the successful supplement it is. When the supplement becomes the substitute, however, the complex choreography of the meal is lost from view, and fast food becomes but a mechanical mode of consumption, indulged excessively because the other associated satisfactions of the meal—close friends, loved family members, gratitude, humor,

30. See Matt. 26:26–28.

joy—are absent. When we do not know what will truly sate us, we will feed excessively. Plato saw this long ago.[31] No effort to count calories can save us from the indulgence we now wear around our bodies. Our hunger is not for calories; it is for the choreographed, liturgical splendor of the meal. Without it, we feast on crumbs, grow fatter by the day, and wonder why our hunger never retreats. Fast food substitutism is the cause. The condition of our mortal frame will only worsen until we return to the competence that surrounds the meal, for which fast food can be a supplement but not a substitute. In the meantime, global obesity rates will continue to rise.

§80. *Marriages are producing fewer babies and the permutations of having sex preoccupy our imagination.* If we consider what is necessary for civilization to survive the ever-present prospect of death, sex in marriage with a view to childbirth is the competence that needs to be developed, while having sex within the marriage is the supplement. For much of American history, this was the prevailing understanding, although in 1951, Talcott Parsons, the famous mid-twentieth-century sociologist, argued that prostitution was a necessary supplement to functioning marriages in a well-ordered society.[32] After the 1960s, Parsons's once-scandalous claim seemed prudish.

To understand the sexual revolution of the 1960s, we must bear in mind the strange but euphoric moment that happened after the benefits of the sexual revolution, a supplement-turned-substitute, had kicked in but before the world it constructed collapsed. The "high" of the sexual revolution involved turning the supplement of having

31. See Plato, bk. 9, 586b in *The Republic*: "Like cattle, [people who have no experience with wisdom] graze, fatten, and copulate. Greed drives them to kick and butt one another with horns and hoofs of iron. Because they are insatiable, they slay one another. And they are insatiable because they neglect to seek real refreshment for the part of the soul that is real and true."

32. See Talcott Parsons, chap. 3 in *The Social System* (London: Routledge, 1951), 56.

sex within marriage into a substitute not requiring marriage at all. The lead weight of marriage, which linked sex to the lifelong labor of having and raising sons and daughters, was turned into the gold of having sex, anywhere and with anyone, without cost. President Nixon repealed the gold standard on August 15, 1971; fortunately, a new symbolic gold standard by which citizens measured their wealth was ready to replace it: having sex independent of marriage, without regard to generation. Once this happened, a number of self-evident truths appeared in glistening splendor. First, because generative marriage was no longer seen as an institutional venue within which competence was to be developed, no compelling legal ground to confine having sex to men and women within marriage remained. Second, because generative marriage was no longer the referent, getting pregnant became the collateral damage of having sex rather its purpose, which invited not only legal battles over abortion but also the subtle encouragement of it. These are the well-known consequences of the sexual revolution. The legal arrangements by which we now live corroborate and nominally sustain this new golden age.

Let us speculate. What if the fixed law that declares that supplements cannot be turned into substitutes can, in fact, be violated? Would having sex outside of marriage not count as an instance of the *new* meal? If so, would we not expect that supplements to that meal would soon make their appearance—ones whose referent is having sex with someone but, like fast food, would provide something akin to it without the ordeal and preparation necessary for the meal? Like fast food, its referent would be the meal that involves having sex, but without the fuss. Pornography certainly fits into this category, and soon, we are informed, we can expect robotic sex "partners" to be the next vitamin to supplement the meal of having sex.

More generally, the question is this: If supplements can be turned into substitutes, why stop there, at the first transmutation that turns lead into gold? Why not build on the alchemy we have created? Might our substitutes themselves require supplements, which in turn themselves become substitutes requiring additional supplements, ad infinitum? Having reached the limits of our imagination with respect to supplements involving fixed gender orientation, why not explore a supplement involving unfixed and ever-chosen (or never-chosen) gender orientation, which then itself becomes the new substitute? Here would be the new meal of transgenderism that is currently emerging, soliciting us to abandon the male and female pronouns that pertained to the original meal and its supplement (generative marriage and having sex within it) because that quaint arrangement is claimed to have been wholly superseded.

If, on the other hand, there is a fixed law that supplements cannot be turned into substitutes without paying an immense price, then we are living on borrowed time, because generation and having sex within marriage is the meal, and also the healthy supplement from which we cannot continue to depart without dying of hunger. Substitutism in this matter would bring us to a civilizational dead end. Nothing less. Alternatively, if supplements can be turned into substitutes without cost, and these in turn invite new supplements, and so on, and so on, then we should welcome the repudiation of the old meal that poisons us like lead and live in the light of this new golden age. There is, I suspect, no intermediate alternative: Either the fixed law remains intact or it does not. That is the question lurking in the argument we are having today about what *having sex* legitimately means. Either it is the supplement to the meal of generative marriage or it is the means from which an ever-proliferating array of supplements can and should emerge. Meanwhile, marriages in the developed world—which is to say in the regions where substitutism is most pervasive—are producing fewer and fewer children.

I will now take the opportunity to elaborate on a claim I made much earlier, in section 47, to distinguish my stance from that of identity politics; namely, that "erotic longing institutionalized in generative marriage [has] a higher stature in society than other sorts of erotic longing." Within the world identity politics constructs, such a claim must be rejected because it is not sufficiently "inclusive." Within the politics of liberal competence, on the other hand, the generative family is a domain of competence with which society cannot dispense. Erotic longings not implicated in generation—gay marriage comes immediately to mind—may supplement the generative family, but the men and women who undertake the always difficult task of developing competence within the generative family cannot be indicted because they do not endorse the supplement. Identity politics gives us the categories of transgressors and innocents, and continually adds former innocents to the list of transgressors as it discovers new innocents. Thinking through this matter in terms of supplements and substitutes allows us to fix first on the generative meal, the domain of competence that must first be developed if civilization is to survive at all, and then attend to the supplements that may be added or allowed, either by custom or by law. A world thought through in this way will turn out to be more tolerant and pluralistic than the world identity politics constructs, which filters the world through the lens of purity and stain. Can it really be the case, as identity politics increasingly declares, that millions upon millions of men and women who believe in a conventional generative family must count themselves among the transgressors? Should such men and women really feel shame for guiding their sons and daughters in the direction of reproducing the sorts of understandings about generation that they themselves possess? This does not pass the test of common sense in daily life, and is an invitation to political suicide for the Democratic Party. Thinking through the mystery of erotic longing within the framework of supplements and substitutes avoids both problems. Through this framework, supplements can be accommodated without claiming that the meal is impure.

§81. *Facebook has 2.6 billion active users, and citizens are getting lonelier by the day.* I have already cited, in section 20, one of the more important passages from *Democracy in America*, in which Tocqueville wrote:

"Feelings and ideas are renewed, the heart enlarged, and the understanding developed only by the reciprocal actions of men, one upon another." Tocqueville foresaw, as few others did, the grave crisis of loneliness and isolation that would haunt America in the distant future, and thought the most powerful antidote for this crisis would be face-to-face relations. The crisis of loneliness and isolation that is now upon us illuminates all that he wrote about civic associations, local governance, federalism, marriage, and religion.

From the vantage point of the question, how can democratic liberty be saved and loneliness averted? face-to-face relations are the meal wherein competence is developed, and any prosthesis we don to magnify and extend those relations is the supplement. Facebook is such a supplement. Just as the supplement of the fast food "dinner" must have a home-cooked meal as a referent, our Facebook "friends" must have as a referent meal those friendships we have made in face-to-face relations. If, like the courage of Rousseau's warrior, one's actual friendships are strong and durable, then Facebook and other social media can serve to magnify and extend those friendships, just as the weapons of Rousseau's warrior at first magnify and extend his fierceness. As citizens rely more heavily on the supplement, they intimate that they can turn lead into gold by spending nearly all of their time online with their so-called social media friends. Their supplemental friends soon become a substitute, and they even begin to see their face-to-face friends only online or not at all. As this happens, their loneliness and isolation increases proportionately.

I have noted in several places that when we turn supplements to the meal into substitutes for the meal, our hunger grows. In the case of Facebook friends, there is now ample empirical evidence that citizens are starving, so to speak, as a result of the substitute meal that social media provides. This starvation is peculiar, in that we starve not because we have nothing to eat but because what we are voraciously eating cannot sate us. Therefore, we crave more of the supplement—opioids, vitamins, fast food, sex, and social media. The reason the hunger associated with turning supplements into substitutes is so dangerous is that it very quickly leads to an overdose. This problem cannot be remedied without establishing where it is that the real meal lies, where it is that competence lies. Social media substitutism is an ever-growing ailment, which increasingly renders citizens incapable of meeting one another face to face, with all that that involves in the way of goodwill, patience, generosity, forbearance, compromise, and risk. Increasingly unable to make real friends, citizens settle for the scant nourishment their online friends provide, and "defriend" those who disturb their Arcadian slumber. They deplore the growing polarization of our world, go to bed empty inside, and wonder why they hunger as they do.

§82. *Brick-and-mortar retailers are struggling because citizens are buying from Amazon.* Our households are the center of our lives, requiring constant attention and a never-ending flow of materials that we must bring through the front door in order to develop competence. Not long ago, citizens would leave their homes and "go shopping" at brick-and-mortar retailers and make expert judgments about whether what they saw, touched, heard, and smelled would or would not be appropriate in their homes. Going shopping turns out to be quite an art, which both depends on our practical judgments and develops those judgments as citizens do more of it. That is why, among other reasons, we do not send our children to the grocery store by themselves. They have not yet learned the art of going shopping. The old saying that a husband provided with a grocery list will inevitably bring home the wrong items illuminates the point: Shopping is an art, requiring connoisseurship that only practice and the full engagement of our evermore refined senses can provide. This connoisseurship is akin to the courage of Rousseau's warrior; it can be supplemented by the "weapon" of online shopping, but for online shopping to continue to work well, its referent must remain the actual act of going shopping, no less than the referent of the weapon must remain the courage that underlies it. The development of liberal competence requires that we always keep the referent in mind.

The evidence that the referent for online shopping must continue to be the actual act of going shopping can be provided by explaining what we might call the "Best Buy problem." If we already know what we need, we can order it from Amazon without worry; but if we do not, we have to go to a brick-and-mortar store to see, touch, hear, or smell the item, so that we can tell if it would work well in our home. Brick-and-mortar stores like Best Buy become, in effect, the showrooms for major online retailers like Amazon: We go shopping in these stores so that we can apply and further develop our connoisseurship; we then make our purchase through a major online retailer, which reaps the profits. Amazon depends on the connoisseurship we develop by going shopping at actual retail outlets, but it does not incur the cost of assisting us in developing our connoisseurship in the way the brick-and-mortar stores do. Amazon purports to be a substitute for going shopping, but the real source of its revenue is not its warehouses, but rather the referent: the brick-and-mortar stores that Amazon is slowly but irrevocably pricing out of existence. If and when these stores finally shut their doors for good, Amazon will for a time play the part of the substitute it now claims to be. Then we will discover what Rousseau's courageous warrior discovers when he turns his supplemental weapons into substitutes for courage—namely, that he has been living on borrowed time. If ever online shopping becomes a full-fledged substitute and stand-in for the actual act of going shopping, our connoisseurship will wither, and Amazon will be of little use to us—no less than the warrior's weapons are of little use to him if he has lost his courage.

It has not escaped our collective notice that the founders of both Amazon and Facebook are among the world's richest men. But before rising to that height, each of these companies was a supplement: Amazon was the supplement whose referent was going shopping in brick-and-mortar stores, while Facebook was the supplement whose referent was face-to-face friendship. Each company is now monetizing our temptation to turn supplements into substitutes. They understand our temptation and they encourage it. Nevertheless, it is important that we remind ourselves where the root of the problem lies. It is *us* who choose to be believe that through online shopping our households can effortlessly become homes. It is *us* who choose to believe that through our Facebook friends we can have substantive and enduring associations. Today, Amazon and Facebook are perhaps the best examples of the online substitutism through which we attempt to bypass the fixed order of things. Supplements cannot be turned into substitutes without cost, however. The cost we are bearing today is the erosion of liberal competence. The stock price of these two companies continues to soar in proportion to the "high" their online substitutism produces in us, a high that only increases as our hunger grows.

§83. *Online education is supplanting the real-time classroom.* Is the knowledge citizens need mere information that can be transmitted, or is it wisdom that must be developed in conversation with wise teachers and fellow students? Online education defends the former answer; the understandings of our best teachers insists on the latter. The debate is an ancient one, dating back to the antipathy between Socrates and the sophists. Today, to be called sophisticated is high praise. Socrates thought otherwise. The sophists with whom he disagreed claimed, as online education does today, that education could be conveyed directly from teacher to student; in our own day, that type of education is said to produce "measurable outcomes." Socrates believed education was a more mysterious affair, requiring the degree of patience and encouragement of a midwife, who could provide the level of assistance in the birth of a child that real education amounts to, but who did not bring that birth about by preaching to the mothers, drawing diagrams, and providing them with birthing manuals—the equivalent of lecturing, sending out PowerPoint slides, and providing so-called study guides that take place in online learning today. In a real "academy" (a word dating back to the school Plato founded in Athens in 387 BC), students wrestle with the difficult questions no mere textbook can answer: Who are we? What is our place in the cosmos? There are indeed measurable outcomes that can come from this enterprise—but they are ones that we must wait to discover in the adult lives of our citizens who have undergone this type of real education. Having educated their students well, academic institutions will be measurably rewarded by the loyalty and generosity of their alumni. The reward in a liberal society, in turn, is having enough wise citizens to be able to justify self-government.

Online education may be new, but the sophistic view of education has been pushing aside the Socratic understanding in our academic institutions for some time—a development that not coincidentally corresponds with the ever-diminishing significance of the humanities in the academic curriculum. The humanities—philosophy, literature, theology, and history—cannot be conveyed from teacher to student in informational packets. The humanities must be discussed, because the wisdom the subjects purvey "is hard to accept, but also hard to reject."[33] The real-time classroom is the only venue in which discussions of this important sort can occur. As the study of the humanities dwindles, the need for the real-time classroom will diminish. History tells us that the education of the leaders of every literate society has required the classroom. Under the banner of "educational access," educational substitutism is on the way, however. Without much imagination, we can anticipate an educational future in which the vast majority of citizens in the making receive their education, and the credentials that attend it, through online education. A fortunate minority in elite academic institutions will have the real thing—classroom discussions guided by knowledgeable teachers focused on questions that are perennial

33. Plato, bk. 7, 532d in *The Republic*, 226.

and difficult to answer. This class of elites for whom online education is a supplement rather than a substitute will become our citizen-leaders. The rest will endure the educational substitutism of online education. A society organized around the principle of permanent stratification might be satisfied with this sort of arrangement. But a liberal society, intent on developing citizen competence by posing the enduring questions that no society can long pretend to escape, must recognize that educational substitutism is the opioid high that precludes the development of citizen competence that liberal societies must count on to endure and thrive. The meal of the real-time classroom offers real nourishment, is not expensive, and can be made available to all. Teachers who love their calling, a modest number of primary texts, students enthralled by the questions they cannot escape, desks, and a blackboard are all that is needed. Rousseau's warrior does not incur great expenses to develop courage; the expense comes when those without courage don weapons as a way to hide the fact that they are devoid of courage. Wisdom, Plato says, is "beyond price."[34] The costs mount only when the sophists appear—when the supplement is turned into a substitute.

§84. *We are unable to navigate the streets and roads without Google Maps, and the promise of driverless cars captivates our imagination.* Reading a map to figure out how to get to our destination and driving to that destination require competence. That competence takes years to develop. Maps do not tell us what to do just by looking at them. Until we conjoin reading a map with driving to and reaching our destination, we have not yet learned how to use a map. Similarly, automobiles do not teach us how to drive them. The proper use of the accelerator, brakes, steering wheel, and signals; the protocols and decorum drivers must show one another; and the judgment needed to ascertain

34. Bk. 2, 374d in ibid.

safe distance, weather conditions, and the adjustments one must make for each situation must all be learned. They are the meal. Google Maps and driverless cars can supplement these competences, but they cannot substitute for them. If we *can already* read a map and drive a car, we can imagine any number of circumstances in which these supplements would be beneficial. They could save us from having to learn the quirks of the street configuration and traffic patterns in other neighborhoods or cities by heart, as we have in our own, for example. And the safety features of driverless cars could avert the danger of driving too close to the car in front of us or not seeing a car that is passing us. These benefits would extend our already existing competences. If they become substitutes for those competences, however, we will have a nation of infantilized citizens without the capacity to understand where they are and how to get to where they are going. If Rousseau's warriors attend solely to their weapons and lose sight of the courage needed to use them, when they suddenly do not have them, the courage they need to defend themselves will be lacking. Similarly, if the substitutism of Google Maps and driverless cars undermines and diminishes citizen competence in map reading and driving, then when these digital supplements *go dark*, citizens will be left utterly helpless and immobile, wherever they happen to be.

§85. *We are entranced by digital technology, and believe we can supplant the analog world altogether*. Google Maps and driverless cars are immediate examples of the digital world supplanting the analog world, but to understand the extraordinary threat to competence they pose, more must be said about digital substitutism. The digital world renders the world we actually inhabit—a world of qualities it takes competence to distinguish between, let alone reproduce—as informational quantities, or "bits."[35] Map reading and driving are ordinary competences.

---

35. Hobbes was among the first to argue, in 1651, that the perceived world of qualities are actually quantities. See Hobbes, pt. 1, chap. 1, sec. 5 in *Leviathan*, 7.

Nearly everyone is capable of developing them. Because musical competence is so difficult to achieve, an illustration involving music will bring us closer to understanding the peril of digital substitutism. Consider the inimitable sounds of B. B. King on the electric guitar[36] and of Leo Kottke on the twelve-string acoustic guitar.[37] Digital sampling of their music renders what is inimitable about them as encoded bits, which musicians everywhere around the globe can, without effort, now invoke and incorporate into their own sound. That it took a lifetime for King and Kottke to develop their respective sounds matters little; the sum of their labors—their musical competence—is available with the click of a mouse. Musical competence, like many other competences, takes a lifetime to develop. Continual practice is necessary. Such practice is analog, in the sense that what a musician creates one day he cannot exactly reproduce the next. With each passing day, his competence increases and his connoisseurship develops. The music can be "freeze-framed" along the way with digital sampling, but the ever-developing practice of producing music is the source of the wealth we find in the digital sample. This phenomenon of freeze-framing predates digital sampling, of course. Anyone who has watched a master craftsman at work knows that although a few tricks of the trade can be relayed, those shortcut entrées into the craft are, so to speak, the interest on the principal. We are happy to receive them, but we also intimate the chasm that exists between the interest we receive and the principal that remains locked behind the theft-proof bank vault of long-developed competence that is not available to us. Digital sampling instantly offers tricks-of-the-trade freeze-framing to the entire world; it samples competence and pro-

36. See "B.B. King—Lucille," YouTube video, 10:13, posted by TexasStrat, n.d., https://www.youtube.com/watch?v=-Y8QxOjuYHg.

37. See "Leo Kottke—Eggtooth," YouTube video, 5:52, posted by jpiir, n.d., https://www.youtube.com/watch?v=E4BOSZQw-TY&list=RDgJvm6sl6u-Og&index=39.

vides shortcuts for those without it. Digital substitutism promises a shortcut to competence for nearly everyone; the peril is that it bypasses the meal of developing competence. A civilization lives on borrowed time if it proceeds in this way. Digital sampling in the arts shifts the burden of activity from the first-order artist who develops his musical competence to the second-order artist who samples and rearranges that music. Much of the music we hear these days is of this latter sort. Because substitutism sunders the relationship between the meal and its supplement, nothing new can emerge from the music it produces. Like opioid addiction, this sort of music only uses up what remains of the meal that competence once produced.

We can argue about whether this development in the musical arts is fatal. Perhaps the world does not need music or, less strikingly, it does not need new music, and can live comfortably in the museum housing the artifacts of the world that musical competence once created. At the other end of the spectrum, in a broken world such as ours, the world does need a competent military. In the race to compete with China, the American military has made its bet that the best way to do this is by going digital with its military operations. China is already doing this. Must we not follow, indeed catch up and surpass, our new adversary?[38] To accomplish this, actual military competence is being "sampled," rendered digitally, and activated in the form of a complicated array of software algorithms. This, we are told, is the future of warfare. Actual military competence, achievable only through never-ending practice, will consequently recede. Why train warriors when we can have warrior algorithms instead?

38. Huawei's near monopoly on 5G technology has settled attention on the need for America to push ahead toward complete digital substitutism. The latency of 4G technology meant that digital competence could not wholly supplant analog competence. By overcoming the latency effects, 5G will be the technological venue in which America and China attempt digital substitutism. Let us hope that China gets there first.

We can only expect this gambit to end in catastrophic failure.[39]

The digital substitutism China seems to be on the verge of achieving is new, but the habit that underlies it is not new to China at all. Tocqueville wrote in 1840 of this Chinese disposition to supplant actual competence with algorithms. Because doing this amounted to turning the supplement to developed competence into a substitute for it, China could never be a global power:

> Three hundred years ago, when the first Europeans came to China, they found that almost all the arts had reached a certain degree of improvement, and they were surprised that, having come so far, they had gone no further. The nation was a hive of industry; the greater part of its scientific methods were still in use, but science itself was dead. That made them understand the strange immobility of mind found among this people. Following in their father's steps, they had forgotten the reasons that guided them. They still used the formula without asking why. They kept the tool but had no real skill to adapt or replace it. . . . They had to copy their ancestors the whole time for fear of straying into impenetrable darkness if they deviated for a moment from their tracks.[40]

39. Nowhere has the peril of digital substitutism been more clearly revealed than in the various vessel crashes the US Navy has endured in the past few years, resulting from a digital system failing and the officers on the bridge not actually knowing how to navigate and steer their ships. See Lieutenant Commander Erin Patterson, "Ship Collisions: Address the Underlying Causes, including Culture," *Proceedings* 143, no. 8 (August 2017), https://www.usni.org/magazines/proceedings/2017/august/ship-collisions-address-underlying-causes-including-culture: "Computer-based training is not a substitute for real training evolutions. Conducting *operations*—the norm for Japan-based Forward Deployed Naval Forces—is also not training. JO SWOs [junior officer surface warfare officers] need *training* evolutions where they can learn how to handle their ship in a safe and controlled environment. Proficiency in seamanship comes from practice. Repetition of the basics is vital."

40. Tocqueville, pt. 1, chap. 10 in *Democracy in America*, vol. 2, 464.

The provocative question today is whether this caricatured account of China still holds. There is ample evidence that it does not,[41] and that analog competence is alive and well. The deeper question is how the Chinese—and now American—embrace of digital substitutism will end. Perhaps the reason China is winning the race[42] has as much to do with the state of its technology as it does with the explanation Tocqueville suggested—namely, that it does not have a long history of analog competence to *overcome*, as the Americans do. Tocqueville thought that the secret of America's success was that its citizens were a practical people trusting in their own direct experience. Ralph Waldo Emerson, writing a few years after Tocqueville in 1844, declared that "experience is the hands and feet of any enterprise."[43] The federal political arrangements wisely established by the Founding Fathers, America's long history with a frontier, which forced the development of competence upon the pain of death, and the fact that the formation of the state came long after local communities had developed—all these encouraged the development of the enduring habits[44] of analog competence among Americans that now militate against their full-on embrace of digital substitutism. In America, we are on the verge of discovering—in every domain, from art to the military, from beauty

41. See David P. Goldman, "Inside China's Plan for Global Supremacy," *Tablet*, March 19, 2019, https://www.tabletmag.com/jewish-arts-and-culture/281731/chinas-plan-for-global-supremacy.

42. See Kai-Fu Lee, *AI Superpowers: China, Silicon Valley, and the New World Order* (New York: Houghton Mifflin Harcourt, 2018).

43. Ralph Waldo Emerson, "Experience," in *Essays and Lectures* (New York: Library of America, 1983), 482.

44. See Tocqueville, pt. 1, chap. 2 in *Democracy in America*, vol. 1, 31–32: "Peoples always bear some marks of their origin. Circumstances of birth and growth affect all the rest of their career. If we could go back to the elements of societies and examine the very first records of their histories, I have no doubt that we should there find the first cause of their prejudices, habits, dominating passions, and all that comes to be called the national character."

to war—whether the temptation of digital substitutism is more powerful than the habit in this country of putting liberal competence first. The ever-growing tensions between China and America will put that temptation to the test. I have indicated why I do not believe digital substitutism can work. I suspect, nevertheless, that the American military and, indeed, American citizens in their own domains will try. The analog world of liberal competence is the time- and space-bound world—the world of things made, of neighborhoods long lived in, of property owned, of long-laboring citizenship, of actual experiences had, of music sung and played, of military competence developed through practice, and of the competences achieved in every domain from art to war. It is, in short, the face-to-face, real-time world that digital substitutism dares to replace, but cannot.

§86. *The federal government continues to expand, our social problems grow worse, and our political parties are locked in mortal and impotent opposition to each other.* Governmental substitutism is a problem no less pathological than the other substitutisms I have considered thus far. The problem of governmental substitutism is obscured, however, because members of both political parties think they need go no further than declare that they are "pro" or "anti" *this* or *that*. They are "pro-government" or "anti-government"; "for" affirmative action or "against" it; and the list goes on. This sort of thinking can resolve itself only by one side overpowering the other. No wonder American politics grows uglier by the day. When politics devolves into pro and anti sloganeering, we no longer see members of the opposite party as fellow citizens with whom we disagree, but rather as the embodiment of dark forces that need to be purged so that our own light may shine brightly. *Why should we look at our seemingly intractable political and social problems through the lens of substitutism, when it suffices to consider members of the other political party as evil? Let our rage prevail, so that the other side may be defeated, and all will be well. Politics is not the venue in which we establish the areas where government can properly sup-*

plement the difficult but necessary labor citizens undertake together within society; it is the venue through which the righteous and pure find their scapegoat. That is the blinding political sentiment that guides us in these harrowing times.

To think clearly about the proper role of government, Tocqueville helps us distinguish between the meal, the supplement, and the maladies that arise when supplements become substitutes. One of the axioms of liberal political thought is that society logically comes before the state, just as the meal logically comes before the vitamin supplement. Tocqueville had this view. The meal is to be found in society—in the face-to-face relations our civic associations, our families, and our religious institutions provide. These are the institutional locations where we build our world, together with our neighbors. The state can supplement the meal we find in society, but it cannot become the substitute for it. Tocqueville was not pro government or anti government. In *Democracy in America*, he prophesized that Americans of the future would be tempted to turn the state into a substitute. That is why he wrote, "I praise [democracy] much more on account of what is causes to be done than for what it does."[45] In the hands of everyday citizens, democracy is inefficient and feckless. Elites will always be more sober-minded and farseeing. In the hands of everyday citizens working with their neighbors, democratic institutions "spread throughout the body social and restless activity, superabundant force, and energy never found elsewhere."[46] The state can supplement those institutions, Tocqueville noted, but it cannot substitute for them without cost. We have not heeded his counsel. Everywhere we look, governmental substitutism prevails.

The deep wound of slavery and its aftermath, which I have considered a number of times throughout the pages of this book, is healing but still needs our attention. The state can surely supplement the

45. Pt. 2, chap. 6, in ibid., 243.
46. Pt. 2, chap. 6, in ibid., 244.

efforts we ourselves must make to heal the wound of slavery in the institutions of society; but during the last half-century, the Great Society programs inaugurated during the Johnson administration (1964–65) have become substitutes for our efforts rather than supplements to it. Little wonder that the high that democrats experienced during the Obama administration, which seemed to vindicate governmental substitutism, has yielded to the withdrawal symptoms they now experience as the Trump administration calls governmental substitutism into question. We shall see whether the Trump administration and those that follow it actually put an end to governmental substitutism. Our presidents and their administrations cannot heal this wound because the problem is deeper than politics can reach. Everyday citizens are the ones who are going to have to heal the wound within the institutions of society. The state can supplement that work, but cannot substitute for it.

Governmental substitutism is also the root cause of the metastasis of Title IX, which now dares to establish the protocol between citizens that anticipates and culminates in *having sex*. A mystery since before civilizations began commenting on them, the relations between men and women are something that a legally binding algorithm produced by the state will never comprehend. In the institutions of society, we learn just enough to reproduce civilization—often well, but sometimes not. In those delicate and never fully adequate institutions, which provide an interlocking network of cues about how men and women should comport themselves, we somehow work out the awkward choreography that we need. Governmental substitutism cannot heal the wounds that emerge from the failure of those institutions, though the state can step in, temporarily, to clear out the poison that keeps the social body from healing. Governmental substitutism, however, is never a temporary measure; it stands in for the institutions of society, and causes them to whither from disuse. That means we can expect more Harvey Weinsteins in the world, not fewer, as governmental substitutism grows.

Beyond these two glaring examples of governmental substitutism, the overreach of the EPA during the Obama administration, animated by the zero-tolerance "environmentalism" that began to emerge decades before he took office, provides a third example. If our relationship to nature is to be salutary, we must recognize that what constitutes the meal is stewardship, not environmentalism. Stewardship is the connoisseurship we develop through our living relationship with nature. It emerges through the daily questions we must pose about how to exercise our dominion over nature with the technologies we have on hand and culminates in the judgments we develop about what and how much we really need from nature to compose a household and build a home. The steward with his tools is always already in nature; the environmentalist wishes to place himself outside of nature, except when he is a tourist. The steward knows that moral immunity is impossible, that mistakes will be made, and that lessons will be learned; the environmentalist achieves the appearance of moral immunity by outsourcing the dirty tasks necessary for life to proceed—mining, electronics manufacturing, and the like—to other nations of the world, so that he can sleep well at night. The steward humanizes nature by responsibly drawing from it to fill a household and make a home; the environmentalist denaturalizes man by denying him the opportunity to be a steward. Here, the defenders of governmental substitutism believe that citizens are not up to the task. Therefore, the state has to substitute for capacities that either never existed or once existed but now no longer do. In *Democracy in America*, Tocqueville anticipated our ailment when he wrote, "Nothing is more difficult than the art of being free."[47] Like Plato's doctor who does not understand the proper use of medicine, and administers his irksome treatments until the patient finally dies without recovering

47. Tocqueville, pt. 2, chap. 6, *Democracy in America*, vol. 1, 240. Tocqueville also uses the phrase "the art of being free" in three other places in the book: pt. 2, chap. 9, 290; pt. 2, chap. 10, 354; and pt. 2, chap. 10, 359.

his health, the man who believes in governmental substitutism does not believe that the (social) body can be healthy without never-ending intervention. And like Rousseau's modern soldier, he does not understand that without courage, no amount of added weaponry can help him. The height of this folly is the assertion, made by those who believe in governmental substitutism, that the only way to "save the planet" is through the Paris Agreement or some future equivalent. They get high on this governmental substitute for stewardship, suffer withdrawal and its associated rage when anyone casts doubt on the idea that governmental substitutism can "save us," and promptly conclude that death is near. Something else is happening here besides frustration and discouragement that the latest science is being ignored or disparaged.

The 7.6 billion people currently living on the planet place immense pressures on our natural world. Governmental substitutism will not remedy this ailment. If we are not stewards of nature *first*, and during each day of our lives, no array of governmental constraints and stipulations—set to kick in decades from now—is going to save the planet. The government can supplement, but it cannot substitute for, the meal that is stewardship. Similarly, no comprehensive array of governmental constraints and stipulations can heal the wound of slavery and its aftermath, or stop the Harvey Weinsteins of the world from emerging in large numbers. Those who believe that such constraints and stipulations can remedy these ailments are no less self-deceived than opioid addicts, who no longer think the meal is necessary. Both experience the euphoria of believing they have discovered a golden truth that eludes their dull and sober neighbors—namely, that supplemental medicine can be transformed into a substitute, on which we may exclusively live, without cost. Government substitutism supposes that stewardship with respect to nature; charity, goodwill, and faith with respect to the wound of slavery; and the civilizing of men and women within the institutions or society are not competences liberal citizens can develop. Therefore, state competence must compensate. The more the state steps in, the less competence the citizen will develop—in turn, requiring the state to step in evermore prominently. The remedy for this vicious circle[48] is painful but effective: citizen competence. There will be blunders, embarrassments, and collateral damage along the way to its redevelopment, but the alternative—governmental substitutism—would be worse.

§87. *National borders are ferociously defended by some and recklessly abandoned by others.* The question of national borders has become a flash point indicator of support or opposition to globalism. Considered within the framework of management society and selfie man, globalism is the concession made to managerial elites by democratic citizens who believe themselves to be "less than men," who believe that the problems they face exceed their competence. Considered within the framework of identity politics, globalism invites atonement for past national transgressions. Those who have abandoned their nations and borders are the innocents who understand the price that must be paid to unburden the present and future from the transgressive past. Those who continue to defend their nations are transgressors who are unwilling to renounce the stain that taints them and their history. The former are the cosmopolitans who claim they sleep well at night; the latter are the populists. Considered within the framework of supplements and substitutes, national borders represent the framework within which the justice of law operates.[49] Citizens from other countries who do not enter the country legally are illegal aliens—not, as cosmopolitans claim, "undocumented immigrants." Justice is the meal, so to speak, without which citizens

48. See part 1, n. 91.

49. See Max Weber, "Politics as a Vocation," in *From Max Weber*, ed. H. H. Gerth and C. Wright Mills (London: Routledge, 1948), 77: "A state is a human community that (successfully) claims the *monopoly of the legitimate use of physical force* within a given territory" (emphasis in original).

starve. The meal of justice, however, is supplemented by mercy, as I indicated some pages back (in sections 30–33). When justice is supplemented by mercy, national borders—the meal—must come first. The mercy that liberal polities demonstrate to asylum seekers and others who wish to become competent liberal citizens is possible because the justice of law is in place. Open borders purports to be a merciful policy, but it is not. Mercy is the supplement to justice, not a substitute for it. No justice; no mercy. Open borders—a world without the justice of law—returns us to the state of nature. Hobbes saw the problem long ago. In his great work *Leviathan* (1651), he wrote:

> [Without the security of the state] there is no place for industry, because the fruit thereof is uncertain, and consequently, no culture of the earth, no navigation, nor the use of commodities that may be imported by sea, no commodious building, no knowledge of the face of the earth, no account of time, no arts, no letters, no society, and which is worst of all, continual fear and danger of violent death, and the life of man, solitary, poor, nasty, brutish, and short.[50]

The competence of citizens, Hobbes understood, can only be developed within the framework of the justice of law. Open borders is a substitutism that is no less disastrous than opioid addiction. Both transform a supplement into a substitute, and live on borrowed time.

§88. *Paper money is no longer a supplement to gold money but, as fiat currency, it has become a substitute for it.* I will not enter into the interminable debates between "gold-bugs" who believe we must return to a gold standard and sophisticated economists who believe that fiat currency has put an end to the need for "that archaic relic."[51] I indicated a while back, in section 74, that Plato was the first to think through the problem of turning sup-

50. Hobbes, pt. 1, chap. 13, sec. 9 in *Leviathan*, 76.

51. Keynes, chap. 4, sec. 3 in *A Tract on Monetary Reform*, 172.

plements into substitutes, so it is fitting that I turn to his *Republic* to explore what he says there about the monetary regime oriented by gold and about what comes after that regime is inevitably cast off.

The relevant passages are to be found in book 8 of *The Republic*, in which Plato traces the successive phases of decline from the regime based on honor (timocracy), to the regime based on wealth (oligarchy), to the regime based on freedom (democracy), to the regime based on power (tyranny).[52] The oligarchic soul who predominates in the oligarchic regime, Plato tells us, is the man oriented by the love of gold.[53] Both the democratic soul who will later predominate in the democratic regime after the oligarchic regime collapses and the oligarchic soul are ruled by their appetites. The oligarch, however, is a stingy soul,[54] who represses[55] most of his appetites, so that he can amass a fortune in gold. The oligarch is, in short, a saver. The world in which he lives has limits: Gold money and everything it buys are scarce. In such a world, the oligarch opines that he must be disciplined and competitive to get his share.

The oligarch's golden world, however, is difficult to hold together. He and others around him must continually repress their appetites—an unlikely prospect if, *in secret*, their appetites really do rule. And they do. Eventually, Plato writes, the oligarchic chatter about

52. For a more complete exposition of the passage from timocracy to tyranny, see Joshua Mitchell, chap. 2 in *Plato's Fable: On the Mortal Condition in Shadowy Times* (Princeton, NJ: Princeton University Press, 2006), 75–110.

53. See Plato, bk. 8, 548a, 551a, 553c, and 554a in *The Republic*.

54. See bk. 8, 548b, 554a, 554e, 555a, 558c, 559d, 560c, and 572c in ibid.

55. See bk. 8, 554d and 555a in ibid. It is not a coincidence that Freud discovered "the pleasure principle" (see chap. 2 in *Civilization and Its Discontents*, 25) and the need to repress and redirect this pleasure during the age of bourgeois liberalism. "Eros and Annake [love and necessity] have become the parents of human civilization," he writes (chap. 4, 55). What Freud discovered is the psychic profile of the oligarchic man about whom Plato had written 2,400 years earlier.

necessary scarcity, difficult discipline, winners and losers, and enduring deprivation becomes too much to bear. Then, driven by their insatiable appetites, citizens look to opinion leaders, who tell them that they need not restrain themselves at all.[56] They want a freer, happier world that encourages the expression of their spontaneously emerging appetites, and believe themselves entitled to such a world. There is opposition to these opinion leaders and those who follow them, but the enticement of ever-increasing gratification of the appetites eventually prevails. When oligarchic repression, discipline, and deprivation are finally abandoned, the democratic regime emerges. The democratic citizens that predominate within this regime want liberation from the stingy constraints of their oligarchic fathers. "All appetites are equal," they proudly declare. All have an equal right to be expressed, and all should be expressed. They should, in fact, be celebrated. Democratic citizens do not wish to save money. They wish to consume, to spend, to gratify "any appetite that comes to mind."[57]

Gold, the "archaic relic," will not suffice as a currency for the expanding desires of the democratic soul, however. When the ever-expanding and ultimately infinite appetites are constrained by the use of gold money, which is finite, something must give: either the appetites must be repressed or the gold money must be supplemented by paper money to accommodate the appetitive expansion that char-

---

56. In the context of my earlier remarks in sec. 56 about the prominent twentieth-century figures Sanger, Keynes, and Rawls, it could be said that each figure in his or her own way justifies the emergence of democratic desire. Sanger focuses on the constraint on a woman's desire that having children entails, and wishes to remove that constraint. Keynes focuses on the constraint that allowing market cycles to unfold without government intervention produces, and wishes to intervene in those cycles. Rawls focuses on the distributive justice that makes the expression of desire among the least advantaged possible, and offers a theory of justice that insists those expressions be registered.

57. Plato, bk. 8, 561c–d in *The Republic*, 253.

acterizes the democratic regime. At first, this paper money still has as its referent the meal (gold) for which it is the supplement. If that were not so, it would just be paper, having no value. The supplement has value, we must always remember, only when it has a meal as its referent. In the language of economics, paper money, in order to have value as money, must be exchangeable at "the gold window."[58] The only thing that keeps the paper money supplement from becoming a substitute for gold is, in fact, its exchangeability at the gold window. If opioid use and the subsequent addiction is the analogy, opioids can be important pain-relieving supplements if dispensed responsibly through the pharmacy window, but can become addictive substitutes if the patient bypasses the pharmacy window and, instead, *decrees* when he wants the drugs and how much of them he wants.

This supplemental relationship between gold and paper money befits democratic souls who are still *somewhat able* to restrain their appetites. This supplemental relationship can endure, however, only as long as this transitional, strange, and unstable intermediate between the stingy oligarch and the profligate democrat remains in the picture.[59] He eventually succumbs, because there is no way to constrain the appetites once they begin to rule the soul. When the profligate democratic soul finally supplants the still somewhat-disciplined democratic soul, as it must, the demands of the appetites expand even further. If the ever-expanding appetites are to be gratified, paper money

58. The "gold window" is a figurative expression for the location where gold and paper money can be exchanged, one for the other, at a fixed ratio.

59. Plato seemed to think this intermediate stage between the oligarch and democrat was important enough to give it special treatment. See Plato bk. 8, 560a–c in *The Republic*. Why does he invoke what I am calling "intermediate stages"? In book 8, Plato gives us four types of regimes—timocratic, oligarchic, democratic, and tyrannical—with each regime having a kind of soul associated with it. Between each type, Plato pauses to explain a strange intermediate hybrid, who is not the type that is either collapsing or emerging. I have proposed here that paper money is the strange and unstable intermediate between gold money and fiat currency.

must be delinked from its earlier supplemental relationship to gold. Because the constraint that gold imposed on paper money is no longer endurable, the gold window must now be closed.[60] After the gold window is closed, paper money no longer has gold as its referent. The meal (gold) has been bypassed.[61] The supplement has become a substitute.

In the most precise sense, the transformation from supplement to substitute corresponds to the transformation of paper money into fiat currency. A couple of paragraphs ago, I mentioned the opioid addict who bypasses the pharmacy window and simply decrees that he must have his opioids, and suggested that this decree that turns his supplement into a substitute inaugurates a headlong spiral toward death. The Latin word *fiat* means "decree." The substitute for gold, and its paper money supplement that *cannot* be printed out of thin air, is fiat currency, which *can* be printed out of thin air by Federal Reserve decree. Just as the opioid addict's decree that he will bypass the pharmacy window turns his opioid supplement into a substitute, so the profligate democratic soul, with his ever-expanding appetites, depends on the decree that makes fiat currency available for him—on Plato's account, in a headlong spiral toward tyranny.

I indicated earlier that when the stingy oligarch fully gives way to the profligate democrat, there is a visible shift from saving to consuming. Economic growth for the former is savings driven, while for the latter it is debt driven. Not wanting to constrain their appetites like their stingy

60. The gold window was closed by President Nixon, on August 15, 1971 (see sec. 80). The expanding appetites in America that required that the gold window be closed were the massive domestic spending on the Great Society programs and the massive foreign spending to fend off communism abroad. The impossibility of doing both has never been addressed; both sides still get what they think they want. Our official national debt now stands at $26.5 trillion.

61. On the question of whether gold is money, see "Ron Paul vs Bernanke: Is Gold Money?," YouTube video, 5:32, posted by Campaign for Liberty, July 13, 2011, testimony of Ben Bernanke before Congress, https://www.youtube.com/watch?v=2NJnL1ovZ1Y. Relevant comments begin at 4:30.

oligarchic fathers did, when economic crises occur, profligate democratic souls conclude that the economy must be reflated immediately by pumping fiat currency into the economy to gratify their existing and ever-emerging appetites. This adds to the debt load democratic souls bear. Crisis begets crisis, and debt piles upon debt. The cycle ends, Plato writes, when a tyrant emerges out of nowhere, and promises citizens that all their debts will be forgiven.[62] Nothing more befriends a citizenry exhausted by debt than a tyrant who promises to lift its burden.

Taking the broader view of economic history, when the disciplined oligarchic soul for whom gold was money predominated, wealth increased. Afterward, when discipline gave way to indiscipline, as it must because man's appetites are infinite, gold money could no longer service the growing demand for the gratification of these desires—but paper money linked to gold as a supplement could. This, too, made us stronger, healthier, wealthier, and more, as supplements do. When the democratic appetites were fully unleashed, however, the supplemental relationship between gold and paper money could no longer service the now inordinate demand. The gold window was closed, and fiat currency became a substitute for gold.

How has our reliance on fiat currency—on money by decree—affected the citizens of our country? Rather than have us endure natural and jarring economic downturns that would have disciplined the appetites, the Federal Reserve has flooded the economy with fiat currency to soften or avert any downturn. This has protected the value of the stock portfolio and real estate assets held by the well-to-do from bottoming out. Those without these assets, in turn, have gained nothing. The economic recovery that has followed the attenuated downturn, such as it is, has been fueled by the injected fiat currency that asset owners, but never the least among us, can draw upon at a low rate, and invest in the reflating economy. As it reflates, asset holders reap windfall profits, and attend singularly to signals from

62. See Plato, bk. 8, 566a, 566e in *The Republic*.

the Federal Reserve that the party will soon be over and it will raise the cost of borrowing the fiat currency it has printed out of thin air. Until it does, the stock market will go up, and so, too, will the cost of housing, because asset holders will bid up the price. Housing affordability therefore will decrease—except for those whose homes have increased in dollar value because of the reflation. The least among us, wage earners without stock portfolios or real estate, have suffered through the economic downturn and have often lost their jobs and had to take lower-paying ones. In short, they have gained nothing from the economic reflation that the injection of fiat currency has accomplished.

Mere wage earners have been hit in another way as well. Federal Reserve policies guided by the Phillips Curve[63] have deliberately kept wages low. Each time "wages heat up," the Federal Reserve has raised the interest rate, and therefore the borrowing cost, of the fiat currency it has decreed into existence. Anticipating a downturn, companies dutifully lay off workers. The Federal Reserve's orchestrated "cooling of the economy" causes wage earners to be laid off; when, after an economic downturn, the Federal Reserve reflates the economy with fiat currency, only the well-to-do have the purchasing power to benefit.

How can liberal competence be developed and sustained when wage earners fall further and further into debt? In Plato's *Republic*, the profligate democratic soul lives on borrowed time, then falls into servitude. In our own day, we can predict that fiat currency substitutism will continue to pile up debt and impoverish ever-growing numbers of wage-earning citizens, whose competence we must count on if our liberal polity is to be healthy. Substitutisms of every

63. The Phillips Curve, named after William Phillips, is an equation that describes the inverse relationship between unemployment and inflation. Since increasing wages produce inflation, to keep inflation down wages must be kept low—something that can be accomplished when the Federal Reserve raises interest rates to "cool" the economy.

sort undermine the development of liberal competence. It is time we paid attention to how fiat currency substitutism does this as well.[64]

§89. *Globalists mind the business of the world and lose sight of their own business.* I have already considered globalism in a number of different ways.[65] Here, I will focus on global substitutism. The idea that justice involves minding our own business and, paradoxically, that injustice is the result when we start looking outside our purview, can be found as early as Plato's *Republic*,[66] but there are more recent accounts as well. In 1759, Adam Smith put the matter in the following way:

> The administration of the great system of the universe . . . the care of the universal happiness of all rational and sensible beings, is the business of God, and not man. To man is allotted a much humbler department, but one much more suitable to the weakness of his powers and the narrowness of his comprehension—the care of his own happiness, of that of his family, his friends, his country: that

64. In a remarkable *60 Minutes* interview with Federal Reserve Chair Jerome Powell conducted on March 10, 2019, Powell stated, "The opioid crisis is millions of people. They tend to be young males. It is a very significant problem. And it is part of a larger picture of low labor force participation, particularly by young males." ("Full 60 Minutes Interview with Fed Chair Jerome Powell," interview by Scott Pelley, *60 Minutes*, March 10, 2019, https://www.cbsnews.com/news/full-transcript-60-minutes-interview-with-fed-chair-jerome-powell/). Fiat currency substitutism, as I have already indicated, harms the lower and middle classes. Families fall apart, well-paying jobs become scarce, and inflation erodes the purchasing power of the money that is earned. Little wonder that a "boy crisis" should emerge from this configuration of problems.

65. In sec. 23, I considered the relationship between "anywheres" and "somewheres." In secs. 65–72, I considered the relationship between management society and selfie man. In sec. 87, I considered the relationship between justice and mercy.

66. See Plato, bk. 4, 443c–d in *The Republic*: "The reality is that justice is not a matter of external behavior, but the way a man privately and truly governs his inner self" (137).

he is occupied in contemplating the more sublime, can never be an excuse for his neglecting the more humble department.[67]

Smith did not suggest that we should be unconcerned about global matters but rather that global matters should not come first. Global concerns must be a supplement to minding our own business, not a substitute for it. At first blush, this seems to be a recipe for the narcissism that afflicts delinked man in the democratic age, which is so corrosive to a liberal polity.[68] As the sequence in Smith's passage indicates, personal happiness for him, and for liberal thought in general (see sections 13–16), cannot be severed from the happiness we discover and make our own through our family, friends, and our nation. Attending responsibly to our "humbler department" does not nourish narcissism; it provides the meal—family, friends, and country—we cannot live without for long. Liberal competence can only be developed from that starting point. Once developed, then we may ponder the "sublime" question that I noted early on, in section 26, has always occupied the West: Why are the scales of justice perpetually out of balance?

The liberal answer to this question does not take the form of a morally dreamy insistence that the imperfections of the world can be overcome, immediately or within a single generation, with this or that plan to achieve social justice. Having developed competence in an imperfect world, it will occur to the liberal that in repudiating the imperfect world, we do not draw nearer to perfection but rather remove the occasions for developing competence altogether.

The liberal answer will instead take the form of a morally sober recognition that, by virtue of living in history, we cannot escape the meal and its imperfections; and that, by virtue of the ready availability of supplements to the meal, we intimate that the meal points us toward

67. Smith, pt. 4, sec. 2, chap. 3 in *Theory of Moral Sentiments*, 237.

68. See Christopher Lasch, *Culture of Narcissism: American Life in an Age of Diminishing Expectations* (New York: W. W. Norton, 1979).

a more nourishing feast. If we had *only* the meal, we would intimate there was nothing more. Here are the lesser creatures of creation, who *are* their existence and nothing more.[69] With the supplements that we administer with the meal, we imagine we can bypass the meal itself. The moral trial of life involves the dilemma that the supplementary antidote that lifts us above the lesser creatures can become a poison if, in the hope of complete liberation from the meal of our merely historical lives, we turn that supplement into a substitute. Globalism is that poison. Whether we like it or not, to be mortal is to forever sit at the table, in our home, where the meal is served. Let us develop our competence there. Nations may make bilateral and multilateral treaties with other nations; and international organizations backed by a few or many nations can undertake important projects together. These projects, however, have no standing independent of the nations that underwrite them—nations that are impermanent, fragile, and held together and strengthened only by the competence their respective citizens develop. As the prominent twentieth-century theologian Reinhold Niebuhr once put the matter:

> The task of building a world community is man's final necessity and possibility, but also his final impossibility. It is a necessity and possibility because history is the process which extends the freedom of man over natural process to the point where universality is reached. It is impossible because man is, despite his increasing freedom, a finite creature, wedded to time and place and incapable of building any structure of culture or civilization which does not have its foundations in a particular and dated locus.[70]

69. See Marx, "Economic and Philosophic Manuscripts of 1844," 76: "The animal is immediately identical with its life-activity. It does not distinguish itself from it. It is its life-activity."

70. Reinhold Niebuhr, chap. 5 in *The Children of Light and the Children of Darkness: A Vindication of Democracy and a Critique of Its Traditional Defense* (Chicago: University of Chicago Press, 2011), 188.

§90. The various substitutisms I have considered, and those I have not, undermine liberal competence or preclude it from emerging in the first place. Substitutism is not a problem that is restricted to one political party, although governmental substitutism has been a cornerstone of the Democratic Party, by virtue of its twentieth-century legacy of progressivism. Substitutism runs deeper than politics, and animates our actions within it and beyond it. That substitutism is a pathology of American life today, appearing nearly everywhere, is beyond dispute. If, after identity politics has runs its course, our country is to return to the liberal politics of competence, we will need to identify all the manifestations of substitutism and soberly ask, in each case, what the referent meal is for which the supplement emerged in the first place. Then, we will need to declare our allegiance to supplementism rather than substitutism. Only through such an allegiance can competence be redeveloped. In taking this task upon ourselves, we will rediscover the meal that provides the "daily bread"[71] needed for a sober life. From those fixed-referent meals, we can add supplements that do not merely cause us no harm but actually work to our advantage—whether they be in social media, online shopping, or any other form. This was the lesson of Plato's good doctor and Rousseau's courageous warrior. It can be our lesson, too. The way we have been proceeding, the way of substitutism, leads to an unsustainable euphoric high that promises much but, finally, delivers little. The addict often discovers this too late. Alas, we are the addict. Our country is ill. The evidence is everywhere. In performing the reverse alchemy that turns substitutes back into supplements, we can undertake the necessary operation to return us to the liberal politics of competence.

71. See Matt. 6:11.

Patient and Unending Labor

P. THE CREATURE MAN, WHO ALWAYS LOOKS FOR SHORTCUTS

And God shall wipe away all tears from their eyes; and there shall be no more death, neither sorrow, nor crying, neither shall there be any more pain: for the former things are passed away.[1]

§91. Someday the lion will lay down with the lamb.[2] Someday the wheat and the tares, good and evil, the clean and the unclean, will be separated.[3] Someday, we will find the security for which we long.[4] Someday, the end of history will arrive, and our labors will end.[5] Someday—not today. Man is a creature who always looks for shortcuts to that distant someday. *Homo, ex ingenio celeritas quaesitor.* These four hopes—a second innocence after long immersion in a broken world, a justice that is clean and without ambiguity, a security that cannot be undermined, and a world wherein there are no more difficult labors—are the shortcuts identity politics promises but cannot deliver. Identity politics cannot deliver them because these are religious longings, which man by himself can never bring about.[6]

1. Rev. 21:4.

2. See Isa. 11:6.

3. See Matt. 13:24–30, cited in part 1, n. 116.

4. See Matt. 13:12: "For whosoever hath, to him shall be given, and he shall have more abundance: but whosoever hath not, from him shall be taken away even that he hath."

5. See Matt. 24:36.

6. See Daniel J. Mahoney, *The Idol of Our Age: How the Religion of Humanity Subverts Christianity* (New York: Encounter Books, 2018).

§92. What is the shortcut that identity politics promises to the second innocence? The seldom stated but always presumed mythical first innocence posited by identity politics provides a clue. The first innocence is to be found everywhere that is devoid of the white, heterosexual man who gave us "Western civilization." The first innocence existed in the pristine natural world before Western civilization emerged, and it still exists today in those regions of the globe where nature remains unstained by Western civilization or where other civilizations resist Western civilization. Pristine nature and non-Western civilizations are innocent. They always have been and they always will be, no matter how many people die of natural disasters among them, and no matter what tyranny, slavery, or cruelty non-Western civilizations have authored or may cause in the future. Adherents of identity politics believe that because Western civilization destroyed the first innocence, it owes a debt to nature and to other civilizations that it cannot repay except by extinguishing itself. From this point of departure, is it not difficult to discern the shortcut adherents take to the second innocence. First: The technology and industry that have disrupted pristine nature must be removed or supplanted. Nature is not never-ending, unpredictable, emergent evolution, as Charles Darwin's theory of evolution proposed in 1859.[7] Nature is a wounded victim to be healed. Replace dirty fossil fuel technology and industry that caused the loss of the first innocence with clean solar and wind technology, or deindustrialize altogether, and the second innocence is in our grasp. Second, with respect to other civilizations: Renounce Western history, institutions, states, borders, and privilege by relentlessly attacking them until they succumb. Renarrate history; upend the inherited institutions of family and religion; shift the task of politics from developing liberal competence to purging transgressors and revealing heretofore voiceless

7. See Charles Darwin, *The Origin of Species by Means of Natural Selection* (Cambridge, MA: Harvard University Press, 2001).

innocents; supplant economic competition, indeed all competition, with social justice and so-called "cooperation" that includes some but excludes mavericks, original thinkers, earnest competitors, and those who are impatient or disgusted with the folly of man—do these things, say the defenders of identity politics, and the second innocence will be in our grasp.

§93. The identity politics shortcut to the second innocence supposes that the transgression that needs to be addressed is *out there*, to be grasped and worked on, and therefore that the second innocence requires of us a "work," an activity—and perhaps even activism. This strategy is not unique to identity politics; it has been a Christian temptation right from the beginning. At the dawn of the Reformation in 1535, Martin Luther identified its sweet temptation:

> But such is human weakness and misery that in the terrors of conscience and the danger of death we look at nothing except our own works, our worthiness.... Human reason cannot [in fact] refrain from looking at active righteousness, that is, at its own righteousness.[8]

This shortcut to the second innocence bypasses the longer way, the harder way, the almost impossibly difficult way—not of looking outward but of looking inward, to where the arrow of condemnation leaves us wounded and without defense against the words and deeds we have "done and left undone."[9] Proponents of identity politics aim the wounding arrow of condemnation outward toward other groups, rather than inward, to save themselves from the terrors of conscience, as Luther called them, and the need for contrition, repentance, atonement, and—hardest of all—the forgiveness of others.

8. Luther, "Lectures of Galatians," in *Luther's Works*, vol. 26, 5.

9. Episcopal Church, *Book of Common Prayer*; see part 1, n. 77.

"If we say we have no sin, we deceive ourselves, and the truth is not within us."[10] Who, today, has the strength to endure the wound that that admission would cause or reveal, to start each day bearing it, because the wound is in us and we cannot alone heal it? Here is the Cross the mainline churches in America found too difficult to bear. Identity politics offers a shortcut; it retains the categories of transgression and innocence, but purports to solve their inscrutable riddle by looking outward at others rather than into the internal abyss we can never fully fathom or fully command. I stated the problem long ago. We are all Adam. "I did not do it; it was Eve's fault."[11]

§94. What is the shortcut that identity politics promises to a clean and unambiguous justice? Human relations are never clean; motives are never pure. There are never "solutions" to "problems," only never-ending trade-offs between lesser evils and partial goods. The cleanliness we achieve in one place is always achieved at the price of leaving a stain elsewhere. Justice in the world is never clean. Impatient with impurity and ambiguity because they confirm that there are no quick, opioid-like fixes to free us from the sober world as it is, identity politics tries to separate the wheat from the tares before the harvest. Each person *is* his identity group, replete with prescriptive ethnic or racial[12] confessions to which he must adhere or be silenced. Therein lies the shortcut identity politics takes to cleanliness in human relations. Mixed motives are not an ineradicable aspect of life; they are evidence of lurking microaggression or privilege, which must also be silenced. The pure of heart alone are allowed to speak. Therefore, in addition to them, the only others who will take the stage are the abject

10. 1 John 1:8.

11. Gen. 3:12–13, cited in part 1, n. 192.

12. See Mohamed Ali, "Prescriptive Racialism and Racial Exclusion," *Quillette*, April 1, 2019, https://quillette.com/2019/04/01/prescriptive-racialism-and-racial-exclusion/.

sinners who wreck everything they touch while deluding themselves about the purity of their own dark motives. The American Founding Fathers did not make terrible and necessary compromises to hold together states with vastly different inheritances; they were racists who justified slavery. Identity politics recognizes no terrible and necessary compromises, only pure "solutions," against which all compromise is a betrayal that must be resisted, routed out, and purged.

Insisting that the world must be clean, identity politics hides away the stain of the world through bookkeeping sleights of hand or by removing stain from the books altogether. Nowhere is the problem more evident than with respect to energy production and use. We must have environmental justice! Clean solar and wind energy must replace dirty fossil fuels! How dreamy this all is. The rare-earth minerals that facilitate the production of electricity in solar panels are produced in strip mines almost entirely located in China,[13] because the American landscape must remain unsullied, and its environmental bookkeeping kept spotless. Carbon dioxide–producing explosives are used to blast through hard rock. Carbon dioxide–producing diesel machinery, of a gigantic scale, is used to remove the debris. To process and refine the debris into an industrially usable material requires harsh chemicals that pollute rivers and groundwater. The refined rare-earth metals are incorporated into the solar cells in manufacturing plants using electricity still largely produced by burning coal, which produces yet more carbon dioxide. Then, diesel-burning cargo ships transport the solar panels across the ocean before they are conveyed by diesel truck to the sites where they will be used here in America. No one yet knows how many millions of these solar panels, containing biologically damaging rare-earth metals, will be disposed of at the end of their life cycle. No recycling system is yet in

13. See Michael Silver, "China's Dangerous Monopoly on Metals: Control of the Rare-Earth Supply Gives Beijing Both Economic and Military Advantages over the U.S.," *Wall Street Journal*, April 14, 2019, https://www.wsj.com/articles/chinas-dangerous-monopoly-on-metals-11555269517.

place to address the matter. Will diesel trucks transport the waste, or will electric trucks whose batteries are charged by coal-fired power plants perform the task? Where will the waste go? In a landfill where the rare-earth metals will pollute the groundwater? If solar panels are recycled, how much electricity from petroleum-based fuels will be necessary to melt them down and extract the valuable rare-earth metals from them? Turning to the other purportedly clean-energy source, what about the generation of electrical power produced by wind turbines? With these, too, rare-earth minerals are needed for the magnets in the rotors. What about the immense amount of coal that must be burned to produce the lime for the roughly 30,000 tons of concrete that form the base platform on which large wind turbines are positioned? How much coal is necessary to produce the steel for the tower and turbine blades?

I raise these questions not to indict solar and wind technology. If we are to build a world together, the technology of energy production will have to advance. Nuclear fission, hydrocarbon, solar, wind, and, in the future, fusion technologies will all be in the dirty mix. So-called clean energy can be seen as a "solution" to the "problem" of dirty fossil fuels only by performing bookkeeping sleights of hand or by removing the stain from the books altogether. *What we now call clean energy is better understood as energy made possible by mining heavy metals from our planet rather than by extracting liquid and gaseous petroleum from it.* In the bookkeeping of mortal life, there is no cleanliness. Christianity proposed a Divine resolution to that problem, a shortcut by which God takes upon Himself man's stain. Identity politics gives man a shortcut to the problem as well; namely, *deny* that uncleanliness is inscribed into your world, and use bookkeeping as a way out of facing the dirty truth about yourself and your world.[14] Visible cleanliness in one place

14. See Mark P. Mills, *The "New Energy Economy": An Exercise in Magical Thinking* (New York: Manhattan Institute, March 26, 2019), https://www.manhattan-institute.org/green-energy-revolution-near-impossible.

is *always* purchased at the price of invisible uncleanliness in another. American environmental fastidiousness has contributed to turning other parts of the world into environmental wastelands.

§95. What is the shortcut that identity politics promises to a security that cannot be undermined? Nothing characterizes identity politics better than the overriding insecurity of its adherents, which often takes the form of oscillating back and forth between righteous certainty and debilitating insecurity. Insecurity has always been man's lot. Death is always near; and even when we deceive ourselves that we will live forever, there is always the worry that what we have will be taken from us. Identity politics is peculiar in that it proposes a shortcut that allows us never to be haunted by insecurity.

How does it do this? Identity politics provides the security of confidently knowing who we are. We are *our identity*, perhaps even our intersectional identity—but our identity, nevertheless. Our identity is foundational; it is immovable rock, not shifting sand. It is prior to reason and speech; therefore reason and speech cannot cast doubt on it. Once we greeted each other with a handshake to indicate that we posed no threat to the other person; now we greet each other and announce our identity—to indicate to others what they *cannot* question, doubt, or in any way threaten. Identity politics divides citizens into groups, yet the security it purports to offer is a *personal* security that no other person may disrupt. If we imagine one day that we are *this* identity and the next day we are *that* identity, no one can tell us otherwise. If by material means, we alter our bodies from one day to the next, no one can raise questions or have doubts about the alterations we have made, or what they may indicate about our titanic internal struggles that are unlikely to resolve without the help of those we love. In the world that identity politics constructs, we do not begin each day with humble cognizance of our mortal insecurity and, in a world with others, attempt to establish wherein a workable but never permanent security may lie. Rather, we begin each day with a security that cannot be abnegated, and associate only with those who "affirm" and "honor" the identity to which we cling. "Everybody is special,"[15] but nobody really needs anyone. In Genesis it is written: "It is not good for man to be alone."[16] But in the world identity politics constructs, we are alone. The theology undergirding the purported security our identity offers cries out for consideration. God stands in need of nothing; man, made in the image of God,[17] improperly ascribes this attribute to himself. Like God, man wishes to be sufficient unto himself. His *identity* is the cheap imitation that grants him that.

To what insecurity would man be exposed if his identity could not provide the shortcut to the security he desires? Above all, the insecurity of working and living with others—not those who affirm and honor us, but those who find our identity either irrelevant to their labors or anathema to their convictions. The liberal politics of competence requires that we live in just this sort of world. The fellow citizens who surround us, should we lift our gaze from our mobile phones and tablets to recognize them, are *not* there to affirm or honor us; they are there so that together we may build a world despite our differences.

The insecurity of working and living with others gives rise to a second insecurity, more terrifying than the first: the insecurity of asking for forgiveness and of forgiving. I have indicated throughout the book that identity politics invokes the Christian categories of transgression and innocence, but makes no room for the God who reconciles the imbalance of payments—the injustices—that all of history chronicles. Nor is there a need, in the world identity politics constructs, for forgiveness. When citizens have impervious identities and need not build a world together because state competence promises cradle-to-

15. See "Barney — Everyone Is Special (SONG)," YouTube video, 1:30, posted by Barney, February 23, 2012, https://youtu.be/k_t7pTfdYts.

16. Gen. 2:18.

17. See Gen. 1:26.

grave security, it is not required that there be any intercourse between them. No grievous mistakes will be made, no reckless pride will be exhibited, no injurious words will be uttered, and no "bullying" will be endured. In such a world, to the great relief of the proponents, forgiveness will neither be asked for nor given. Therein lies their purported security against the mystery and terror of a world in which the imbalance of payments between the transgressor and the innocent will always be with us. So deep is this need for what could be called "the security of just compensation" that even when they themselves are forgiven, they immediately lose sight of the luminous lesson that the mercy of forgiveness exceeds the justice of payment, and refuse to forgive others. Man: the forgiven servant who does not forgive.

Then came Peter to him, and said, Lord, how oft shall my brother sin against me, and I forgive him? till seven times? Jesus saith unto him, I say not unto thee, Until seven times: but, Until seventy times seven. Therefore is the kingdom of heaven likened unto a certain king, which would take account of his servants. And when he had begun to reckon, one was brought unto him, which owed him ten thousand talents. But forasmuch as he had not to pay, his lord commanded him to be sold, and his wife, and children, and all that he had, and payment to be made. The servant therefore fell down, and worshipped him, saying, Lord, have patience with me, and I will pay thee all. Then the lord of that servant was moved with compassion, and loosed him, and forgave him the debt. But the same servant went out, and found one of his fellow-servants, which owed him an hundred pence: and he laid hands on him, and took him by the throat, saying, Pay me that thou owest. And his fellow-servant fell down at his feet, and besought him, saying, Have patience with me, and I will pay thee all. And he would not: but went and cast him into prison, till he should pay the debt. So when his fellow-servants saw what was done, they were very sorry, and came and told unto their lord all that was done. Then his lord, after that he had called him, said unto him, O thou wicked servant, I forgave thee all that debt, because thou desiredst me: Shouldest not thou also have had compassion on thy fellow-servant, even as I had pity on thee? And his lord was wroth, and delivered him to the tormentors, till he should pay all that was due unto him. So likewise shall my heavenly Father do also unto you, if ye from your hearts forgive not everyone his brother their trespasses.[18]

The liberal politics of competence supposes that when citizens labor together, there will be grievous mistakes made, reckless pride exhibited, and injurious words uttered. Transgressions will occur for which compensation will be absent or imbalanced. Without asking for, and granting, forgiveness, the liberal politics of competence cannot develop or be sustained. Citizens must be able to endure the mystery and insecurity of a world in which not all payments will be made, a world that is not entirely fair.[19] Once Christian hope anticipated that the ledger books would be balanced at the end of time, and in the interim we were charged to forgive one another, no matter what we have endured. Christian hope having been ruled out, the imbalance of payments that forgiveness provokes is now too difficult to endure. That is why identity politics demands that the ledger books be balanced immediately. The accumulated debt that transgressors owe must be paid—but because there is no forgiveness, the debt can never be erased. Heavy laden and without hope of ease,[20] all forward movement is arrested and tomorrow never arrives.

Identity politics is frightened by a future that can only be discovered through forgiving and being forgiven; that is why it only recov-

18. Matt. 18:21–35.

19. Cf. John Rawls, "Justice as Fairness," *Philosophy and Public Affairs* 14, no. 3 (Summer 1985), 223–51. See also secs. 56–58 in this book.

20. Cf. Matt. 11:28: "Come unto me, all ye that labour and are heavy laden, and I will give you rest."

ers and eternally reenacts transgressions that *have been*. The short-cut to security that identity politics promises comes at the cost of a future; the currently imagined grim contours of which can only be annulled when the inconvenient accounting that forgiveness entails dismantles the edifice of transgressions that have been. Therein lies the longer way, the way inscribed in the liberal politics of compe-tence, which presupposes that if citizens are to build a world togeth-er, and therefore have a future together, they must not only attend to money and the world of payment, as I called it earlier in section 30, they must also forgive and be forgiven. Identity politics wishes to bypass the broken world in which harm is perpetrated and received. Hence the fragility of its adherents. Alas, the broken world in which we live provides the only available path to the future, and we must make our way through it, not around it. There are no shortcuts.

§96. What is the shortcut identity politics promises to a world in which there are no more difficult labors? I have anticipated the an-swer in my assessment of the significance of forgiveness in a broken world. In the world that identity politics constructs, evidence of a broken world must be eliminated in order to bring about a world that is not broken. Competition between persons, business enterprises, and nations must be eliminated so that the sting and humiliation of failure are no longer felt. Our sons and daughters must be taught to share and care, to please others, to collaborate; and if they are to compete at all, it cannot be on the unsupervised playground, for fear of what that might unleash, but in the venue of parent-coordinated "activities" that domesticate them and prepare them for further do-mestication in our colleges and universities. If the 2.28:1 ratio of boys to girls who are diagnosed with ADHD[21] is one of the consequenc-

21. See Ujjwal P. Ramtekkar, Angela M. Reiersen, Alexandre A. Todorov, and Richard D. Todd, "Sex and Age Differences in Attention-Deficit/Hy-peractivity Disorder Symptoms and Diagnoses: Implications for DSM-V and ICD-11," *Journal of the American Academy of Child & Adolescent Psychiatry*

es of this domestication, then our boys have been disproportionally harmed by this innovative education intended to end the harm competition causes.

This cargo cult–like endeavor—in effect, of building a noncompetitive runway so that noncompetitive airplanes might someday land there—indulges in the fantasy that we have reached the end of history. Quick to point out that Western civilization has oppressed and marginalized non-Western civilizations, proponents of identity politics have not noticed that their attempt to put an end to relentless competition can only be indulged because Western civilization is currently without competitive peers. That will change. China and perhaps India will see to that in this century. If America survives the twenty-first century, there will be other national rivalries in centuries to come. The identity politics of innocence, as I indicated back in section 23, can only be indulged when the competitive world that compels us to develop competence or die—figuratively and literally—has been suspended. We know from history that no civilization or nation endures forever. The end-of-history narrative identity politics constructs, which justifies the replacement of the politics of competence with the politics of innocence, confuses the end of history with the momentary interlude of Western ascension in which we still find ourselves. The broken world, however, allows no one to rest. The shortcut identity politics promises to a world without difficult labor undermines personal, economic, and national competition—not least by identifying them as mere artifacts of the transgressive white, heterosexual man. If its enterprise succeeds, difficult labors will not come to an end; they will remerge, now without those "transgressive" artifacts of liberty, market commerce, representative government, rule of law, and the fantastic achievements in scientific understanding and techno-

---

49, no. 3 (March 2010), 217–28.e3, https://www.jaacap.org/article/S0890-8567(09)00052-5/abstract.

logical advancement that have made Western ascendency possible. Instead of prevailing over a world in which competition has been rendered obsolete, the enterprise of identity politics will place us all among the losers in that competition. *Put an end to competition, and you do not achieve a postcompetitive world; you get failure and death*. Pondering the entire world for a moment, not a single civilization or nation outside of Europe and the Anglo-sphere is being deliberately and mercilessly torn apart from within by its own people. Only once-Christian nations, haunted by Christian categories of transgression and innocence but unable to return to Christianity so that they may understand the deeper meaning of these categories, are doing this. Identity politics promises to the contrary, there will no end to competition and to difficult labors.[22]

§97. The search for shortcuts is not unique to identity politics. Throughout history, man has sought to avoid the longer ways his humble station requires him to walk. What is unique about identity politics is the shortcut it proposes. In an ironic twist befitting the creature man, who always looks for shortcuts, identity politics finds the Christian shortcut too difficult to endure, for it demands that man be hard on himself and admit both his stain and his inability to remove it without Divine assistance. The various shortcuts identity politics offers do not require that man be hard on himself. They require only that white, heterosexual man be hard on himself. The rest are innocents, who find a shortcut to purity by scapegoat-

22. Reflecting on the aftermath of the 1968 Paris uprising against stringent university testing, French liberal Raymond Aron wondered in a now famous essay whether any society calling itself democratic could endure if its youth were not subject to competition. See Raymond Aron, "After the Barricades: The Meaning of the French University Crisis," *Encounter* 31, no. 2 (August 1968). The Marxists who opposed bourgeois competition in 1968 have been replaced by adherents of identity politics, who oppose competition because they see it as an artifact of transgressive Western civilization.

ing him. It is he who stands in the way of a second innocence after long immersion in a broken world, a justice that is clean and without ambiguity, a security that cannot be undermined, and a world wherein there are no more difficult labors. Alas, once he has been purged, some other group of former innocents must take his place. Group after group will be placed on the sacrificial altar to bear the sins of the world and to give the ever-dwindling groups of innocents the shortcut they need. If we strain our imagination, we can envision a distant future in which a few remaining innocents—who have read in the ancient archives the chronicle of the successive purging—begin to wonder aloud why transgression and debt still haunt them at night. Then, with the devastating clarity that seems so often to emerge only in the aftermath of needlessly inflicted suffering, they will perhaps begin to grasp that the shortcut that purging other groups promised will never in fact relieve them of their burden, which arises from causes within themselves they can barely name let alone command. Man always "misses the mark." "Hamartia" was the name given for this by the ancients. "Original sin" is the Christian term for this mystery. *Identity politics declares that there is no original sin, only an original sinner.* That is its shortcut.

§98. What is the shortcut offered by management society and selfie man? I have characterized management society and selfie man as an arrangement befitting citizens who feel themselves to be "greater than kings and less than men."[23] When ensnared by this setup, citizens look upward to global managers to solve all their problems, inward to themselves for self-satisfaction, but not outward to their fellows—their families, civic associations, churches and synagogues, and local and federal political bodies—to develop competence in the mediating institutions in which they live. What looking upward and inward have in common is that they involve no risk. They are shortcuts that bypass the diffi-

23. See sec. 71.

cult labor of building a world with others. Management society and selfie man is the configuration befitting the Arcadian shepherd,[24] who remains just as he is because he does not need others and because others do not need him. This much I considered earlier in sections 65–72.

There is more. The mediating institutions that are most needed to pull our Arcadian shepherd out of his slumber are the very institutions that identity politics indicts. Living in accordance with them, therefore, invites derision and scorn. Adherents of identity politics who live conventional lives within these institutions, as so many do, must therefore demonstrate their identity politics credentials by publicly endorsing lifestyles they themselves do not choose, and by attacking the institutions and ideas by which they themselves live.

The upper classes, whose very success has always depended on embracing these conventional mediating institutions, can and do disparage them, but their critique does not appreciably alter how they themselves live. They speak of the heavy burdens to be borne, but they themselves do not bear them. If biblical language were used to describe them, their lives could be summed up with this verse: "For they bind heavy burdens and grievous to be borne, and lay them on men's shoulders; but they themselves will not move them with one of their fingers."[25] They recycle in order to save the planet—but still fly to exotic vacation destinations on greenhouse gas–emitting airplanes. They speak compassionately about the evil of racism—but live in segregated neighborhoods. They insist that climate change is causing the oceans to rise, but spend vast sums of money for pristine oceanfront vacation homes.[26] They declare they

24. See part 1, n. 35. Kant suggests that man prefers to remain alone and self-satisfied, like an Arcadian shepherd. Nature, he claims, will not allow it, and forces man into a world of competition with others. Tocqueville's insight is that democratic social conditions may, in fact, allow man to live without others, as the Arcadian shepherd does.

25. Matt. 23:4.

26. On September 22, 2009, President Obama addressed the United Nations on the subject of climate change: "No nation, however large or small,

are "uncomfortable with" the prejudices that are supposedly inscribed into conventional mediating institutions, but they themselves do not like being uncomfortable. They live at a safe distance from what they say—and from what they watch. They are fierce critics of gun violence, but will binge watch television series whose plots are based on it. Their sons play violent video games and their daughters listen to rap music, but unlike the sons and daughters from lower social strata who have no inoculation against the abhorrent acts such games and music glorify, these things are, for them, bracketed indulgences and cathartic escapes, rather than poisonous exemplars. Educated to be unapologetic critics of Western civilization and its institutions, the sons and daughters born into these classes will maintain their harsh posture toward Western civilization and its institutions long after they marry and settle into conventional lives of their own. The fig leaf of their commitment to identity politics covers over their participation in the conventional mediating institutions identity politics denounces; and their innocence-signaling defense of identity politics offers a shortcut to purity, which they adopt to avoid impugning themselves. At one time, the upper classes in America demonstrated their standing through the luxury items they owned. Thorstein Veblen made light of their conspicuous consumption in his now classic 1899 book *The Theory of the Leisure Class*.[27] Less than a century later, in 1977, Ronald Inglehart declared that the era of postmate-

---

wealthy or poor, can escape the impact of climate change. Rising sea levels threaten every coastline. More powerful storms and floods threaten every continent. More frequent drought and crop failures breed hunger and conflict in places where hunger and conflict already thrive. On shrinking islands, families are already being forced to flee their homes as climate refugees" (Barack Obama, "Obama's Speech on Climate Change" [speech, UN Climate Change Summit, New York, September 22, 2009, https://www.nytimes.com/2009/09/23/us/politics/23obama.text.html]). In August 2019, former president Obama purchased a $15 million estate on the small island of Martha's Vineyard.

27. See Thorstein Veblen, *The Theory of the Leisure Class* (Oxford: Oxford University Press, 2009).

rialism was upon us.[28] If conspicuous consumption could no longer distinguish the upper classes from the rest, *a new distinction was needed*, one that the rest could not afford to indulge. That new distinction is the *luxury beliefs* the upper classes alone can afford to profess.[29] However much the upper classes may drift toward the configuration of management society and selfie man that undermines and impugns conventional mediating institutions, their robust practices and habits check their drift in that direction. Fathers and mothers teach their sons and daughters one thing and expect of them another. In the event that their sons and daughters become entranced by those teachings and depart significantly from the conventional path laid out for them, fathers and mothers must deny their screaming inclinations to pull their sons and daughters back to the well-worn path for fear of being exposed as a "racist," "misogynist," "homophobe," "transphobe," "Islamophobe," "fascist," "Nazi," "hater," or "denier."

Our sons and daughters belong to a future for which we cannot fully prepare them, and which we will never fully understand. To suggest, therefore, that fathers and mothers are *right*, and that their sons and daughters are *wrong*, is surely misplaced. In the world that identity politics constructs, however, fathers and mothers can never be right, and sons and daughters can never be wrong. The collateral damage caused by this default posture is immense, not least to those sons and daughters whose anxieties seldom disappear—and are often amplified—after they leave convention behind. Because identity pol-

---

28. See Ronald Inglehart, *The Silent Revolution: Changing Values and Political Styles among Western Publics* (Princeton, NJ: Princeton University Press, 2009).

29. See Rob Henderson, "'Luxury Beliefs' Are the Latest Status Symbol for Rich Americans," *New York Post*, August 17, 2019, https://nypost.com/2019/08/17/luxury-beliefs-are-the-latest-symbol-for-rich-americans/. More recently, Rob Henderson wrote, "Thorstein Veblen's Theory of the Leisure Class—A Status Update," *Quillette*, November 16, 2019, https://quillette.com/2019/11/16/thorstein-veblens-theory-of-the-leisure-class-a-status-update/.

itics informs them that only those who consider themselves among the innocents count, sons and daughters are understandably eager to embrace identities they believe will relieve them from the unredeemable burden of transgression they would otherwise carry. The moment they take this shortcut to innocence that turns out to bring no rest, fathers and mothers must renounce their authority over them altogether, and hand their sons and daughters over to therapists or doctors whose livelihood depends on this staggering transfer of authority.

A surer path to a premature and permanent extraction of sons and daughters from their families, compelled by state-sanctioned experts, has yet to be devised. The Frankfurt School that arose in the aftermath of World War I and reached its apogee after World War II, with the publication in 1951 of *The Authoritarian Personality*,[30] dreamed of ways to undermine the conventional family, but failed. Identity politics accomplishes this goal effortlessly, by denying fathers and mothers the authority to doubt and guide their sons and daughters once they have cloaked themselves with innocence. The modern state, always intent on shifting power from mediating institutions to itself, is more than happy to certify their innocence. A great battle looms just over the horizon; it will be fought over whether the conventional generative family is so implicated in transgression that it obstructs the emergence of the next generation of innocents. When this battle commences in earnest, the upper classes, who often live conventional lives and purchase the purity they lack by innocence-signaling the sentiments identity politics requires, will lose their cover and have to choose one side or the other—the conventions of the mediating institutions by which they live or the iden-

---

30. See Theodor W. Adorno, Else Frenkel-Brunswik, Daniel J. Levinson, and R. Nevitt Sanford, *The Authoritarian Personality* (New York: W. W. Norton, 1993). For an excellent overview of the Frankfurt School, see Martin Jay, *The Dialectical Imagination: A History of the Frankfurt School and the Institute for Social Research, 1923–1950* (New York: Little, Brown, 1973).

tity politics of innocence they profess. Therein lies the next great struggle between state and society in America.

The consequences of the identity politics indictment of mediating institutions has been catastrophic for the least among us.[31] While the safe harbor of their intact mediating institutions generally protects the upper classes from the buffeting winds of identity politics they themselves contribute to whipping up, fragile and exposed citizens who struggle alone without the luxury of being protected by such institutions have little hope of building a world in the rubble that is left when those institutions are undermined.[32] Regardless of their identity category, the effort the least among us make to reanimate or defend those institutions is rebuffed. If they are white, they will be mocked as "clingers"[33] or deplorables; if they are black, Hispanic, or anyone other than white, heterosexual men, they must censure themselves. Innocents dare not express admiration for the conventional mediating institutions so many of them know lead to personal and familial success. They keep silent, understanding that in the world identity politics constructs, they will be scapegoated with the "C" word—conservative—if ever they renounce the narrative role assigned to them.

The shortcut promised by management society and selfie man offers a moral pass to members of the upper classes who attack the conventional mediating institutions of society while also benefitting from

31. See Charles A. Murray, *Coming Apart: The State of White America, 1960–2010* (New York: Crown Forum, 2012).

32. See J. D. Vance, *Hillbilly Elegy: A Memoir of a Family and Culture in Crisis* (New York: Harper, 2016). See also the fine essay by R. R. Reno, "War on the Weak" (in *First Things*, August 2013, https://www.firstthings.com/article/2013/08/war-on-the-weak).

33. "Barack Obama's Small Town Guns and Religion Comment," YouTube video, 1:38, posted by potus08blog, April 11, 2008, https://www.youtube.com/watch?v=DTxXUufI3jA. President Obama's ideas fall well within a strand of Enlightenment thinking that asserts that adherence to premodern ideas, like religion, will drop off as standards of living increase.

them, and makes the stability and ascent of the least among us well-nigh impossible. Indicting conventional mediating institutions does not free citizens from transgressive structures so that all may live happy, liberated lives. It divides society into two hostile camps—the well-to-do who are able to cover their privilege with garlands of righteousness and the least among us whose suffering can only be ameliorated if conventional mediating institutions are intact and robustly defended. The shortcut of management society and selfie man, which proclaims that nations and the mediating institutions within them are the cause of inequality around the globe, contributes to the devastating inequality we see around us today.

§99. What is the shortcut offered when supplements become substitutes? Management society and selfie man promises liberation from the stain and impurity of conventional mediating institutions. Turning supplements into substitutes promises a drug-like fix that relieves citizens of the need for the figurative sobriety that liberal competence presupposes. In the case of the opioid epidemic sweeping America (see section 74), the problem is literal and figurative. While I did not develop the idea earlier, in every case of substitutism I considered, from section 70 to section 89, *three distinct phases* are present: life without the supplement; life with it; and life with the supplement now turned into a substitute.

Whatever their difficulties, the first and third phases are, strangely, easier to bear than the second phase, in which liberal competence develops and sobriety is tested. The first phase knows no supplements; this is the simple life, the life that figuratively comes before the loss of the first Edenic innocence.[34] Alternatively, if Rousseau's description is more palatable, this is the life of natural man before being enfeebled

---

34. In the biblical account, immediately after their fall, God gave Adam and Eve animal skins to protect them from the thorns outside the Garden of Eden (see Gen. 3:21). These were the supplements to their own skins. There were no supplements during the first innocence.

by the trappings of society. Because the latter are unavailable to him, in this first phase man is shielded from the temptation to turn supplements into substitutes. That so many of us have the recurring dream of returning to an earlier simplicity—of eating non-GMO foods, of living authentically, of downsizing, of outlawing plastic bags and plastic straws, of only using clean energy, and so on—is salutary at least in one respect: it confirms that we know the peril of losing sight of the "meal," as I called it in section 76, even if we do not quite know what to do with the insight we have. This attempt to return to the Edenic, natural condition is not a shortcut but rather a *contrived innocence*. It less resolves the temptation of turning supplements into substitutes than precludes the temptation from emerging in the first place. That is why this first phase is easier to bear than the second phase—and why the attempting to return to the first phase is a stopgap measure that cannot permanently shield us from facing our post-Edenic world.

The second phase, which involves the never settled question of whether the supplements at our disposal are helping us build liberal competence or undermining our efforts, I will turn to shortly. The third phase, in which we turn supplements into substitutes, is the dangerous shortcut that deludes us that we have achieved a second innocence, because the difficult labor associated with creating the meal no longer concerns us. We look back at the meal, assuring ourselves that it is no longer necessary. Many who today call themselves global citizens look back, for example, at the meal that is our national home and no longer believe it is necessary. In this, they have succumbed to the third phase, that of "global substitutism," as I called it in section 89. Evidence that the nation is the meal to which we must return is dismissed by simply increasing the dosage—by doubling down, as European Union elites are now doing, at the very moment when citizens within its group of countries declare that the supplement to the nation that the European Union was supposed to be has been turned into a substitute. The escalating addictive cycle I am describing is well known, and self-reinforcing, which is why it is so extraordinarily difficult to arrest before the patient dies. Europe today is in this dangerous third phase. It cannot end well—not only for Europe but for all instances where supplements have been turned into substitutes. Closer to home, the crisis of loneliness in America, which should direct us to the meal of friendship and neighborliness, is being responded to by increasing the dosage of social media substitutism,[35] as I called it in section 81. This is as predictable as it is fatal.

It is in the second phase, in which the responsible use of supplements is always in question, that liberal competence can be fully developed—and will be most threatened. That is why it is the most difficult of the three phases to bear. Plato's doctor and Rousseau's warrior, who first introduced us to the distinction between supplements and substitutes (see sections 74–75), can both use supplements at their disposal to amplify and extend their competence as a doctor and a warrior. Alternatively, by turning supplements into substitutes, they will undermine their competence altogether. Such is the case, too, with liberal citizens in all that they do. Some thoughtful conservatives argue that there is a fixed, discernable human nature, that the welcoming embrace of scientific and technological advances within liberal thought recklessly disregards human nature, and that further advances point to an impending transhumanism that will erase human nature altogether. Formulated in this way, what is the remedy? Scientific and technological advances will only accelerate, and the supplements they offer will cause each successive generation to look back on the previous one with puzzlement and incredulity. Many of the arguments on behalf of a fixed, discernable human nature amount to enticing encomiums to return to a world without supplements—in short, to a first-phase contrived innocence. We live, however, in a post-Edenic world, a providential world whose historical

35. See Eileen Brown, "Americans Spend Far More Time on Their Smartphones than They Think," ZDNet, April 28, 2019, https://www.zdnet.com/article/americans-spend-far-more-time-on-their-smartphones-than-they-think/.

unfolding no one can anticipate or arrest. Scientific and technological advances are an ineradicable aspect of that world. Our challenge
as liberal citizens must be met in a different way. The way to meet it—
the way that avoids first-phase contrived innocence and third-phase
substitutism—requires, first, that we develop competence with the
meal; second, that we amplify that competence through the addition of supplements; and third, that we exercise unwavering vigi-
lance against taking the shortcut that substitutism offers. We must
develop competence as citizens of our respective nations; only then
can global concerns be adequately addressed. We must develop that
mysterious competence called friendship; only then can the supplement of social media vastly extend that competence. History will not
stand still. Scientific and technological advances will put new and undreamed-of supplements into the hands of future generations. *What
will remain fixed is the configuration of the meal, the supplements to the
meal, and the dangerous shortcut involved in turning those supplements
into substitutes*. On this reading, imminent transhumanism is a consequence not of the reckless liberal embrace of scientific and technological advances, but rather of a fatal substitutism that abrogates
the relationship between the always human meals through which we
live, know, and find joy, and the supplements that can amplify but not
replace them.

Q. THE THREE PILLARS OF RENEWAL

§100. I have considered the enticing but ultimately deadening shortcuts that tempt citizens away from liberal competence. What possible future might lie ahead if we have the fortitude and faith to take
the longer way, the way that invites us to develop such competence,
and to live out the sober satisfactions that attend it? In this matter,
we should first heed Tocqueville's observation in *Democracy in America* that thinking along party lines will not help us see very far:

> I did not intend to serve or combat any party; I have tried not to
> see differently but further than any party; while they are busy with
> tomorrow, I have wished to consider the whole future.[36]

The party of the Left today invites us to embrace the identity politics of innocence, which, for all the reasons I have considered, is a political and theological dead end. The party of the Right has given us an
untempered defense of purportedly free global markets, to the detriment of our middle class, and an unsavory commitment to democracy
exportation abroad, to the detriment of our national security. The Left
has shamelessly exploited the deep wound of slavery as a template to infinitely extend its power, by gathering together, and inventing,[37] groups
of innocents it purports to protect and serve. This has turned it into a
festering cauldron of grievance and resentment in which what matters is
not the illuminating and productive ideas citizens and candidates might
generate but the number of identity politics debt points it can amass.
The Right, fearful that any reference to the deep wound of slavery
would derail its commitment to a color-blind society, ignores the wound
entirely, or speaks euphemistically about using "enterprise zones" as a
way to "combat the problems of our inner cities." Rightly or wrongly,
this elision invites suspicion that it is the party that harbors racism. A
renewed America will require more than either party can now provide.

§101. Liberal competence in America cannot develop and flourish
unless we renew our commitment to the middle-class commercial
republic our country was established to be. No middle class, no liberal competence. This must be the first pillar of a renewed America.
The party of the Left speaks incessantly of the poor—not with a view
to how they can become competent members of a vibrant middle

36. Tocqueville, author's introduction in *Democracy in America*, vol. 1, 20.

37. See part 1, n. 50 on Mora's description of the invention of the category
"Hispanic."

class but with a view to how state programs may provide them with "assistance." For every problem, there is another government "service." If such assistance does more than supplement the existing mediating institutions already around them, if it becomes governmental substitutism (see section 86), it invariably produces debilitating, drug-like dependency that is difficult to cure. If we really are concerned with the poor, we must do everything in our power to fortify the middle class, so that the poor may swell its ranks. The party of the Right has done no better on behalf of the middle class. A monomaniacal focus on market efficiency and profit, on the "principles" of a free market, the contention that money is the measure of all things, the attempt to reduce to one single measure the necessarily multiple and conflicting goods a competent commercial enterprise must keep in mind—these are the ways, paradoxically enough, that Karl Marx talked about "capitalism."[38] Adam Smith, supposedly one of the great luminaries of the Right, never argued, as Marx did, that money is the measure of all things. The very title of Smith's magisterial work, *The Wealth of Nations*, alerts its readers that commerce and politics are two distinguishable domains. Smith's apprehension, in fact, was that the productivity gains generated by the global division of labor and globally extensive markets would undermine the geographically circumscribed political unit that is the nation.[39] The political economist, he believed, must understand that there are trade-offs between what market efficiency demands and what political community requires—we do not live *in* a market, but rather go *to* the market; we

38. See part 1, n. 147.

39. See Smith, bk. 1, chap. 11 in *Wealth of Nations*, 275–78. In this short but extremely important passage, Smith asks who will look after the good of the nation. Of the three groups that Smith considers—landowners, workers, and businessmen involved in foreign trade—he concludes that only the landowners can have a deep and abiding concern for their nation. Workers could have that same concern, but they are too exhausted by their work to be able to demonstrate it.

are not "workers," but rather "citizens who work." Money is not the measure of all things. Our challenge today is precisely the challenge Smith worried about in his 1776 masterpiece: how to square the circle of global commerce and political health. The Right has ignored Smith's difficult proposition for decades. It has its economists, but no political economists. This means—we should be clear on this point—there are some in its ranks who so revere market efficiency that they would be untroubled if the destruction of the American middle class was the necessary collateral damage of market efficiency. That was the recipe for the certain implosion of the Right, which Donald Trump set in motion during his 2016 campaign when he quipped, "Free trade is stupid trade."[40]

Squaring the circle of global commerce and political health will require more than rejiggering trade deals to shrink our balance of payments with China, more than rebooting the manufacturing sector here in America. America-centric trade deals, American net-export status, and a booming manufacturing sector will not, by themselves, generate liberal competence. Economists are concerned with *market value*: the patriotic among them want to square the circle by shifting the global balance sheet of market value in our direction. Liberal competence, however, requires that we be concerned with *use value*.[41] Market value is one metric; use value is another. The former is a supplement to the latter, not a replacement for it. That is why squaring the circle will be such a challenge.

Why is the concern for market value not enough? A few examples will suffice. First, consider those citizens who live in the world identity politics constructs. In order to cover themselves with the fig leaf

40. "STUPID TRADE: Donald Trump Says There Is No Such Thing as Fair Trade (FNN)," YouTube video, 0:20, posted by NewsNOW from FOX, July 17, 2017, https://www.youtube.com/watch?v=5xHzcbq-3_4.

41. The distinction between use value and market value is integral to Smith's analysis. See Smith, bk. 1, chap. 4 in *Wealth of Nations*, 32–33.

of innocence, venture capitalists and commercial enterprises today, also smitten with identity politics, underwrite or make products that they market to those citizens who are seeking to cover themselves with the fig leaf of innocence. These products have market value, but they will be of little use to liberal citizens intent on developing competence. Identity politics innocence-signaling may add market value to GDP, but it has little use value. America-centric trade deals, American net-export status, and a booming manufacturing sector that makes these sorts of products will not help restore the liberal politics of competence.

Second, consider those citizens who have given up developing liberal competence altogether, satisfied with living within the configuration of management society and selfie man. Believing themselves to be greater than kings and less than.men, the middle-class commercial accoutrements of house and automobile ownership have little appeal. These citizens travel extensively rather than settle down, rent in cities rather than buy in suburbia or exurbia. When they do make their purchases, they consist less of "big-ticket items" that bind them to a place and community, and more of expensive gadgets with which they can peruse social media, play games, and otherwise distract themselves.[42] The market value of these purchases may suggest robust economic health, but a world of liberal competence cannot be built with these purchases, because they are of little use in that undertaking.

Third, consider those citizens who are captivated by various substitutisms, through which they bypass the meal entirely and live exclusively on what should be only a supplement. The opioid crisis is illustrative, even if extreme: purchasing opioids may add market value to GDP, but it will not help restore liberal competence.

42. See Fluent, *Devices & Demographics 2017* (New York: Fluent, 2017), http://www.fluentco.com/wp-content/uploads/2017/01/Fluent_DevicesandDemographics_2017.pdf.

If we are to fortify our middle-class commercial republic, fixing our attention on market value is not going to be enough; we must instead ask the difficult question no one wants to raise: What will have use value for competent liberal citizens? To answer this question, we will have to proceed inductively, by living as competent liberal citizens, and rediscovering, as we go, what is useful and what is not. Liberal competence cannot be measured by market value quantities, only by use value qualities. That is a political rather than economic matter, because we cannot establish what is useful without at the same time asking the political question, How are we to live well with others and build a world together? To save liberal competence, we are going to have to make qualitative judgments about use value, rather than pretend that when the market value of what we bring into our country balances the market value of what goes out, all will be well.

§102. The earnest effort to heal the legacy of the wound of slavery is the second pillar on which a renewed America must rest. Throughout *American Awakening: Identity Politics and Other Afflictions of Our Time*, I have insisted that the wound of slavery is a singular wound in American history, and that identity politics has recklessly exploited that wound for the purpose of extending the political franchise of the Democratic Party. The argument here? Civil rights for black Americans leads to women's rights, to gay rights, to transsexual rights, to rights claims by innocent group identities in the future that we cannot currently imagine. This is scandalous. Legalized slavery deprived slaves of the one institution without which civilization grinds immediately to a halt: the generative family. No other American group underwent that deprivation, generation after generation. Going further, and adding insult to injury, in the world that identity politics constructs, the generative family that civilization needs to reproduce itself is neither necessary nor worthy because it is not sufficiently "inclusive." Racism is a charge thrown about so frequently that it has lost its meaning. In an effort to clarify its deeper meaning, I proposed earlier that it involves the scapegoating of one group by another.[43] Surely, such scapegoating includes the ability of one group to determine the terms of engagement by which another group must live. By that definition, identity politics *is* racist—for it demands of black Americans that they sit in silence as identity politics castigates the generative family (and the churches that defend it), without which the legacy of the wound of slavery has no hope of healing. That is not all. Identity politics is guilty of cultural appropriation, by virtue of invoking the suffering of black America as a template to be used by other purportedly monovalent and innocent identity groups.[44] The supposed solidarity between black Americans and identity politics innocents who want to dismantle the generative family is contrived; the appearance of accord and unanimity has been purchased by the racism that silences black American voices.

There is more to say about healing the legacy of the wound of slavery. Identity politics, as I have suggested, requires a transgressor who will be used to cover over the transgressions of the innocents so that their own stains may remain hidden—to others and perhaps even to themselves. The deeper Christian foundation of identity politics would have it that all are stained, and that no mortal group can relieve us of our burden. Theologically compelling though this account may be, if we are all stained, then no distinctions or judgments about specific historically inflicted wounds can be made. If we are all stained, then our culpability can never be mitigated or erased by the wounds we have received at the hands of others. With this insight, we stumble toward a theology of the Cross, on the basis of which we would conclude that the glory of God is revealed through

43. See part 1, n. 20.

44. See "Dr. Umar Johnson Confronted by LGBT Feminist during Xseed in Life Program KC 2015," YouTube video, 12:59, posted by Xseed in Life, February 20, 2015, https://www.youtube.com/watch?v=MBpu_MWxYt-M&feature=youtu.be.

the afflictions that we have patiently endured, regardless of the fact that the transgressions of others have been their proximal source.

> And as Jesus passed by, he saw a man which was blind from his birth. And his disciples asked him, saying, Master, who did sin, this man, or his parents, that he was born blind? Jesus answered, Neither hath this man sinned, nor his parents: but that the works of God should be made manifest in him.[45]

Looking down from the Divine height, it may be true that suffering itself, however great or small, without distinction, testifies to the glory of God; but from man's point of view, it does not. Distinctions must be made. Some have been harmed by the transgressions of others. The merely mortal man asks, "Why must I look to my own culpability when I have suffered at the hands of another?" Then he settles in with his wound and goes no further.

The legacy of the wound of slavery in America will not be overcome unless *both the Christian and the merely mortal view* are given their due. The haunting, paradoxical truth is that while we grow and are deepened by suffering, we must also mitigate the harm and suffering caused by transgression, by redressing the imbalance in the ledger book of justice where possible. With respect to this latter matter of redressing the imbalance, there is the additional problem that without humility, man's monstrous pride, which makes him blind to any cause but his own,[46] precludes us from clearly establishing just where the scales of justice *can* balance.

Setting aside the immense obstacle pride presents to balancing the scales of justice, who are the transgressors? And who are the innocents? There is no slavery in America today on the basis of which we can identify the specific parties to the crime. Slavery ended in 1865. If reparations are to be offered, to whom, and on what basis? By

45. John 9:1–3.
46. See Hobbes, pt. 1, chap. 5, sec. 3 in *Leviathan*, 23.

whom, and on what basis? If only these matters could be established! Yet they cannot. And even if they could be, what then? *Would the account be settled once the checks have cleared?*

Our problem is more intransigent, more ineffable. America lives with the legacy of slavery—an *aftermath* in which suspicions linger and trust is too often lacking. This has left America in limbo, neither indelibly stained nor without spot or blemish. This difficult intermediary condition must be given its due. The party of the Left tells us that America is indelibly stained, and that citizens must stand back and let government programs do their work. The party of the Right tells us we are without spot or blemish, and that citizens need do nothing at all. The one thing on which both parties agree is that citizens themselves are not accountable in this matter. That is not true. The truth is that the legacy of the wound of slavery must be addressed as all deep wounds must be addressed: with long and patient labor, goodwill, and a prayerful longing to heal what has been broken. Only through the liberal politics of competence can this be done. The identity politics of innocence, which calls out transgression and declares innocence but goes no further, cannot accomplish this. Nor, does it really intend to. Words echo in our dreams, but in the morning, we awaken to a world that is still stiff and unaltered. The identity politics of innocence promulgates those dreams. In the Hebrew Bible, Joseph is sold by his brothers into Egyptian slavery; then, through demonstrated competence, he helps restore his people.[47] Therein lies the way forward. In Robert Woodson's words:

> The Josephs of our own day do not need charity. They need to be considered as 'friends.' The relationship of friends in every arena of society, working to pursue common goals, is a relationship that will allow Americans to heal and prosper.[48]

47. See Gen. 37:2–50:26.

48. Woodson, chap. 5 in *Triumphs of Joseph*, 137. See also Shelby Steele,

Wounds are healed by *doing*, not by *sayings* that give citizens comforting dreams. There are no shortcuts. Let us all be those Josephs—or find them, work with them, and give them all the support we are able to provide.

§103. The third and final pillar on which a renewed America must rest is a modest foreign policy, of the sort that defenders of the "liberal world order" today find so unpalatable. "Liberal," for these defenders, is universal. Anything that is not universal is its opposite—namely, parochial, local, and prejudicial; in short, authoritarian.[49] This simple, facile opposition has set the stage for the great battle of our time, between so-called liberal universalists and all others, without distinction.

Have we not been through variants of this Manichean-like struggle before; and each time we have, has it not amplified our military presence abroad and centralized our political power at home? Our two great military failures of the post–World War II period—the Vietnam War and our ongoing unsettling, ill-defined military engagements in the Middle East—have been justified on the basis of simple oppositions. Ponder Vietnam: Our leading lights were so entranced by the opposition between liberal universalism and communism that the idea that Vietnam was a postcolonial war of national independence was inconceivable. And the Middle East? Our leading lights have been so enamored by the opposition between liberal universalism and Islamic fundamentalism that the idea that the nations of the Middle East are involved in an internal wrestling match with modernity, which we cannot successfully referee, is unthinkable. Liberalism: the abstract universal "idea" against which the forces

"The Right and the Moral High Ground," *Wall Street Journal*, March 31, 2019, https://www.wsj.com/articles/the-right-and-the-moral-high-ground-11554057729?mod=e2two.

49. See Robert Kagan, "The Strongmen Strike Back," *Washington Post*, March 14, 2019, https://www.washingtonpost.com/news/opinions/wp/2019/03/14/feature/the-strongmen-strike-back/?utm_term=.f142d096f611.

of darkness align, and because of which never-ending wars must be authorized—against Vietnam after World War II; against Islamic fundamentalism after 2001; and soon, against authoritarianism in its various guises, from Trump and his deplorables to various figures in Britain and Europe who challenge the liberal world order. *Everyone* who does not believe in so-called liberal universalism is an authoritarian at heart. They differ among themselves only with respect to the political power they have at their disposal to implement their wretched prejudices.

What does so-called liberal universalism really amount to? Often the idea is not worked out in detail, but the general account of it is unmistakable: Liberal universalism is the fruit of the Enlightenment, and is taken to be synonymous with the French Revolution, and the "All men are created equal" clause of the American Declaration of Independence, which itself emerged from the writings of John Locke. This is an intellectually dubious genealogy. The Enlightenment was not one intellectual movement; it was many, each having distinct national characteristics. John Locke, perhaps the first great liberal thinker, wrote a century before the French Revolution, and *never* would have endorsed a revolution on the basis of abstract and universal rights, as the French Revolution was. The French Revolution sought to overthrow everything, even the Gregorian calendar. Locke remained a Christian throughout his life, and sought to defend property and the integrity of the (Christian) family. If Locke must be painted as a universalist, it ought to be as a Christian universalist—which is to say, he believed that God would unify His kingdom at the end of history.[50]

---

50. Later, purportedly secular Enlightenment figures tried to strip away Locke's Christianity and develop a universal theory of history based on the development of reason—notably, those ideas put forward by Hegel. In regard to his project, have we forgotten Nietzsche, who in the 1870s demonstrated, to the embarrassment ever afterward of German idealism, that Hegel's universal history was Christianity, deformed and in disguise (see part 1, sec. 56)? The bitter fruit of Nietzsche's revelation is the postmodern morass in which we now find ourselves.

What about America? Liberal universalists claim that she is a proposition that can be reduced to a single clause in the Declaration of Independence. The American Revolution, however, was unlike the French Revolution, not least because it did not end with the Terror—in which anyone who believed in particular truths rather than universal ones was subject to execution by guillotine. The American Revolution was undertaken with a view to citizen self-government, property rights, national self-determination, and the bourgeois prejudices by which universalists are repulsed. Edmund Burke, a conservative, defended the American Revolution and heaped scorn on the French Revolution.

Is liberalism really committed to abstract universal ideas? Perhaps *neoliberalism* of the sort so many of our global elites defend is, but the French and Anglo traditions of liberal thought are not. Neoliberalism is a sleight of hand that betrays its deeper origin. Alexis de Tocqueville, perhaps the greatest liberal thinker of all, had the French Revolution in mind when he wrote his unsurpassed masterpiece, *Democracy in America*. His father was imprisoned and narrowly escaped the guillotine during the Terror. He went into the dungeons with black hair and came out enfeebled and gray. Innumerable passages in *Democracy in America* speak to the danger of abstract universal ideas. Everything Tocqueville wrote about mediating institutions and about federalism was informed by what could be called the French Revolution problem—namely, that as social bonds get weaker, people have little reason to gather together or to count on one another. Their attention therefore drifts upward to abstract universal ideas (see section 68), and they become incapable of building a world with their neighbors and fellow citizens—those deplorable creatures who actually believe in the particular ideas that are always necessary if we are going to build a durable world together. Contemplating the challenge this would pose to liberty in the democratic age, Tocqueville wrote:

> A nation can always establish great political assemblies, because it always contains a certain number of individuals whose under-

standing will, to some extent, take the place of experience in handling affairs. But the local community is composed of *coarser elements*, often recalcitrant to the lawgiver's activities. The difficulty of establishing a township's independence rather augments than diminishes with the increase of enlightenment of nations. A very civilized society finds it hard to tolerate attempts at freedom in the local community; it is disgusted by its numerous blunders and is apt to despair of success before the experiment is finished.[51]

Real liberalism is not universal. It is *plural*. It acknowledges that the existence of "coarser elements" does not mitigate against the development of liberal competence, but rather is the occasion for its development. Neoliberals who believe in universalism are appalled that this might be so, and express their contempt for anything that falls short of their own supposed universal measure. Authoritarianism *does* fall short of this measure, which is why they justifiably oppose it. But so, too, does Tocquevillian liberalism, which recognizes that plurality, from the local to the international level, is the only healthy and viable alternative to the bludgeoning soft authoritarianism of neoliberals on the left and the more hard-edged authoritarianism on the right, about which we should all be concerned. The profound error, indeed the profound danger, is to declare that all who oppose the abstract universal ideas are authoritarian without distinction.[52] If we wish to understand precisely why global neoliberal elites were deposed in 2016, and why

51. Tocqueville, pt. 1, chap. 5 in *Democracy in America*, vol. 1, 62 (emphasis added).

52. See Yoram Hazony, *The Virtue of Nationalism* (New York: Basic Books, 2018). Unable to make the necessary distinctions, many neoliberals have failed to see that Hazony and the national conservative movement he is leading intend to recover a healthy understanding of nationalism that has been lost. The intellectual project underlying the national conservative movement involves retrieving the covenantal thinking of early modern authors such as the fifteenth-century author John Fortesque and the seventeenth-century author John Selden. The intellectual roots of authoritarianism cannot be found there.

they will continue to be deposed, we should look no further than this reckless and irresponsible claim, which proves beyond doubt that they are clueless about why they are being vigorously opposed and called out as charlatans who hover over the world and sleep well at night. Real citizens live in nations; they have particular understandings of family, politics, religion, and themselves. A truly liberal world order, unlike the *faux* liberal world order that neoliberals have constructed at great cost to everyday citizens but at no cost to themselves, can only be built around the ineluctable plurality in the world. When so-called enlightened universalists call such real citizens out with scorn and derision, eventually those citizens say, "Enough!"

Neoliberal universalism is not merely a conceptual problem; it inspires immodest military incursions abroad in the name of banishing the forces of darkness. A righteous empire can proceed along this course, but a middle-class commercial republic cannot. Presidents Washington and Jefferson were apprehensive about military engagements involving the affairs of Europe[53] because they understood them to be a threat to the republic they helped establish. So, too, did President John Quincy Adams, perhaps the last (and largely unrecognized) Founder:

> [America] goes not abroad, in search of monsters to destroy. She is the well-wisher to the freedom and independence of all. She is the champion and vindicator only of her own. She will commend the general cause by the countenance of her voice, and the benignant sympathy of her example. She well knows that by once enlisting under other banners than her own, were they even the banners of foreign independence, she would involve herself beyond the power of extrication, in all the wars of interest and intrigue, of individual avarice, envy, and ambition, which assume the colors and usurp the standard of freedom. The fundamental maxims of her

53. See Tocqueville, pt. 2, chap. 5 in *Democracy in America*, vol. 1, 227–28.

policy would insensibly change from liberty to force.... She might become the dictatress of the world. She would be no longer the ruler of her own spirit.[54]

Liberal competence cannot develop when foreign threats, real or imagined, require that political and economic power be centralized and managed from above in order to gather together and coordinate the resources that war requires. For a time, the enterprise of centralization can succeed, but in the end it cannot, because the world is not ours to manage. The future is emergent, as I indicated early on in section 69. The prideful ambition of man is to know the future and direct it. The humbler course requires that we do all in our power to avoid endless military engagements abroad that tempt that prideful ambition, unless such engagements are necessary for national security, and declared so by the Constitution. The War Powers Act, passed by Congress in 1973, is not bulwark enough.[55] We do not live in a post-war world. Wars will have to be fought in the future. Let us have the finest, fiercest military available to engage with our enemies, one characterized by courage, and supplemented with strength. But let us deploy it with the humility that has long been absent.

A perennially ambitious military also poses a domestic threat, which we cannot ignore either. Military engagements abroad invariably produce a top-down domestic management enterprise that

54. John Quincy Adams, "Speech to the US House of Representatives on Foreign Policy" (speech, Washington, DC, July 4, 1821), https://millercenter.org/the-presidency/presidential-speeches/july-4-1821-speech-us-house-representatives-foreign-policy.

55. See Jeff Phillips, "Bring Back the War Declaration," *Washington Examiner*, July 27, 2019, http://www.washingtonexaminer.com/opinion/op-eds/bring-back-the-war-declaration: "While the War Powers Resolution was designed to prevent similar end-runs around the legislature, the law all but killed formal declarations of war, replacing them with authorizations of the use of military force. The United States hasn't had a declaration of war since."

stifles the liberty of citizens at home; domestic management "excels at preventing, not at doing."[56] We stifle the emerging future by establishing such an enterprise. Without such a future, liberal citizens will have limited opportunity to rise to the challenge of newly emerging problems and demonstrate their competence. Perhaps, in the end, the question we must pose is this: Do we have the faith—perhaps even the courage—to try out the liberal politics of competence? Our current experiment with the identity politics of innocence has provided us with a way to avoid the difficult labor of working with our fellow citizens by placing as an insuperable obstacle between us—*our identities*. Management society and selfie man, along with various forms of substitutism, provides us with further shortcuts that avoid this difficult labor. Neoliberal universalism—a friend of management society and a form of substitutism—has neither the faith nor the courage to stand back and let the world be plural and emergent, at home or abroad. That is why the achievement of a modest foreign policy will be both cause and consequence of the revitalization of the liberal politics of competence at home.

§104. Looking to the future, I can dimly imagine an America that builds securely on the three pillars of renewal I have proposed here: refortifying our middle-class commercial republic; healing the legacy of the wound of slavery; and establishing and sustaining a modest foreign policy. That we are almost unable to imagine this future does not surprise me. The trails set before us—identity politics, the configuration of management society and selfie man, and substitutism in its multiple guises—are each a manifestation of man's pride, which must be humbled if we are to see clearly. *Identity politics is the pride of believing that we ourselves are clean, that transgression is someone else's problem, and not our own. The bipolar configuration of management society and selfie man is the pride of believing that we may live out our lives as Arcadian shepherds, without the need, really, of anyone who might trouble*

56. Tocqueville, pt. 1, chap. 5 in *Democracy in America*, vol. 1, 91.

us. Addictive substitutism in its multiple guises is the pride of believing that we may bypass the humble condition of sharing a meal together around the table. Pride is our shortcut; by indulging it, we dare to evade the difficult labors that beset our lives, which remind us of our frailty and culpability. All of the pillars of renewal I have proposed will involve difficult but necessary labors if the promise of America is to be fulfilled, and if the citizens of this country are to recover the sobriety and humility we so dearly need to live well, with a modest but justified hope for the future.

American Awakening:
Wuhan Flu Edition

§1. Throughout *American Awakening*, I proposed that identity politics involves the mortal attempt to purge the political community of its uncleanliness, so that its adherents can pronounce themselves pure and without spot or blemish. The Christian claim that precedes identity politics, as I indicated on so many occasions throughout the book, is that *all of us* are stained, and that only the Innocent Lamb of God, the Divine Scapegoat, can take away the stains—the sins—of the world. The correlate of this Christian proclamation, which I emphasized not often enough, is that because of our stain, *all of us* are also condemned to die; and only the innocent Lamb of God, the Divine Scapegoat, can free us from the death that, by virtue of our stain, we cannot through our own effort escape. I will say more about this shortly. With respect to the stain that marks our transgression, identity politics *accepts* the Christian claim that the world is impure and must be cleansed, but *rejects* the Divine Scapegoat through whose self-sacrifice man's transgressions are covered over. Identity politics fixates instead on a mortal scapegoat through whom the pure are separated from the impure, or, more boldly (as I indicated in section 10 of the preface), identity politics seeks to purge the scapegoat and *all* that he has wrought in history, so that the world itself may be cleansed of its impurities.

In the light of the prevalence of this quasi-religious longing of identity politics for purity by mortal means, we should expect that the prejudices that inhere in identity politics about the problem of worldly stain would color judgments about the Wuhan flu pandemic. In fact, they have. The term "quarantine," now heard everywhere, for example, has taken on this identity politics coloring, which has added a layer of meaning to its otherwise innocuous medical definition. For adherents of identity politics, the word quarantine indicates a separate "safe space" of purity and life, marked off from a region that is stained and prone to death—strangely akin to the distinction Christians might make between life *inside* the Garden of Eden before the fall of man and life *outside* of it after the fall, where stain and death prevail. Whatever coronavirus may be *biologically*, in the political world on whose categories we rely to address it, identity politics prejudices about purity and stain are causing us to stumble into the future with distorted vision, at great cost.

§2. The alternatives I set out in *American Awakening* are the identity politics of innocence and the liberal politics of competence. In various places (notably in section 23 of part 1 and section 96 of the conclusion), I suggested that the identity politics of innocence can only be indulged when the never-ending competition and struggle that characterize mortal life seem to have been temporarily suspended, either through delusion or because of social privilege. Competition and struggle, and the *death* they portend, I said, would reappear one day, and with them, the need to return to the liberal politics of competence. The spread of the Wuhan flu *has* brought death near. Should we really be surprised, then, that as panic set in and every government in the world mobilized for the battle against death, we heard few outcries that the people and institutions that were to save us are irredeemably stained because their ranks are not proportionally filled by marginalized identity groups?[1] When death comes near, we see things in their true light. That is why we have focused on the competence of the people and institutions who are keeping death at bay, rather than on their innocence. The darkest moments of the Wuhan flu pandemic have handily confirmed my thesis about the narrow conditions under which identity politics can supersede the liberal politics of competence.

§3. Although the Wuhan flu has now brought death near enough for us to understand the need to attend to the liberal politics of competence, *before* it became a pandemic, a number of European countries refused to suspend flights from China for fear of being called racist. This appears

1. See Robert L. Woodson Sr., "What the Coronavirus Reveals about the Race Grievance Industry," *Hill*, April 6, 2020, https://thehill.com/opinion/ civil-rights/490975-what-the-coronavirus-revals-about-the-race-grievance-industry.

to have been the case in Italy, for example, where the number of deaths from the Wuhan flu has been quite high. At roughly the same time in early 2020, the Trump administration shut down flights to America from China—and immediately was declared racist for doing so. At least in the short run, that decision probably averted a great many American deaths. Identity politics declares that political borders are archaisms belonging to the age of nations, and that they must be repudiated by those who wish to sleep well at night. As human carriers were unwittingly spreading the Wuhan flu around the globe, adherents of identity politics *were* sleeping well at night—until death came near and woke them from their slumber. Borders suddenly mattered a great deal. The urge to sleep was not entirely overcome, however. The long-standing medical convention of naming contagious diseases by their cities or regions of origin, so that the vectors of their transmission can be mapped and the disease better understood, was avowed to be racist. Rather than calling it the Wuhan flu, adherents of identity politics insisted, from the sleepy comfort of their quarantined living rooms, that it be called COVID-19.[2]

§4. As I write this epilogue, our attempt to keep death at bay is fully underway. A civilization cannot long endure if it forgoes the routines by which it regenerates itself. In the coming months, we will have to redirect our attention toward these routines. The question of the moment nevertheless must remain firmly in our mind for future reference: What do we think we are accomplishing by this extraordinary effort to keep death at bay, and what are its likely consequences?

Consider the unprecedented political experiment we have undertaken, and its foreboding anticipation of future tyranny. In the space of a few short weeks, the global-world-without-boundaries heralded by so many since 1989 collapsed in upon itself. The dream of a border-

---

2. See "New Rule: Virus Shaming | Real Time with Bill Maher (HBO)," YouTube video, 5:28, posted by Real Time with Bill Maher, April 10, 2020, https://www.youtube.com/watch?v=dEfDwc2G2_8&feature=youtu.be.

less world was supplanted by the nightmare of imminent death that prompted many to mark their front door as the outer limit of their habitation. Daily life was reduced to *limiting contact* to those immediately around us at home; *seeing*, but not really connecting with, others in Zoom-like virtual meetings or passing them, at a distance, in stores that provide daily bread; *listening* to government authorities who informed us of what we must do next; and *watching* Netflix at home for entertainment, to dispel boredom and anxiety. Are these activities not the ones that Tocqueville more or less predicted would characterize the kinder and gentler despotism that awaits us at the end of history?[3] Is not "social distancing" the prerequisite for the emergence of the bipolar arrangement of management society and selfie man that I chronicled in sections 65–72 of part 2? When death comes near, just what sort of political arrangements are we willing not simply to endure but to *advocate*? If Wuhan flu, or some future iteration of it, becomes a permanent feature of life, would we be willing to live this way *permanently*? If we believe we can succeed in keeping death at bay

---

3. See Tocqueville, pt. 4, chap. 6 in *Democracy in America*, vol. 2, 692: "I am trying to imagine under what novel features despotism may soon appear in the world. In the first place, I see a multitude of men, alike and equal, constantly circling around the pursuit of petty and banal pleasures with which they glut their souls. Each of them, withdrawn into himself, is almost unaware of the fate of the rest. Mankind, for him, consists in his children and his personal friends. As for the rest of his fellow citizens, they are near enough, but he does not notice them. He touches them but feels nothing. He exists in and for himself, and though he may still have a family, one can say that he no longer has a fatherland. Over this kind of man stands an immense, protective power, which is alone responsible for securing their enjoyment and watching over their fate. That power is absolute, thoughtful in detail, orderly, provident, and gentle. It would resemble paternal authority if, father-like, it tried to prepare its charge for a man's life, but on the contrary, it only tries to keep them in perpetual childhood. It likes to see citizens enjoy themselves, provided that they think of nothing but enjoyment. It gladly works for their happiness but wants to be the sole agent and judge of it. It provides for their security, foresees and supplies their necessities, facilitates their pleasures [and] manages their principal concerns. Why should it not entirely relieve them for the trouble of thinking and all the cares of life?"

through state-enforced social distancing, then we will have chosen the path marked out for us in *Brave New World*, Huxley's dystopian novel in which in order for citizens to be protected from suffering and death, they must renounce their political liberties altogether and bow without opposition to a world-controlling elite. Social distancing purports to keep one kind of virus at bay; but let us not forget that social distancing is, as well, a *political* virus that destroys liberal competence by removing altogether the occasions for citizens to build a world together, face to face. There is more than one way to die. Physical death is one of them. A dystopian future is another. For the moment, the death *of* man is our singular concern; what of the death *in* man that these political arrangements produce?

The disturbing political arrangements that now shape our lives should not be our only concern. What of the psychological and social consequences of our attempt to keep death at bay through social distancing? One class of citizens has been able to remain safely ensconced behind the firewall that separates the digital world into which the Wuhan flu *cannot* penetrate from the analog world into which it *can*. This class of citizens (about which I wrote in section 23 of part 1 and section 85 of part 2) meets their friends through social media, and meets for work over Zoom-type video-conferencing software. For how long will such arrangements be viable? After working through the technical glitches of the software, many members of this class now feel strangely comfortable, and ponder with some satisfaction a future in which they will gather with others only in this way. A digital future of this sort cannot sustain us, however. Social media "friends" are supplements to actual friendship, not substitutes for it. They are the supplements to the meal (see part 2, section 81), but they cannot be a substitute for it. While we still have the meal of pre-pandemic social communion firmly with us in our minds and hearts, social media and Zoom-type meetings can work as robust supplements, on which we can rely during a crisis that someday will pass. But proof that in the long run these cannot be a substitute for the meal of social communion is already appearing:

depression and suicide are on the rise, and citizens are beginning to act out in willful disregard of governmental edicts. We grow strong with supplements, but die when we turn them into substitutes. Life lived digitally—the experiment now underway by the class of people who live behind the firewall that the Wuhan flu cannot penetrate—cannot substitute for life lived on the ground in the analog human world that we must build together in real time. The emerging proof is that the experience of this class of people is now strangely bifurcated: as a *supplement*, their digital world amplifies what they were able to accomplish in the analog world that currently brings death near; as a *substitute*, their digital world makes them ill. Amid this strange paradox, we can only hope that once they have overdosed on the digital world, they will recognize the importance of the meal of real-time human association. There is no assurance of this happy outcome, however. Digital substitutism, as I call it in the main text of *American Awakening* (see part 2, section 85), is an addiction; as such, it is a seductive death sentence we neither want to admit has befallen us nor renounce.

What of the economic consequences of our attempt to keep death at bay? The battle lines have been drawn in the way I specified in part 1, section 33 of this book: on the one hand, there are those who pronounce that human life is priceless. On the other, liberals remind us that this pronouncement misunderstands the very order of things: Commerce—the "world of payment," as I called it—cannot be annulled. The *merciful* understanding that human life is priceless can be a supplement to the world of payment but not a substitute for it. That is why commerce cannot be shut down in the name of mercy. Living in the world of payment means that human life *does* have a price, which we calculate whether we have universal health care or free-market health care. If the resources of a nation are deliberately directed toward saving people from dying from the Wuhan flu, those resources will not find their way to curing cancer or any other number of mortal afflictions. If state-enforced lockdown orders save people from death by Wuhan flu, those same lockdown orders will contribute to death by other causes. We cannot judge a course of action against the imaginary standard of a deathless world, in which *if* we mobilize the resources of the nation, *then* we can count the number of people we save through our efforts. Not by accident is the world of payment also the world of justice, the scales of which always set one thing against another, in an effort to find the difficult and ever-shifting balance between them. Mercy supplements justice, but cannot supersede it. We live in a world of never-ending trade-offs and balancing acts. Supplementing this balancing act is *mercy*, which is, in its highest form, *religious*. By our invocation of the term "mercy," we mean to illuminate those mysterious instances in which the world of payment is eerily suspended by the infinite outpouring of God's grace. These outpourings overwhelm the paltry but necessary calculations and balancing acts that constitute human justice. In this sense, those who pronounce that human life is priceless are surely right to alert us that the world of payment is not enough. *God's* mercy is seldom on people's minds these days, however. All too many of us have decided to be *heralds of infinite mercy ourselves*. If the world of payment grinds to a halt as a consequence, so be it.

Just who is it that can indulge in such a fancy? I have already introduced them. They are the class of people who have been able to remain safely ensconced behind the firewall that separates the digital world into which the Wuhan flu cannot penetrate from that analog world into which it can. They are the class of people who insist that only a strict quarantine implemented around the globe can keep death at bay. Bolting their front doors is a sign of universal human benevolence, they claim, because they are protecting others from the harm they might otherwise bring should they go to work or visit their friends, neighbors, children, parents, or others in need.

There is something to this claim, but let us acknowledge its real implications. If we are at war, we surely are not showing that we care for those we love by bringing enemy combatants with us on our visits. In these strangely warlike times, however, visitors bringing death *there will be*. For those who profess the universal benevolence of a worldwide quarantine, these death-bringing visitors are the analog workers who grow our food, truck it to market, stock the shelves of our grocery stores, and deliver the food to our front door in the vast analog economy of things that undergirds the digital economy. If those who perform these services were to show the same universal benevolence *and themselves not show up for work*, what would be the consequences for those who are digitally privileged? They would soon perish, not from the Wuhan flu, but from starvation. So-called universal benevolence is always partial. It gives those who practice it license to sleep well at night, and it tramples on "the least among us"—currently those in the analog world whose work does not allow them the privileged distinction between a safe space of purity and life, on the one hand, and a region that is stained and prone to death, on the other. The analog world of work will *never* be free from death.[4] "Distrust those cosmopolitans who go to great length in their books to discover duties they do not deign to fulfill. The philosopher loves the Tartars so as to be spared loving his neighbors."[5] So wrote Rousseau in 1759. Our version of Rousseau's cosmopolitans are the digitally privileged, who quarantine in the name of universal benevolence toward humanity as a whole, so as to be spared facing the inconvenient fact that exposed analog workers *in plain view* are servicing the safe space in which they securely dwell.

§5. There is more to say about the privileged delusion that death can be kept at bay. For those who are safely quarantined, the somber task ahead is uncontestable: remain in the lockdown that *insulates* them from death until a vaccine can be developed that *inoculates* them from

---

4. See Gen. 3:19: "In the sweat of thy face shalt thou eat bread, till thou return unto the ground; for out of it wast thou taken: for dust thou art, and unto dust shalt thou return."

5. Rousseau, bk. 1, *Emile*, 47.

death. In that way, they can move seamlessly from the safe space their quarantine provides to the safe space a vaccine insures. Under what conditions might we dare to conceive that a proposal like this would work? Does not the whole of human history bear witness to the fact that there is no safe space that keeps death from coming near?[6]

The answer is digital substitutism in conjunction with the configuration of management society and selfie man. These mutually reinforcing delusions make it possible to believe that *for the very first time in human history*, we actually can keep death at bay. Digital substitutism purports to reduce the entire analog world of qualities and indeterminate relations to informational bits—hence the desire to test and continuously monitor everyone on the planet for the Wuhan flu in order to unambiguously designate them as either "positive" or "negative." The configuration of management society and selfie man specifies the necessary division of labor for this project to succeed. Armed with the informational bits that global testing and monitoring will provide, the global managers will be able to develop and coordinate *a plan* to vaccinate the whole world. Until they develop a vaccine, citizens should stay indoors, get their work done with the computer operating systems provided by Microsoft, Apple, and Google; browse

6. The safety that we *have* found from viruses has been largely a consequence of herd immunity, which is to say it has been thanks to nature rather than to technology. The 1953 movie of the H. G. Wells book of the same name, *The War of the Worlds*, is worth revisiting in light of the Wuhan flu pandemic. In the movie, Martians invade and threaten to destroy human life on earth. The world's most powerful technology is put to use to try to stop them. In the end, it is not man's technology that saves the human race but rather invisible nature that is responsible, neutralizing the invading force with microbes. The debate over how to fight the Wuhan flu pandemic sets up the same opposition between the believers in technology, who say only vaccines can save us, and the believers in nature, who say only herd immunity can save us. See Martin Kulldorff, "Delaying Herd Immunity Is Costing Lives: The Current Lockdown Is Protecting the Healthy instead of the Vulnerable," *spiked*, April 29, 2020, https://www.spiked-online.com/2020/04/29/delaying-herd-immunity-is-costing-lives/.

the Internet with Microsoft Edge and Google Chrome; order their quarantine supplies online from Amazon; meet their friends on Facebook; have work meetings using Zoom or its equivalent; learn everything they need to know through Google; and entertain themselves with Netflix.[7] Citizens are not, after all, competent enough to exercise prudential judgment about how to care for themselves, their families, or their neighbors. They must leave that to the global managers. God once pronounced that should Adam and Eve ever "eat from the tree of knowledge of good and evil, they will surely die."[8] Global managers—our new idols—offer a novel variant of that eternal decree: everyday citizens will surely die if they dare attempt to figure things out by themselves or together with those around them.

The current epicenter of this frame of mind is the Bill & Melinda Gates Foundation, which never met a crisis that more digital technology and greater global coordination could not solve. Vaccines have been an incontestable blessing to humanity. The debate between those who are "for" them and those who are "against" them misses the mark. The issue is not whether we should be for them, but rather the *way* in which we should be for them. Bill Gates asserts that the world must be inoculated against death by Wuhan flu *before* our lives can be rebooted.[9] This claim is plausible only within the seductive framework that digital substitutism provides. In the analog human world, we can *never* eradicate impurity. Death is ever present. Vaccines are ameliorative; they mitigate death by particular causes but do not remove its general curse. They allow life to carry on as normal, which is to say, *with the general curse of death ever near*. To assert that we must await a vaccine

7. See Joel Kotkin, "The Pandemic Road to Serfdom," *American Mind*, May 1, 2020, https://americanmind.org/essays/the-pandemic-road-to-serfdom/.

8. Gen. 2:17.

9. See Bill Gates, "Here Are the Innovations We Need to Reopen the Economy," *Washington Post*, April 23, 2020, https://www.washingtonpost.com/opinions/2020/04/23/bill-gates-here-are-innovations-we-need-reopen-economy/.

to cure us of the Wuhan flu as a *precondition* of life carrying on as normal is to misunderstand the insoluble problem man is up against. A quarantine that insulates us from death while global managers develop a vaccine that inoculates us from death: this is not medical science; this is a quasi-religious dream of an Edenic paradise we can create to quarantine ourselves from the post-Edenic world of stain and death. This sort of paradise, or any other sort that *cures* the world of its other injustices, rather than ameliorating them, can never exist on earth.

§6. How are we to respond to the fact that we are compelled to live in a post-Edenic world? Consider first how we have responded to the Wuhan flu. Based on now largely discredited models that predicted a roughly 2.5 percent death rate, the world was locked down; social, political, and economic life ground to a halt; and unprecedented surveillance was employed to trace those who were, or might have been, carriers of death. Now imagine the following: We discover a virus that is 100 percent fatal. To make matters worse, unlike the Wuhan flu, which takes about two weeks to incubate, this flu-producing virus generally takes about sixty-nine years to incubate before taking its victims. Moreover, this virus does not come from one place, which means we cannot locate its geographical origin or study its transmission vectors, as we can with the Wuhan flu. Rather, everyone seems to be born with it. Although person-to-person contact does not transmit it, the fear of death that it produces is always on the verge of reverberating through society in a "war of all against all" for self-preservation. Researchers ironically give it the name "Adam 69 flu," because like original sin bequeathed by Adam to his progeny, everyone inherits it, regardless of their genetic makeup, the group to which they belong, or where they live on planet earth. Would we go to *even-greater lengths* to cure ourselves from the Adam 69 flu than we have for the Wuhan flu? Or—heaven help us—would we understand this flu to be a *constant and tragic reminder* that we live in a post-Edenic world in which we should take prudent measures to protect those whose age and/or preexisting conditions make them especially vulnerable, all the while continuing to build a liberal world of competence together?

The thoughtful reader will have anticipated where I am heading: If every human being who will ever live is born with the Adam 69 flu, civilization must accommodate this curse or itself perish. Accommodation is not to be confused with recklessness. We must cherish life as a gift. Life for its own sake, however, is not the highest good. Life has merit and worth only through its rich relations and through its elegant composition, to which we contribute, sometimes in subtle and beautiful ways, notwithstanding the fact that we will have all inherited the Adam 69 flu. We come into the world and then we perish; in addition to the curse of death that we will inherit and pass on to our children, we will receive and pass on a civilizational inheritance of which we are stewards. If we are not earnest and joyous caretakers of that inheritance, there will be neither children nor civilization. Yet what can our relationship to our children and our civilizational inheritance be if, in this post-Edenic world, we are so frightened by death that we are prepared to do anything—yes, *anything*—to keep it at bay? Even renounce the comprehensive labor of the hundreds of generations who came before us, who toiled with the full knowledge that the curse of death had befallen them? Are we really prepared to abandon *all* of this in exchange for the digital substitutism that Microsoft, Apple, Amazon, Facebook, Zoom, Google, and Netflix promise? To be sure, living in a post-Edenic world means that we will witness and endure sometimes senseless suffering and death that will cause us to doubt there is a grander providential plan in which we play a small but important part. Such doubt can easily devolve into nihilism, which welcomes death and prompts us to act imprudently. The more hopeful course requires that we frame all the competence-building challenges we will face in our post-Edenic world around the understanding that we *already have* contracted Adam 69 flu and will never recover from it.

I suspect, but cannot prove, that this understanding will help us to think more clearly about *the death from which no quarantine can pro-*

tect us, and about how we are to live in the interim before we die. A decent civilization protects those who are subject to immediate danger. What is going on around us right now vastly exceeds the prudent wish to protect. It involves nothing less than an effort to enkindle the ember of the fear of death and turn it into a raging inferno that consumes everything, in a futile quest to create a world that is without spot or blemish, a world freed from the curse of death.

Acknowledgments

This book, written in the convulsive aftermath of the 2016 election, began as a modest attempt to draw together into one synoptic essay my thinking about identity politics and several kindred maladies from which we suffer in America today. This attempt came on the heels of fragmentary efforts to capture the current moment in essays of mine published in *American Affairs*, the *American Interest*, *Providence Journal*, POLITICO, *City Journal*, *First Things*, *National Affairs*, and the *American Mind*. To the editors of those publications, I wish to express my thanks.

I had not anticipated that my synoptic essay would grow into a book, nor that the bulk of it would be written in half a year. To that, I owe my providential good fortune to being surrounded by a group of fellow travelers and discontents, all of whom have seen that the well-formed post-1989 world, of both the left and the right, is collapsing. Some I have known for decades; some have recently appeared. Some are academics; some are journalists. Some are in business; some are public intellectuals. They include John Agresto, Richard Avramenko, David Azerrad, Sietske Bergsma, Peter Berkowitz, Patrick Deneen, Eldon Eisenach, David Goldman, Joseph Hartman, Yoram Hazony, Rebecca Heinrichs, Brad Hill, Joel Kotkin, Yuval Levin, Robert Lieber, Laure Mandeville, Daniel McCarthy, Arthur Milikh, Jeffrey Mitchell, Mark Mitchell, Pete Peterson, James Poulos, Maya Primorac, Rusty Reno, Eugene Rivers, Yossi Shain, Jon Silver, Rich Tafel, George Weigel, and Robert Woodson. None of us quite agrees about how we got here and where we are going. Some, in fact, strongly disagree with one another. In our conversations, I have nevertheless found a model of both citizenship and friendship. For that, I am thankful.

Finally, I wish to thank Roger Kimball, editor of Encounter Books, for his rare courage to take on this provocative project. Almost without exception, every major university press to which I submitted this manuscript responded in the same way: "The book does not fit our list." Whether this judgment speaks to lack of wisdom on their part or on mine, I leave to the reader to decide.

Index

The letter *f* following a page locator denotes a figure.

Abinadab, 131

Adam (biblical), xliii, 8, 55, 58–59, 105, 122–123, 125, 191, 237

Adam 69 flu, 238–240

Adams, John Quincy, 223–224

addiction obstacle to the retrieval of liberal politics, xlviii–xlix

addictive substitutism, xxxiv–xxxv, 147, 151, 179–180, 207, 226

Alt-Right, 104–109, 120–121

Amazon, 160–162

America: analog vs. digital, 37–39, 165–170, 232–234, 237; awakenings in, 41; back vs. front row, 37–38; battle for the soul of, 46; division in, demographics illustrating, 36–37, 37*f*

American Revolution, 221

analog vs. digital America, 37–39, 165–170, 232–234, 237

anthropogenic climate change, 58–59

antinatalism, 112

anxiety, middle-class, 30–31

anywheres and somewheres, 36–37

Aquinas, Thomas, 46

aristocratic age, 30–31, 141

aristocratic cruelty, 109, 112

aristocratic world, 109–110

Aristotle, 61

Augustine, St., l, 35, 137–138

authoritarianism, 219–220, 222

The Authoritarian Personality, 205

awakenings, American, 41

back vs. front row America, 37–38

Biden (Joe) administration, xiii

Biden, Joe, xiii, 66

Bill and Melinda Gates Foundation, 237

bipolarity: of management society and selfie-man, xlvii–xlviii, 230; medical, xlvi–xlvii; obstacle to the retrieval of liberal politics, xlvi–xlviii, 134–147

black America, wound of, xiv–xv

black Americans: betrayal of, 98–104; conservative, as betrayers and adversaries, 82; Democratic Party and, xiv–xvi; group unity among, 78–82, 131; heterosexual men, 71;

"black Americans," cont.
  identity politics, moral authority
  to end, xiv–xvi; innocent victim
  status, 102–103; policies of racial
  proportionality, effects on, 103–
  104; stain upon, 79–81
Black Lives Matter, 71
Black Studies Programs, xv
borders, xl, 17–18, 175–176, 229–231
Brave New World (Huxley), xlviii, 232
broken world, redemption of a,
  58–61, 198–200
Burke, Edmund, xlv, 46, 106, 221
Buttigieg, Pete, 67

Caesar Augustus, xxxiii
Cain, Herman, 82
Calvin, John, 46, 54
capitalism, stain of, 105
cars, driverless, 164–165
Carson, Ben, 82
Catholic Church, 54–58
Catholics, group unity among, 74–75
Central Bank, 138–139
charity, mercy and, 50–51
"The Charlottesville Statement"
  (Spencer), 107–108
China, 167–169, 199, 213
Christ, xxxiii, xxxix, 58, 72, 84, 125,
  196, 217
Christianity, xxxvii–xxxix, 41–44, 120
Christian radical equality, xxxvii–
  xxxviii
Christian universalism, 220
cisgender, 90

citizen competence, 175–176
citizen groups: acrimony
  between, 40–41; conversations,
  requirements for, 28; diversity
  in, desire for, 104; extending the
  wound of slavery to, 71; isolation
  of, 28; need to work together,
  40–41
citizen-idiots, 146
citizens: demanding and deserving,
  49; in the democratic age, 142–144;
  greater than kings, xlvii, 201, 214;
  isolation of, 27–28, 39, 92–95,
  146–147, 159; powerlessness of,
  144; state, dependence on the, 93;
  substitutisms, living on, 214–215;
  working together, results of, 39–41.
  See also liberal citizen
citizenship, self-interested, 16–21
City of God (Augustine), 35
Civilization and Its Discontents
  (Freud), 5
civilizations, renewal of, 112–113
class privilege, 75–76
climate change, 58–59, 105, 122,
  201–203
Clinton, Bill, 68
Clinton, Hillary, xxxv, 9, 64, 64–65
colonialism, wound of, 43–44, 59
commerce, 14–17, 233
Communist Manifesto (Marx), 66
community, l–li, 26–27
competence, liberal politics of. *See*
  liberal politics of competence
competition, 19–20, 198–200, 229

congressional representation,
 patronage-broker model of, 96–97
conservatism, xliv–xlv, 106–109
conservative movement, xvi–xx
Constant, Benjamin, 15
COVID-19, xxvi, 230
cradle-to-grave security, 26–27,
 195–196

Darwin, Charles, 189
David (biblical), 131
dead, prayers for the, xxxii
death: freedom from, 228;
 inevitability of, 89–90, 238–240;
 Wuhan flu pandemic and, 228–238
debt, xvi–xvii; forgiveness in
 discharging, 58, 195–198; of
 transgressors, 55, 59, 119, 197;
 unpayable and permanent, xix, 7,
 47, 59
democracy, 171
Democracy in America (Tocqueville),
 xxxi, 39–40, 125, 145, 171, 173,
 210–211, 221
democratic age, 142–143
democratic man, 141–144
Democratic Party: 1960s, xiii–xv;
 2020 election and the, xiii, 66–68;
 black Americans and the, xiv–xvi;
 group scapegoating in the, 130;
 healing the wound of slavery,
 215–219; identity politics and the,
 xiii–xiv, 13, 62, 211; innocence, focus
 on, 97, 103–104; manufacturing
 sector, abandonment of, 63–64;

mercy-justice relationship, 68;
 middle class, commitment to, 63,
 211–212; patronage-broker model
 of representation, 97; the poor,
 assistance provided to the, 211–212;
 root supposition of the, xxxix–xl;
 scapegoat identity politics of,
 xxxix–xl; scapegoat in the, 71–72;
 stain of whites, belief in, 65, 68;
 white, heterosexual men, place for,
 65–66, 97; white brokers of the
 innocent, 64–69; white candidates,
 requirements for, 65–68; white
 women, place for, 66–67; wound of
 slavery exploited by, 211
Democrats, 65–66, 68
despotism, 230
Dewey, John, 62
digital substitutism, xxii–xxiv, 165–
 170, 232–233, 236, 239
digi-verse, xxii–xxiii
Divine innocent, 58
Divine Scapegoat of Christianity,
 xxi, xxvi, xxxix, xl–xliii, 124–126,
 228
drug substitutism, xxiv–xxv
Dubois, W. E. B., 79, 81–82, 99

economy, two-fold (visible and
 invisible), xxx–xxxiv, 9
education: college students,
 fears of, 75–76; domestication
 through, 198–199; higher, role of,
 xxxvi–xxxvii; online vs. real-time,
 162–164

Elect, the, xxvii

embodiment, strangeness of our, 89–90

Emerson, Ralph Waldo, 169

Enlightenment, 43–44, 112, 220

environmentalism, 173–174, 189

environmental justice, 192–193

Environmental Protection Agency (EPA), 173

equality, achieving, 124–126

Erikson, Erik, 5

"Ethnicity: Three Black Histories" (Sowell), 80

eugenics, spiritual, xxxviii

European Union, 208–209

Eve (biblical), 105, 191, 237

experts, 22

Facebook, 158–160

family, xiv–xv, 48–52, 63, 76–78, 204–205

fast food substitutism, 154–155

fatalism, 139–140

Federal Reserve, 182

feminists, war against, 89

fiat currency substitutism, 180–183

"First Discourse" (Rousseau), 149

First Great Awakening, 41

foreign policy, 219–225

forgetting, path of, xxi, 118–119

forgiveness: asking for, 195–196; debt discharged through, 58, 195–197; in identity politics, xxxvii, 44; political power and, 58; sustaining the liberal politics of competence,

197; for transgressions, 41–42, 58

Frankfurt School, 205

freedom, radical, 135–140

free market, xviii–xix

free-market, 52, 56–57, 211–213

French Revolution, xvii–xviii, xliv–xlv, 106, 108, 220–221

Freud, Sigmund, 5

friendship: face-to-face, xlviii, 158–160, 210, 232; mediating institutions and, xxv; social media, xxiii, xxv. *See also* relationships

future, liberal citizen's knowledge of the, 22–24

genetic testing, xxxv–xxxvi

gift, mercy of the, 48–49, 50–51

globalism, 135–136, 139–140, 144, 175

global substitutism, 183–185

God and man, radical asymmetry between, 126–128

gold money, 176–183

Google Maps, 164–165

Gospel of Luke, xxxiii

Gospel of Matthew, xxxiii

government, 16, 96–97. *See also* state, the

governmental substitutism, 170–175, 212

Green New Deal, 48

group affiliation, requirement for, 73

group identity, 9

groups, citizen: acrimony between, 40–41; conversations, requirements for, 28; diversity

in, desire for, 104; extending the
wound of slavery to, 71; isolation of,
28; need to work together, 40–41
groups, defining the self outside of,
xxxv–xxxvi
group scapegoating, xl–xlii, 121–132
guilt and innocence, xxxviii–xxxix

happiness, xxxi–xxxii, 19–20, 184
Harris, Kamala, 68
Hart, Kevin, 71
Hayek, Friedrich, xviii, 46
Hazony, Yoram, xviii
Hegel, G. W. F., 115–118
heteronormativity, xiv–xv
higher education, xxxvi–xxxvii,
75–76, 198–199
Hispanics, group unity among,
82–84
Hobbes, Thomas, 19, 138, 176
human extinction, 112, 121–123
human relations, shortcut to
cleanliness in, 191–194
Hume, David, 5
Huxley, Aldous, xlviii, 232

identity: categories of, 40; meaning
of, 5–8; providing a shortcut to
security, 194–198; relationship
within, 7–9; search for, xxxv–
xxxvi; term usage, 5
Identity and the Life Cycle (Erikson), 5
identity politics, xix; basis of, xiv–xv,
13, 228; citizens role within, 63; of
competence and innocence, 33–41;

defined, xvi, 225; Democratic
Party and, xiii–xiv; emergence
of, causes underlying, 12; goal of,
124, 228; impetus behind, xl–xli;
introduction to, xxxii, xxxiv–xxxix;
longing for justice answered by, 41–
45; mercy in, 47; moral authority
to end, xiv–xvi; overturning, xx;
penetration into daily life, xvii;
public nature of, xxx; religious
character of, 42–45; theories of
innocent victimhood in, 8–9;
the transgressor and scapegoat
in, xiii, xix, xli–xlii; upper class
dependence on, 201–203
identity politics, shortcuts promised
by: to clean and unambiguous
justice, 191–194; difficult labor
of, l–li; to innocence, 205;
management society and selfie-
man, 201–207; requirements for,
200–201; to the second innocence,
189–191; to a security that cannot
be undermined, 194–198; when
supplements becoming substitutes,
207–210; to a world without
difficult labors, 198–200
identity politics of innocence: in an
divided America, 38–39; liberal
politics of competence vs., xliv,
13, 21; politics transformed, xxxix;
requirements of, 229
identity politics warriors, 46–47
idiots, 146
immigration policy, 17–18

inclusion, 63, 88. *See also* isolation

income tax, 96

India, 199

individualism, 21, 126–127

Inglehart, Ronald, 204

inheritance: Alt-Right defense of, 106; American understanding of, 2–5; attack by the Left on, xliv; defense of, xliv–xlv, 106; Left and Right and, 106; in liberal politics, historically, xlv; nation and, 2–5, 17–18; original sin tainting, 59; of stain and purity, xxxviii; stain of our, 2–13, 53–55; stewarding, 239; Western, indictment of, 53–54, 59

innocence: as basis for political legitimacy, 10–11; of black Americans, 81–82; contrived, 208, 209–210; criteria of, 33; identity politics of, 123–124, 131–132; precondition of, 84; presumption of, xxxviii–xxxix; restoring, 122; shortcuts to the second, 189–191

innocence and transgression, relationship of, xix

innocence signaling, xlii

innocents, the: Democratic Party's search for, 97; the future and, 10–11; hope for the, 118–119; invisibility of, 47; justice, waiting for, 35–36; mortals vs. Christ, 58; as owners of the future, 11; place in identity politics, 71–72; recovering the silenced traditions of, 59–60; redemption of, 35–36; repayment

of debt to, 59; representation by white transgressor-brokers, 64–66, 68–69, 96; scapegoated, redeeming the, 71–72; scapegoating by, l, 53–54, 70–71, 104, 200–201; shortcut to purity, l, 200–201; successive replacement of, 70, 201; suffering of the, 109–111, 116–118; voice of, 9, 30–33, 64–68, 96, 104, 108

innocent-transgressors, innocence rescinded, 113–114

innocent victims, 7–9, 11, 13, 32

institutions, mediating, xxiii–xxv, 205–207

integralism, xx–xxii

invisible economy, xxx–xxxii, 9

invisible spiritual economy, xxxii–xxxv

Isiah (biblical), 46

Islamic fundamentalism, 219–220

isolation, 19–20, 27–28, 39, 92–95, 146–147, 159

Jefferson, Thomas, 223

Jews, 75, 129

Johnson, Lyndon B., 80, 172

Joseph (biblical), xxxiii, 218

Judas (biblical), xxxiii

justice: achieving, 184; environmental, 192–193; longing for, 45; mercy and, 48–52, 68, 176, 234; patriarchal, 48; scapegoating requirement for, 121; shortcuts to a clean and unambiguous, 191–194

justice of payment, xxxii–xxxiii

Kant, Immanuel, 19, 115–118
Kennedy, John F., 56, 117
Keynes, John Maynard, 116, 138–139
King, Alveda, 82
King, B. B., 166
King, Martin Luther Jr., xiv–xv, xliv, 129–131, 134
Kottke, Leo, 166
Ku Klux Klan, 107

language, power of, xl
Last Man, the, 110–112
Leviathan (Hobbes), 176
LGBTQ, 70–71, 84–91
liberal citizen: anxiety of the, 30–31; assurance, longing for, 24; building a world together, xlv, 30, 33–35, 123, 134–135, 185, 221–222; the competent, 14–21, 102–103; future, knowledge of the, 22–24; hearing the voice of the, 30–41; others, knowing, 26–29; self-knowledge, 24–26
liberal citizenship, difficult labor of, l–li
liberal competence, obstacles to return of, xlvi–xlix
liberalism, xx–xxi, 21, 219–222
liberal politics of competence: in a divided America, 38–39; identity politics of innocence vs., xliv, 13, 21; imagining a world of, 134–135; need for a return to, 229; in real time, 146; requirements for a, xx–xxi; requirements of, 13

liberal politics of competence, obstacles to a return to: addiction, xlviii–xlix, 147–186; bipolarity, xlvi–xlvii, 134–147; identity politics of innocence, 134; management society and selfie-man, xlvii–xlviii, 144–147
liberal thought, body of, xlv, 13–18
liberal universalism, 219–221
libertarianism, xviii
life: price of, 233–234; regeneration of, 111–112
Lincoln, Abraham, 46
lion, the: the camel transformed, 109, 112–113, 116; the lamb and, 47; preparing the way for a renewed world, 113–118; transformed to the child, 112
Locke, John, 19, 122, 126, 220
loneliness, xxv, xxxv–xxxvi, 158–160, 209
longing: erotic, 84–87, 157; for justice, 45; of the liberal citizen for assurance, 24
lower class, 63, 102–103
Lowry, Glenn, 82
Luther, Martin, 54, 55, 190

Malcolm X., 81
man: lived paradox of, 134–147; melancholy of, 142–144; stewarding nature, 173–174
man, the creature who looks for shortcuts: to clean and unambiguous justice, 191–194;

"man, the creature who looks for shortcuts," cont.
demands of, l; historical identification of, xlix–l; management society and selfie-man, li; offered by management society and selfie-man, 201–207; problem of, xlix–l; to the second innocence, 189–191; to a security that cannot be undermined, 194–198; supplements becoming substitutes, li; when supplements becoming substitutes, 207–210; to a world without difficult labors, 198–200

man, white heterosexual: brokenness of, 58–59; cathartic rage, escaping, xlii; condemnation of, 42; debt to the innocents, 59–60; Democratic Party and the, 64, 66, 97; guilt, irredeemable, xlii–xliii, xliii; guilt, presumption of, xxxix; innocence, proving, xlii–xliii; invisibility of, xxxiv; Me Too movement, 11, 105; purging, 69–72; redemption of, 105; scapegoating the, xxxix–xliv, l, 42, 200–201; stain upon, 58–59, 105; taking away the sins of the world, xliv; transgressive status, xli–xlii, xliii, 69–70; unearned suffering of, 11; world built by, dismantling the, 58–59. *See also* transgressor, the

management society, liberal citizens in a, 140–144

management society and selfie-man: antidote to, xlviii; bipolarity of, xlvii–xlviii, 225–226, 230; citizen-idiots in, 146; obstacle to the retrieval of liberal politics, 144–147; shortcuts offered by, l–li, 201–207; upper class and, 204; Wuhan flu pandemic and, 236

manic depression, xlvi–xlvii, 137
manufacturing sector, 63–64
maps, paper vs. Google, 164–165
market commerce, 50–51
market efficiency, 212–213
market value, 213–214
marriage, 48–52, 85–87, 155–158
Marx, Karl, 66, 115–118, 212
Marxism, xvii–xviii, 52–53
Mary, xxxiii
masculinity, toxic, xxiv
material economy, xxx–xxxiii
men: black American heterosexual, 71; gay, 88; invisible, 88; Me Too movement, 11, 105; white, unpayable debt owed, xix
mercy, justice and, 47–52, 68, 176, 234
metaverse, xxii–xxv
Me Too movement, men's, 11, 105
microaggressions, 35
Midas, 105
middle class, 30–31, 63–64, 211–215
middle-class anxiety, 30–31
military engagements, 35, 219–220, 224–225
minority, term usage, 74

money: the measure of all things, 212–213; paper vs. gold, 176–183
Montesquieu, Charles de, 15
multiculturalism, 59
Murray, John Courtney, 56
musical competence, 166

national origin, category of, 73–74
nations: American understanding of, 2–4; inheritance within, 2–5, 18; wounds of, 43–44
nature, 173–174, 189, 208
neoliberalism, 221–223
neoliberal universalism, 223
New Elect, xxii
Niebuhr, Reinhold, 34, 185
Nietzsche, 43, 108–109, 112, 114, 118–120, 122, 126
Nietzsche/Nietzscheanism, xxi–xxii
1984 (Orwell), 94–97
"Ninety Five Thesis" (Luther), 55
Nixon, Richard, 156
Northam, Ralph, 113
Novak, Michael, 57

Obama, Barack, 9, 42, 64–65, 67, 79, 172, 173
The Old Regime and the French Revolution (Tocqueville), xvii
oligarchs/oligarchy, 177–178
one drop concept, 79–81
online education substitutism, 162–164
online shopping substitutism, 160–162

opioid addiction, xxxiv–xxxv, 147, 151, 179–180, 207
original sin doctrine, xvi, xix, xxxviii–xxxix, xlii, 8, 34, 59, 201, 238
O'Rourke, Beto (Robert Francis), 67–68
Orwell, George, 94–97

Parsons, Talcott, 155
Passover ritual, xlii–xliii
path of forgetting, xxi, 118–119
patronage-broker model, 96–97
patronage system, 30
Paul, St., 54–55
payments, imbalance of, xxxvi, 233–234
Pelagianism, xxi
Pelosi, Nancy, 70–71
people of color, xix, 70–71
Peter (biblical), 196
pets as substitutes, xxii
pharmacological substitutism, xlviii
Phillips Curve, 182
Plato, xxxvii, xlix–l, 85, 137–138, 148–149, 155, 163, 173, 176–181, 177, 180, 182–183, 209
political activism, 145–146
political legitimacy, basis of, 10
political power, forgiveness and, 58
politics: mercy-justice schism in, 47–52; religion and, 33–34; relocation of religion to, xxxviii, 94; transgression and innocence move into, 34–35

Pontius Pilate, 108

the poor, xxxiii, 51, 103

Porter, Robert, 79

prayer, xxxii

presidential election, 2020, xiii,
66–68

presidents, role of, 42

progressivism, xviii, 46, 52–53, 55–58, 62

property ownership, 86

Protestant Church, 33–34, 54–58

*The Protestant Ethic and the Spirit of
Capitalism* (Weber), 57

Protestants group unity, 74–75

purity: quarantine safe space of, 228;
upper class purchase of, 205

purity and stain: borders between,
xl; derivation of, xxxviii;
inheritance of, xxxviii; Wuhan flu
pandemic and, 228–229

quarantine, 228, 234–238

racial proportionality, 99–103

racism: systemic, xxxiv, 100, 211;
term usage, 129–130

racists, Democrats, 65

radical equality, xxxviii

rage, cathartic, 65, 68, 94–95, 124

Raspberry, William, 82, 103

Rawls, John, 4, 116–118

Reagan, Ronald/Reaganism, 56–58

Reflections on the Revolution in France
(Burke), 106

Reformation theology, xxii

relationships: COVID-19 and,

232–233; face-to-face, xlviii, 20, 29;
identity in, 7–8; permanent debt
in, 7; requirements for, 26–29;
social media substitutism for,
xxiii, 26, 158–160, 209, 210, 232

religion: American's loss of, xxxviii,
34; incomplete, xvii–xix; politics
and, 32–33; relocation to politics,
xxxviii, 94

renewed America, pillars of a:
commitment to the middle-class
commercial republic, 211–215;
foreign policy, 219–225; healing
the wound of slavery, 215–219;
imagining the future, 225–226

reprobate, the, xxvii

Republic (Plato), xlix, 148, 177,
182–183

Republican Party: commerce,
defense of, 46–47; congressional
representation, patronage-broker
model of, 96–97; emergence
of identity politics, response
to, 45; free market, support for
the, 56–57, 211–213; implosion
of the, 213; libertarian freedom,
support for, 56–57; Marxism,
response to, 45–46, 52; middle
class, disdain for, 213; national
conservative movement,
emergence of, 57; patronage-
broker model of representation,
97; post-2016 election schisms, 46;
progressivism, response to, 45–46,
52; scapegoating, fear of, 52–53;

tradition, defense of, 46–47, 52–54, 61; weapons used against the, 45–46; words labeling, 52; wound of slavery ignored by, 211
restoration of creation, 58–59
retail shopping, 160–162
Rice, Condoleezza, 82
Roman Catholic Church, 54–58
Rousseau, Jean-Jacques, xli, 14, 138, 148–150, 159–161, 174, 207, 209, 235

sacrificial offering, xxxix
Sanders, Bernie, 66
Sanger, Margaret, 116, 117
scales of justice, balancing the, xxxii–xxxiii
scapegoat, the: Divine, xxi, xxvi, xxxix, xl–xliii, 124–126; innocent's need for, 70–71, 104; the mortal, xix, 128–129, 228; proving his innocence, xlii–xliii; Republican's fear of being, 53; in secular liberal society, xx–xxi; transferring the stain of the transgressor to, 126; transgressors need for, 64; transgressor standing in for, 8
scapegoating: of black Americans, 81–82; by the Alt-Right, 108; catharsis of, xl–xliv, l; to cleanse the stain of man, 123–124; group, xl–xli, xlii, 121–132; redemption through, 125; relief from, 124–125; requirement for justice, 121; transgressors, 129–130; the two-minute hate in, 94–95; white

brokers of other whites, 64, 81. See also transgressor-scapegoat
scapegoating by innocents: a shortcut to purity, l; of transgressors, 53–54; the white heterosexual man, 200–201
scapegoating of white heterosexual men: as the adversary, 42; by the innocent, 200–201; to cover all transgressions, 84; the innocents shortcut to purity, l; offered for sacrifice, xxxix; proving his innocence, xl–xliv; a shortcut to purity, l; Trump and his supporters, 42
sciences, identity politics and the, xxvi–xxviii
Second Great Awakening, 41
second innocence, shortcuts to the, 189–191
security: against the mystery and terror of the world, 194–198; state-offered, 26–27, 195–196
security of just compensation, 196
segregation, invisible, xv
self, defining the, xxxv–xxxvi
selfie-man, xlvii, 145–146. See also management society and selfie-man
self-interest, doctrine of, 17–21, 35
self-interest, liberal, 16–22
sexual revolution, 155–156
sin, xxii–xxiii, 191. See also original sin doctrine
sins of omission and commission, xli–xlii

sins of the world, 69–70, 105, 126, 228

Sixteenth Amendment, 96

slavery, 59, 79, 83

slavery, wound of: exploiting the, 211; healing the, 43–44, 171–172, 215–219; transgressors defined, 70–71

Smith, Adam, xviii, 46, 138, 183–184, 212

social classes, group unity among the, 75–76

social communion, substitute for, 26, 158–160, 209, 210, 232

social death, xlii–xliii

social distancing, 230–231

social gospel movement, 41

social justice, 13, 22–23, 47, 184

social media substitutism, xxiii, xxv, 26, 158–160, 209, 210, 232, 237

Socrates, 148, 162

soul, needs of the, xxx–xxxii

Sowell, Thomas, 80, 82

Spencer, Richard, 107–108

"The Spirit of Conquest and Usurpation" (Constant), 15

The Spirit of Democratic Capitalism (Novak), 57

The Spirit of the Laws (Montesquieu), 15

spiritual economy, invisible, xxxii–xxxv

spiritual eugenics, xxxviii

stain: of capitalism, 105; of our inheritance, 2–13, 53–55; scapegoating the, 126; upon black Americans, 79–81; upon

Democrats, 66; upon white, heterosexual men, 58–59, 105; upon whites, Democratic belief in, 65, 68. *See also* purity and stain

stain of man, cleansing the, 122–124

state, the: growth of, 39–41; our understanding of the, 2; power of, progressivism's use of, 62; security offered by, 26–27, 195–196; shifting power from mediating institutions, 205–207; struggle between society, 206

Steele, Shelby, 82

strength of man, 109–111

substitutism, xxii–xxv, 151, 207–210. *See also specific substitutisms*

suffering: cultural appropriation of black, 216–217; of the innocents, 109–111, 116–118; material, recompense for, xxxii; unearned, of white, heterosexual men, 11

supplements and substitutes: borders, defended and abandoned, 175–176; digital vs. analog world, 165–170; fast food, fat bodies, 154–155; globalists focus, 183–185; Google Maps and driverless cars, 164–165; government and society, 170–175; money, paper vs. gold, 176–183; online education vs. real-time, 162–164; in person shopping vs. Amazon, 160–162; plastic water bottles, 152–154; sex in marriage for children vs. for not, 155–158; social media vs. loneliness,

158–160; vitamins-meals example, 150; weapons-courage example, 149–151, 161

supplements becoming substitutes, xxii–xxv; consequences of, 49; curing, xlix; examples of, xlviii–xlix; man, the creature who looks for shortcuts, li; manifestations of, xlviii–xlix, 232–233; shortcut offered by, li, 207–210

Swain, Carol, 82

Tech Elect, xxiii, xxv

A Theory of Justice (Rawls), 4, 117

The Theory of the Leisure Class (Veblen), 203

Thomas, Clarence, 82

"The Three Metamorphoses" (Nietzsche), 109

Thus Spoke Zarathustra (Nietzsche), 109

Title IX, 172

Tocqueville, Alexis de, xvii, xxxi, xxxv, xli, xlvii, 3, 16, 20, 22–23, 25, 29, 30–31, 33–34, 39–40, 47, 81, 89–90, 93–94, 108, 125, 129, 139–143, 145, 168–169, 169, 171, 173, 210–211, 221, 221–222, 231

tradition, 46–47, 52–55, 59–61

transgression and innocence: Alt-Right ending the relationship between, 107–108; Christianity resolving the issue of, 123–124; Christian way of understanding, xxxvi–xxxvii; of the colonized, 83; destroying, consequences of, 115; distinguishing between, 73; Hispanics, 82–84; intermixing of, 60–61; invisible economy of, 9; labor of ending the relationship between, 115–118; measuring, xxx–xxxi; migrating from religion to politics, 94; move into politics, 34–35; mystery of, xliv; relation, maintaining the, 71–72; relationship of, in Christianity, xix; West under the spell of, 42–43

transgressions: Christian significance, xliii–xliv; debt of, 59; end of the history of, 59–60; forgiveness for, 41–42, 58; payment to discharge, xxxii, 55; redemption from, 105

transgressor, the: confirming the depravity of, 98; debt of, 55, 59, 119, 197; forgetfulness of, 118–121; hope for the, 118–119; listening to the voice of innocents, 9–10, 64; the past and, 10; purging through cathartic rage, 124; repentences of, 118; standing in as scapegoat, 7–8; voice of, 9; washed clean, 114; white, heterosexual man as, xli–xlii. *See also* man, white heterosexual

transgressors and innocents: hope of the, 118–119; identity and relationships between, 7–8; presidents as, 42; slave owners, 83

transgressor-scapegoat: *1984* (Orwell), 94–95; of the Alt-Right,

"transgressor-scapegoat," cont.
  107; increasing the rage against, 92–98; of the innocent, 53–54; need for, 64; revealing the sins of the, 97; scapegoating others to prove purity, 65
transhumanism, xxv, 121–123
A Treatise of Human Nature (Hume), 5
Trudeau, Justin, 114
Trump, Donald, 42, 65, 71, 172, 213, 220, 229–230
two-minute hate, 92–98

universalism, 222
upper class: black Americans, 103; hypocrisy of the, 42, 201–204; luxury beliefs of the, 204; purchasing the purity lacking, 205; shortcut promised to, 207
Uzzah (biblical), 131

vaccines, 237–238
Veblen, Thorstein, 203
victims, innocent, 7–9, 11, 13, 32
Vietnam war, 219–220
virtue, 21
voice: of innocents, 9, 30–33, 64–68, 96, 104, 108; of the liberal citizen, 30–41
voiceless, the, 88
Voltaire, 14, 17

War Powers Act, 224
Warren, Elizabeth, 66, 68
warriors vs. soldiers, 149
Washington, Booker T., 81, 82

Washington, George, 223
water-bottle substitutism, 152–154
wealth gap, 36–37, 136
The Wealth of Nations (Smith), 212
weapons substituting for courage, 149–151, 161
Webb, David, 82
Weber, Max, 57
We Hold These Truths: Catholic Reflections on the American Proposition (Murray), 56
Weinstein, Harvey, xxiv, 172, 174
welfare state, xlv–xlvi, 50–51
West, the: Christianity in the, 42–43; renewal of, 112–115; transgression and innocence in, 42–44
wheat and the tares parable, 60–61
white broker transgressors, 64–66, 68–69, 81
white identity politics, 107
white liberal guilt, assuaging, 101
whiteness, sin of, xix
whites: group unity among the, 75–76; stain upon, 65, 68. *See also* man, white heterosexual; women
Williams, Walter, 82
Williamson, Marianne, 67
women: enslaved, 79; feminists, war against, 89; group unity among, 76–77; the unfree, 77–78; vulnerability of, 77–78; white, heterosexual, 70–71
Woodson, Robert Jr., 82, 98–99, 218
world: delinked, 141–144; redemption of the, 61, 110

wound of black America, xiv–xv

wound of colonialism, 43–44, 59

wound of slavery: exploiting the, 211; healing the, 43–44, 171–172, 215–219; transgressors defined, 70–71

Wuhan flu, xiii, xxv–xxvii, 228–240

youth: college age, fears of, 75–76; extraction from the family, 204–205; male, lessons learned by, 69–70